Lecture Notes
in Business Information Processing   **257**

Series Editors

Wil van der Aalst
Eindhoven Technical University, Eindhoven, The Netherlands
John Mylopoulos
University of Trento, Trento, Italy
Michael Rosemann
Queensland University of Technology, Brisbane, QLD, Australia
Michael J. Shaw
University of Illinois, Urbana-Champaign, IL, USA
Clemens Szyperski
Microsoft Research, Redmond, WA, USA

More information about this series at http://www.springer.com/series/7911

Boris Shishkov (Ed.)

Business Modeling and Software Design

5th International Symposium, BMSD 2015
Milan, Italy, July 6–8, 2015
Revised Selected Papers

 Springer

Editor
Boris Shishkov
Bulgarian Academy of Sciences - BAS /
  Interdisciplinary Institute for
  Collaboration and Research on Enterprise
  Systems and Technology - IICREST
Sofia
Bulgaria

ISSN 1865-1348   ISSN 1865-1356 (electronic)
Lecture Notes in Business Information Processing
ISBN 978-3-319-40511-7   ISBN 978-3-319-40512-4 (eBook)
DOI 10.1007/978-3-319-40512-4

Library of Congress Control Number: 2016941293

Printed on acid-free paper

This Springer imprint is published by Springer Nature
The registered company is Springer International Publishing AG Switzerland

Preface

The International Symposium on Business Modeling and Software Design – BMSD – is an annual event bringing together researchers and practitioners who are interested in business/enterprise modeling and software generation.

Most software systems being developed need to be integrated adequately in their "enterprise context." Moreover, an enterprise context often includes, among other things, already-running software applications. For this reason, it is essential to have *alignment* and *traceability* between the *enterprise level* and the *software level,* and therefore it seems logical to try identify enterprise systems and software systems and bridge the two on that basis. As is well-known, when speaking of a system, we are interested in what the system components are, how they are related to each other, how they are related to the environment, and what the principles are that guide the system evolution. An architecture is supposed to provide an integrated view of the system under consideration. According to one of the BMSD keynote lecturers (Roel Wieringa): "An enterprise architecture is a coherent whole of principles, methods and models that are used in the design and realization of the enterprise's structure, processes, (possibly) information systems, and infrastructure." Although structure, processes, and data are essential for "software architectures" as well, more complexities occur when developing software (in the analysis, design, and implementation), and according to Leszek Maciaszek, another BMSD keynote lecturer, what lags behind is managing system complexity, expressed in terms of dependencies between system elements. Finally, current enterprises and software applications both need to be adaptable because of the constantly changing real-life environment to which they should conform. This all raises a number of BMSD-relevant challenges, the most important of which are:

a. Identifying the enterprise and/or software system(s) to be considered
b. Building aspect models, accordingly, including models that reflect structure, processes, data, and so on
c. Establishing inter-model consistency
d. Capturing the (possibly different) levels of granularity between enterprise models and corresponding software models
e. Establishing alignment and traceability between enterprise models and corresponding software models
f. Addressing possible dependencies between system elements
g. Allowing for ways to model adaptability

Those challenges bring us together at our annual BMSD editions.

Since 2011, we have enjoyed five successful BMSD editions. The first BMSD edition (2011) took place in Sofia, Bulgaria, and its theme was `Business Models and Advanced Software Systems`. The second BMSD edition (2012) took place in Geneva, Switzerland, with the theme: `From Business Modeling to`

Service-Oriented Solutions. The third BMSD edition (2013) was held in Noordwijkerhout, The Netherlands, and the theme was Enterprise Engineering and Software Generation. The fourth BMSD edition (2014) took place in Luxembourg, Grand Duchy of Luxembourg, under the theme of Generic Business Modeling Patterns and Software Re-Use. The fifth BMSD edition (2015) was held in Milan, Italy, with the theme: Towards Adaptable Information Systems.

The Milan edition of BMSD featured for a fifth consecutive year high-quality papers and presentations as well as a stimulating discussion environment.

In 2015, the scientific areas of interest to the symposium were: (a) Business Models and Requirements; (b) Business Models and Services; (c) Business Models and Software; and (d) Information Systems Architectures. Further, there were two application-oriented special sessions, namely, a special session on IT Solutions for Healthcare and a special session on Intelligent Applications of InterCriteria Decision Making Analysis.

BMSD 2015 received 57 paper submissions from which 36 were selected for publication in the symposium proceedings. From these, 14 papers were selected for a 30-minute oral presentation (full papers), leading to a full-paper acceptance ratio of 24 % (compared with 23 % in 2014) and hence indicating the intention of preserving a high BMSD quality for the next editions of the symposium. The BMSD 2015 authors are from Austria, Belgium, Bulgaria, Greece, Egypt, Finland, Germany, India, Italy, Japan, Kazakhstan, The Netherlands, Poland, Portugal, Slovakia, Spain, Sweden, Switzerland, Tunisia, UK, and USA, indicating the strong international presence at the event.

The high quality of the BMSD 2015 program was enhanced by two keynote lectures, delivered by distinguished guests who are renowned experts in their fields: Barbara Pernici (Politecnico di Milano, Italy) and Marijn Janssen (Delft University of Technology, The Netherlands). Their inspiring lectures were greatly appreciated by the participants, helping them get a deeper insight into architectural and data aspects of enterprise modeling. Further, Barbara's and Marijn's participation (together with other professors) in the BMSD 2015 panel was of additional value.

BMSD 2015 was organized and sponsored by the Interdisciplinary Institute for Collaboration and Research on Enterprise Systems and Technology (IICREST), being coorganized by Politecnico di Milano and technically co-sponsored by BPM-D. Cooperating organizations were the Aristotle University of Thessaloniki (AUTH), the UTwente Center for Telematics and Information Technology (CTIT), the BAS Institute of Mathematics and Informatics (IMI), the Dutch Research School for Information and Knowledge Systems (SIKS), and AMAKOTA Ltd.

This book contains revised and extended versions of ten selected BMSD 2015 papers considering a large number of BMSD-relevant research topics: from business processes-related topics, such as process mining and discovery, (dynamic) business process management (and process-aware information systems), and business process models and ontologies (including reflections into the Business Model Canvas), through software engineering-related topics, such as domain-specific languages and software quality (and technical debt), and semantics-related topics, such as semantic technologies and knowledge management (and knowledge identification), to topics touching upon cloud computing and IT-enabled capabilities for enterprises. Those papers are not only relevant to particular BMSD topics but they also concern the issue of bridging the two BMSD sub-areas (enterprise modeling and software specification), something that is a distinctive feature of BMSD.

We hope that you will find the current LNBIP volume interesting. We believe that the ten selected papers will be a helpful reference in the aforementioned topics.

April 2016   Boris Shishkov

Organization

Chair

Boris Shishkov   Bulgarian Academy of Sciences / IICREST, Bulgaria

Program Committee

Hamideh Afsarmanesh	University of Amsterdam, The Netherlands
Marco Aiello	University of Groningen, The Netherlands
Mehmet Aksit	University of Twente, The Netherlands
Antonia Albani	University of St. Gallen, Switzerland
Ognian Andreev	Technical University of Sofia, Bulgaria
Paulo Anita	Delft University of Technology, The Netherlands
Danilo Ardagna	Politecnico di Milano, Italy
Rumen Arnaudov	Technical University of Sofia, Bulgaria
Colin Atkinson	University of Mannheim, Germany
Paris Avgeriou	University of Groningen, The Netherlands
Csaba Boer	TBA, The Netherlands
Boyan Bonchev	Sofia University St. Kliment Ohridski, Bulgaria
Frances Brazier	Delft University of Technology, The Netherlands
Barrett Bryant	University of North Texas, USA
Cinzia Cappiello	Politecnico di Milano, Italy
Jorge Cardoso	University of Coimbra, Portugal
Kuo-Ming Chao	Coventry University, UK
Ruzanna Chitchyan	University of Leicester, UK
Samuel Chong	Capgemini, UK
Dimitar Christozov	American University in Bulgaria – Blagoevgrad, Bulgaria
José Cordeiro	Polytechnic Institute of Setúbal, Portugal
Dumitru Dan Burdescu	University of Craiova, Romania
Jan L.G. Dietz	Delft University of Technology, The Netherlands
Teduh Dirgahayu	Universitas Islam Indonesia, Indonesia
Lyubka Doukovska	Bulgarian Academy of Sciences, Bulgaria
John Edwards	Aston University, UK
Chiara Francalanci	Politecnico di Milano, Italy
Boris Fritscher	University of Applied Sciences Western Switzerland, Switzerland
J. Paul Gibson	T&MSP – Telecom & Management SudParis, France
Arash Golnam	Business School Lausanne, Switzerland
Rafael Gonzales	Javeriana University, Colombia

Clever Ricardo Guareis De Farias	University of Sao Paulo, Brazil
Jens Gulden	University of Duisburg-Essen, Germany
Markus Helfert	Dublin City University, Ireland
Philip Huysmans	University of Antwerp, Belgium
Ilian Ilkov	IBM, The Netherlands
Ivan Ivanov	SUNY Empire State College, USA
Dmitry Kan	AlphaSense Inc., Finland
Dimitris Karagiannis	University of Vienna, Austria
Marite Kirikova	Riga Technical University, Latvia
José Paulo Leal	University of Porto, Portugal
Kecheng Liu	University of Reading, UK
Leszek Maciaszek	Wroclaw University of Economics, Poland/ Macquarie University, Australia
Jelena Marincic	University of Twente, The Netherlands
Michele Missikoff	Institute for Systems Analysis and Computer Science, Italy
Dimitris Mitrakos	Aristotle University of Thessaloniki, Greece
Ricardo Neisse	European Commission Joint Research Center, Italy
Bart Nieuwenhuis	University of Twente, The Netherlands
Selmin Nurcan	University of Paris 1 Pantheon Sorbonne, France
Olga Ormandjieva	Concordia University, Canada
Mike Papazoglou	Tilburg University, The Netherlands
Marcin Paprzycki	Polish Academy of Sciences, Poland
Oscar Pastor	Universidad Politécnica de Valencia, Spain
Doncho Petkov	Eastern Connecticut State University, USA
Henderik Proper	Luxembourg Institute of Science and Technology, Grand Duchy of Luxembourg
Ricardo Queiros	IPP, Portugal
Jolita Ralyte	University of Geneva, Switzerland
Gil Regev	EPFL/Itecor, Switzerland
Wenge Rong	Beihang University, China
Ella Roubtsova	Open University, The Netherlands
Irina Rychkova	University of Paris 1 Pantheon Sorbonne, France
Shazia Sadiq	University of Queensland, Australia
Valery Sokolov	Yaroslavl State University, Russia
Richard Starmans	Utrecht University, The Netherlands
Cosmin Stoica Spahiu	University of Craiova, Romania
Coen Suurmond	RBK Group, The Netherlands
Bedir Tekinerdogan	Wageningen University, The Netherlands
Ramayah Thurasamy	Universiti Sains Malaysia, Malaysia
Yasar Tonta	Hacettepe University, Turkey
Roumiana Tsankova	Technical University of Sofia, Bulgaria
Marten van Sinderen	University of Twente, The Netherlands
Roel Wieringa	University of Twente, The Netherlands
Fons Wijnhoven	University of Twente, The Netherlands

Shin-Jer Yang   Soochow University, Taiwan
Benjamin Yen   University of Hong Kong, SAR China
Fani Zlatarova   Elizabethtown College, USA

Invited Speakers

Barbara Pernici   Politecnico di Milano, Italy
Marijn Janssen   Delft University of Technology, The Netherlands

Contents

Towards Dynamic Business Process Management: Adapting Processes via Cloud-based Adaptation Processes

Roy Oberhauser[✉]

Computer Science Department, Aalen University, Aalen, Germany
roy.oberhauser@hs-aalen.de

Abstract. Dynamic business process management (dBPM) is contingent on the practical viability of automated process adaptation techniques. Various approaches to support process adaptation have been investigated, yet they typically expect some level of manual interaction or involve some amalgamation of additional modeling paradigms or language extensions. Additionally, cross-cutting process adaptation concerns and a distributed and cloud-based process adaptation capability have not been adequately addressed. AProPro (Adapting Processes via Processes), a flexible and cloud-capable approach towards dBPM, supports adapting target processes using adaptation processes while retaining an intuitive and consistent imperative process paradigm. The evaluation consists of case studies in both a business and an engineering domain and demonstrates the approach in a distributed Adaptation-as-a-Service cloud setting. The results show the viability of the approach across various domains.

Keywords: Dynamic business process management · Dynamic BPM · Adaptive process-aware information systems · PAIS · Adaptive workflow management systems · Process change patterns · Aspect-oriented processes · Cloud-based BPM · Adaptation-as-a-service · Web services

1 Introduction

A trend toward increasing automation is rapidly affecting all areas of business. Correspondingly, business processes are being increasingly modeled and enacted in process-aware information systems (PAIS). Dynamic business process management (dBPM) seeks to support the reactive or evolutionary modification or transformation of business processes based on environmental conditions or changes. The technical realization of business processes, known as executable processes or workflows, are implemented in what is known as either a business process management system (BPMS) [1], workflow management system (WfMS) [2], or PAIS [3].

In addressing process adaptation, many PAISs today lack dynamic runtime adaptation with correctness and soundness guarantees [4]. If such dynamic adaptation is supported, it is typically limited to support for manual change interaction by a process actor [3]. Typical types of recurring modifications to workflows are known as workflow control-flow patterns [5], change patterns [6], or adaptation patterns [3].

© Springer International Publishing Switzerland 2016
B. Shishkov (Ed.): BMSD 2015, LNBIP 257, pp. 1–22, 2016.
DOI: 10.1007/978-3-319-40512-4_1

In light of the dBPM vision, the increasing degree of process automation will necessitate a corresponding need to support adaptation by both human and software agents. Our previous work on an adaptable context-aware and semantically-enhanced PAIS in the software engineering domain [7–9] included automated adaptation work and work on supporting the user-centric intentional adaptation of workflows [10]. However, an open challenge remains in practically expressing and maintaining adaptations in an intuitive manner for process modelers and process actors for a sustainable dBPM lifecycle.

Adapting Processes via adaptation Processes (AProPro) contributes a practical and flexible cloud-capable approach for supporting dBPM in a generalized way that can be readily implemented and integrated with current adaptive PAIS technology. This chapter extends [11] and features case studies in multiple domains (business and engineering) to demonstrate its applicability and domain-independence. The approach maintains the ease and accessibility of the more intuitive imperative paradigm for process adaptations by modelers and process actors or users. It can thus further the reusability, portability, maintainability, and sharing of adaptations, including the cloud-based provisioning of adaptation processes within the community, thus supporting sustainable adaptability by extending an adaptation process's lifecycle. The evaluation demonstrates its viability and its performance in the cloud.

The chapter is organized as follows: Sect. 2 describes related work, which is followed by a description of the solution approach. A technical realization is described in Sect. 4, which is followed by an evaluation. Section 6 then concludes the chapter. Since this chapter focuses on the technical implementation of a process, the terms workflow and process are used interchangeably.

2   Related Work

Various approaches support the manual or automated adaptation of workflows. The survey by [12] provides an overview from the perspective of support for correctness criteria, while [6] provides an overview based on the perspective of change patterns and support features.

Declarative approaches, such as DECLARE [13] support the constraint-based composition, execution, and adaptation of workflows. *Case handling approaches*, such as FLOWer [14], typically attempt to anticipate change. They utilize a case metaphor rather than require process changes, deemphasize activities, and are data-driven [1, 3]. [15] provides a review of case modeling approaches. Case-based approaches towards adapting workflows include [16]. *Agent-based approaches* support automated process adaptations applied by autonomous software agents. Agentwork [17] applies predefined change operations to process instances using rules. [18] applies a belief-desire-intention (BDI) agent using a goal-oriented BPMN (Business Process Modeling Notation) [19] language extension. *Aspect-oriented approaches* include AO4BPEL [20] and AO4BPMN [21], both of which require language extensions. *Variant approaches* include: Provop [22], which supports schema variants with pre-configured adaptations to a base process schema; and vBPMN [23] that extends BPMN with fragment-based adaptations via the R2ML rule language. rBPMN [24] also interweaves BPMN and R2ML. *Automated planning* and *exception-driven adaptation approaches* include SmartPM [25], which utilizes artificial intelligence, procedural, and declarative elements.

AProPro differs in that it is an imperative workflow-based adaptation approach that does not require a case metaphor and is activity-, service-, and process-centric with regard to runtime adaptation. Additionally, neither language extensions nor other paradigms such as rules, declarative elements, or intelligent agents are needed. Furthermore, distributed and cloud-based adaptations to either instances or schemas are supported.

3   Solution Approach

The AProPro approach follows an imperative process style. A guiding principle of the AProPro approach is that adaptations to processes should themselves be modeled as processes, remaining consistent with the process paradigm and mindset. Process models are kept as simple and modular as reasonable for typical usage scenarios, in alignment with the orthogonal modularity pattern [26]. Special cases can either be separated out or handled as adaptations via adaptation processes, thus simplifying the target process. The solution scope focuses primarily on adapting process control structures, and not necessarily all adaptations to processes can be accomplished with this approach. In particular, internal activity changes, non-control and (internal) data structure changes, and implicit dependencies are beyond the scope of this chapter.

The following description of the solution approach will highlight certain perspectives. As shown in Fig. 1, *Process Instances (PI1..n)* are typically instantiated *(1)* based on some *Process Schema (S)* within a given PAIS (filled with diagonal hatching). In adaptive PAISs, *Adaptation Agents (AA)* (shown on the left with a solid fill), be they

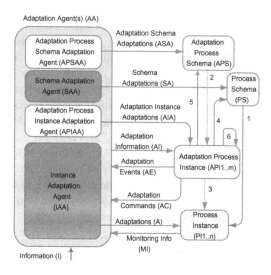

Fig. 1. Conceptual solution architecture.

human or software agents, utilizing or reacting to *Information (I)* (e.g., external information such as context or other internal system information such as planning heuristics) or *Monitoring Information (MI)*, trigger modifications to various process structures. A *Schema Adaptation Agent (SAA)*, such as a process designer or modeler, makes *Schema Adaptions (SA)* to one or more *Process Schema (PS)*. An *Instance Adaptation Agent (IAA)*, such as a process actor or user, may perform *Adaptations (A)* on some *Process Instance (PI)*. Support for such adaptation has been available in adaptive PAISs, e.g., the ADEPT2-based AristaFlow [3].

Workflow-driven adaptations of workflows: adaptations, for instance in the form of adaptation patterns, are specified as workflows that operate on another workflow. For this (see dotted fill), an *Adaptation Process Schema (AS)* is created or modified from which one or more *Adaptation Process Instances (API1..m)* are instantiated *(2)* in the same or a different PAIS. The *(API)* to target *(PI)* relation may be one-to-one, one-to-many, many-to-one, or many-to-many. Utilizing *Adaptation Information (AI)* such as events, triggers, or state, automated instructions denoted as *Adaptation Commands (AC)* can be sent to an *Instance Adaptation Agent (IAA)* that executes *Adaptations (A)* on one or more *(PI)*. Note that in certain PAIS architectures, a direct adaptation mechanism *(3)* that avoids the *(IAA)* intermediary may exist, with *(API)* acting as an *(IAA)*. *(API)* may provide *Adaptation Events (AE)*, e.g., so that an *(AA)* can be aware of the current state of an *(API)*.

Adaptation patterns as workflows: adaptation patterns (insert, delete, move, replace, swap, inline, extract, parallelize, etc.) can be integrated in workflows and applied conditionally based on *Adaptation Information (AI)*, e.g., in the form of process variables or events.

Aspect-oriented adaptations: this is supported by modularizing and constraining an adaptive workflow to operate on one aspect (such as authorization), while having other adaptation workflows address others. The many-to-many relations between *(API)* and *(PI)* or *Schemas (PS)* was previously mentioned. Congruent with the chain-of-responsibility design pattern, adaptations can be modularized and chained.

Variation points: these can be intentionally incorporated via markers for explicit adaptation support during process modeling, e.g., given insufficient modeling information. Adaptation workflows can then dynamically "fill in" these areas during process configuration or enactment.

Adapting adaptation workflows: This concept supports a further degree of flexibility by supporting adaptation workflows operating on (other) adaptation workflows. *Adaptation Process Instances (API)* send *Adaptation Commands (AC)* resulting in *Schema Adaptations (SA)* to a *Process Schema (PS)*, either via a *Schema Adaptation Agent (SAA)* or directly via *(4)*. In a similar fashion, *Adaptation Schema Adaptations (ASA)* can be applied to an *Adaptation Process Schema (APS)* via an *Adaptation Process Schema Adaptation Agent (APSAA)* or directly via *(5)*. Note that in this case, an *(API)* can change its own schema *(APS)* or those of others, and potentially change itself *(API)* or other instances *(API)*, possibly even directly via *(6)*.

Recursive adaptation: instead of separating the *(API)* from its target *(PI)*, if preferable (for instance, to access contextual data), a *(PI)* can include its own *(APS)* fragments and thus become self-modifying.

Exception-based adaptations: (un)anticipated exceptions can be used to trigger the enactment of adaptation workflows within exception handlers.

Reactive and proactive adaptations: in support of dBPM, event- and context-driven changes can automatically trigger and cause automated predictive or reactive runtime adaptations to be incorporated on an as-needed basis, rather than taking all possibilities into process models a priori.

Push-or-pull adaptations: in the push case, the adaptive workflow is triggered outside of the workflow and then applies its changes to the target; in the pull case, the target workflow triggers the adaptive workflow to initiate its adaptations.

Reusability: shared modeled/tested adaptation workflows support the wider reuse of adaptation patterns in the community, e.g., via repositories like APROMORE [27].

Composability: more complex adaptations can be addressed by composing multiple adaptation workflows, e.g., via sub-processes into larger ones.

Process Compliance and Governance: the (AP) can be used to verify expected structural and state conditions (no changes applied), or to additionally apply adaptations when these are not in compliance.

Cloud-based provisioning of adaptation workflows: the concept supports operating in a distributed and PAIS-independent (heterogeneous) manner on other workflows in other clouds, making these adaptation workflows readily available to operate on others as needed. Shared tenancy and pay for use could reduce infrastructural costs.

Service-oriented adaptation services: the approach supports the ability to provision and support adaptations-as-a-service (AaaS) in the cloud.

AProPro supports the goals of dBPM by enabling desired automated or semi-automated adaptations, while allowing process modelers and users to remain in their current imperative process paradigm and modeling language without requiring language extensions. Empirical findings that support such an approach includes: [28] who empirically investigated understandability issues with declarative modeling, and found that subjects tended to model sequentially and had difficulty with combinations of constraints; [29] determined that imperative models have better understandability and comprehensibility than declarative ones; [30] suggests that process modularity via information hiding enhances understandability; and [31], which showed that process complexity affected maintenance task efficiency for process variant construction - here subjects preferred high-level change patterns to process configuration.

4 Realization

To verify the feasibility of the AProPro approach, key aspects of the solution concept were implemented utilizing the adaptive PAIS AristaFlow. The solution approach required no internal changes to this PAIS, relying exclusively on its available extension mechanisms via its generic Java method execution environment. RESTful web services were used for cloud interaction. Adaptation workflow activities utilize a `StaticJavaCall` to invoke the extension code contained in a Java ARchive (JAR) file, which sends change requests to a REST server in the same or another PAIS.

To support heterogeneity, both the communication and the change requests are PAIS agnostic. They could thus be invoked and sent by any PAIS activity in any adaptation workflow located anywhere. Only the actual workflow change operations require a PAIS-specific API. Other PAIS implementations can be relatively easily integrated via plug-in adapters.

4.1 Adaptation Patterns and AaaS

The initial realization focused primarily on demonstrating key AProPro and AaaS capabilities. One such capability is realizing *adaptation patterns as workflows*, specifically those basic to typical adaptations: inserting, deleting, and moving process fragments. On this basis, more complex adaptation workflows can be readily built. For instance, the replace change pattern was realized as a subprocess consisting of an insert and a delete operation, demonstrating the *composability* capability.

The AristaFlow application programming interface (API) expects various method input parameters in order to modify a workflow. Thus, pattern implementations were designed to include these expected values even if some are optional.

The *insert process fragment pattern*, shown in Fig. 2(a), takes the following input parameters:

- *procID*: ID of the target process instance;
- *pre*: ID of the predecessor node;
- *suc*: ID of the successor node;
- *activityID*: ID of activity assigned to node;
- *newNodeName*: name of the new node;
- *staffAssignmentRule*: of this node;
- *description*: of this node;
- *readParameter*: input parameters for the new node;
- *writeParameter*: output parameters of the new node.

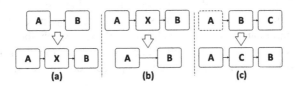

Fig. 2. (a) Insert, (b) delete, and (c) move process fragment patterns.

The *delete process fragment pattern*, shown in Fig. 2(b), takes the following input parameters:

- *procID*: ID of the target process instance;
- *nodeID*: ID of the node to be deleted.

The *move process fragment pattern*, shown in Fig. 2(c), takes the following input parameters:

- *procID*: ID of the target process instance;

- *pre*: ID of the new predecessor node;
- *suc*: ID of the new successor node;
- *nodeID*: ID of the node to be moved.

The *replace* pattern was realized as a subprocess that uses the insert and delete patterns as shown in Fig. 3.

Fig. 3. The Replace process fragment sub-process.

RESTful web services were created in Java according to JAX-RS using Apache CXF 2.7.7, with Java clients using Unirest 1.4.5. For basic pattern AaaS services, the following corresponding REST operations were provided at the target PAIS containing the target workflows to be modified, with procID passed in the URI and the rest of the inputs described above passed as parameters:

- `PUT /procID/{procID}/insert`
- `PUT /procID/{procID}/delete`
- `PUT /procID/{procID}/move`

The following REST operations provide examples of the interfaces for more advanced domains-specific AaaS services that invoke specific adaptation workflows that modify a separate target workflow instance. Such processes are explained later in the evaluation section, while example technical interface parameters of certain adaptation service implementations are given here:

- For quality assurance:
- `PUT/procID/{procID}/adapt/qa` with the string parameters urgent, high risk, junior engineer, and targetIP;
- For test-driven development:
- `PUT/procID/{procID}/adapt/tdd` with the string parameters testDriven and targetIP.

4.2 Implementation Details

The AaaS client-side adaptation process nodes internally invoke static methods in the `ChangeOperations` class for that change pattern (`doInsertProcessFragment` or equivalent). This method invokes a REST client that sends the corresponding request to a REST server. A class diagram of the server-side implementation is shown in Fig. 4. The service determines the type of *Request*, on which basis a corresponding (e.g., *InsertProcessFragment-*) *Command* object is instantiated and passed to a *Controller*, which determines when and in what sequence to execute a given command.

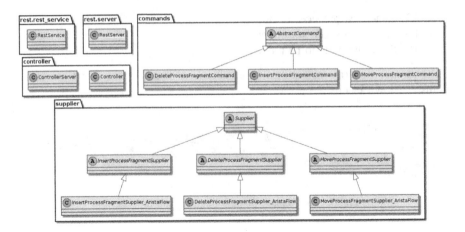

Fig. 4. Class diagram showing key implementation packages and classes.

To support heterogeneity, the commands utilize the corresponding *Supplier* classes which utilize PAIS-specific APIs for the operations.

A lock is acquired for the AristaFlow target process instance and a *ChangeableInstance* object is generated. All changes are first applied to this *ChangeableInstance* object. When the changes are committed, the entire instance is checked by AristaFlow for correctness. If the changes are correct, the actual process instance is modified accordingly. If errors were found, the changes are rejected and the actual process instance remains unchanged.

5 Evaluation

The evaluation focused on the solution concept and a prototype realization thereof. The case studies focused on demonstrating key process adaptation capabilities supported by the concept and its domain independence. The solution concept envisions provisioned adaptation workflows in the cloud that are available to operate on other workflows. Since certain reactive dBPM scenarios may be sensitive to delays, the technical evaluation encompassed cloud performance measurements. In this regard, workflows operating across geographically separate PAISs utilizing a basic cloud configuration would represent a worst case area of the performance spectrum.

As the solution concept is domain independent, a case study in the business domain and the software engineering (SE) domain are used to illustrate the capabilities and adaptation effects. For brevity and readability, certain branches and loops that would likely be involved in realistic models are omitted. Moreover, to maintain readability some screenshots are possibly cropped to remove obvious start and end nodes, while wide horizontal screenshots were cropped and stacked with a curved connector included to indicate the continuation of the workflow.

Figure 5 shows the evaluation setup. System A, which ran the adaptation workflows, was an Amazon AWS EC2 t2.micro instance eu-central-1b in Frankfurt,

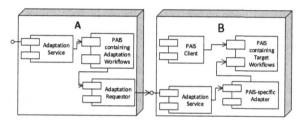

Fig. 5. The evaluation setup.

Germany consisting of an Intel Xeon E5-2670 v2@2.50 GHz, 1 GB RAM, 1 Gbps network, AristaFlow PAIS 1.0.92 - r19, Windows 2012 R2 Standard x64, and Java 1.8.0_45-b15. System B was an equivalent Amazon AWS EC2 t2.micro instance on the US West Coast (Northern California) us-west-1b containing the target workflows. A remote configuration means A is active and communicates with its target on B. A collocated AWS configuration implies that the Adaptation Process is collocated with the Target Process within the same PAIS in the cloud. In a local PC configuration testing adaptations in the first case study, both A and B were collocated on a single PC but commands are still sent via REST.

5.1   Case Study in the Business Domain: Travel Booking

The common conventional approach towards process modeling is restricted in its ability to consider the complexity and reality of real-life workflows, both in the model and its execution. In our view, many of the business process models are artificially simplified in order to be viable.

Therefore, to demonstrate the adaptation capability of the AProPro approach, we chose to model an adaptive variant based loosely on the BPMN 2 Travel Booking Example [32] executed in a local PC configuration. To simplify the diagrams and description for this case study, a limited set of factors, variants, constraints, and assumptions affecting the adaptations are shown, while other basic data such as name, travel dates, etc. are ignored. The following six transportation options exist: rental car, taxi, train, plane, company plane, and helicopter. We also assume that the different transportation options will require different booking steps, and thus we differentiate these workflows rather than assuming that one generic one will do.

5.1.1   Initial Travel Booking Workflow

The initial basis for the *travel booking* workflow is shown in Fig. 6. At the point in time when the process is modeled, the preferences and contextual information are unknown. Conventional process models must consider all possible combinations. Additional (contextual or preferential) factors that could still be integrated include severe weather risk, maximum layover duration preference on connecting flights, etc. The workflow will be described below.

1. The *Set Preferences* node in Fig. 6 takes the preference values shown in Fig. 7. The fields targetIP and ProcessID can be used for remote adaptations. The following preferences can be set:

   - Company executive (yes/no): yes expands the available transportation options with company plane and helicopter.
   - Driver's license (yes/no): if the person has a valid and unsuspended license then rental car is enabled.
   - Urgent (yes/no): if yes, then avoid train. If executive and less than 2 h and not overseas, then enable helicopter option.

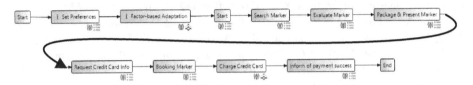

Fig. 6. *Travel booking* initial workflow basis.

Set Preferences

Avoid flying*	○ Yes ○ No	⊗
Car Travel Time (h)*		⊗
Company Executive*	○ Yes ○ No	⊗
Drivers License*	○ Yes ○ No	⊗
Hotel*	○ Yes ○ No	⊗
ProcessID*		⊗
Urgent*	○ Yes ○ No	⊗
targetIP*		⊗

Confirm	Suspend	Reset	Fail and discard

Fig. 7. Screenshot of the *Set Preferences* user interface.

- No fly list (yes/no): if someone has a flying phobia or is not allowed to fly then air transportation options are disabled.
- Duration of travel (hours): If car travel duration time is greater than some threshold (e.g., >=1 h, then disable taxi option; >=2 h car travel, then enable train option; if >=4 h, then enable airplane).

The following environmental context is determined automatically:

- Unavailability of certain travel options (here due to airline/airport strike or train strike): for simplicity, we assume that a strike affects all transportation of that type (this could of course be adjusted to affect only a single airline or single region).
- HotelMoreDifficult (yes/no): if due to high expected occupancy rates, e.g., due to a convention or event in the city (e.g., Oktoberfest) reserving a hotel is likely more difficult than reserving a flight, then attempt to book a room first, and then base the flight dates on the available.

2. The *Factor-based Adaptation* node in Fig. 6 triggers the enactment of the adaptation workflows as a subprocess and is described further in Sect. 5.1.2.
3. The second *Start* node in Fig. 6 waits for a data variable to determine that all adaptations have completed before proceeding.
4. The *Search Marker* node in Fig. 6 is a variation point that is replaced with search nodes applicable to the search criteria for this process instance (e.g., train and rental car only)
5. The *Evaluate Marker* node in Fig. 6 is a variation point to filter and calculate the best offers.
6. The *Package and Present Marker* node in Fig. 6 is a variation point to present the offers and allow an automated or human agent to make its selection.
7. The *Request Credit Card Info* node in Fig. 6 takes in the information required for payment.
8. The *Booking* marker node in Fig. 6 is a variation point to book the reservations.
9. The *Charge Credit Card* in Fig. 6 invokes a subprocess to charge the credit card with the actual amount. This area could also have been adapted based on a payment type preference (which we left out for simplicity).
10. The *Inform of Payment success* in Fig. 6 node notifies the appropriate parties that payment occurred. To demonstrate error-triggered adaptation, if payment was unsuccessful, an error-triggered adaptation replaces the node with a *Inform of Payment failure* node, but could just as well insert a retry loop or offer alternative payment types. Moreover, instead of explicitly invoking the adaptation subprocess as it is here, this adaptation workflow could be placed in an error handler and triggered via a process exception.

5.1.2 Travel Booking Adaptation Workflows

The *Factor-based Adaptation* workflow in Fig. 8 was implemented as a subprocess and triggered by the *travel booking* workflow as described above. As such, it demonstrates the pull adaptation capability, since the adaptations are pulled-in by the target workflow itself. A triggering and "push" of these adaptations on the target workflow, for instance via some external event such as the end of a train strike, would also be feasible, but would require further checks on the process instance state and its progress relative to the adaptation locations to ensure that it has not progressed beyond the adaptation locations. The contextual factors were simulated using a random number generator. The nodes of the workflow are described below:

1. The *Check if hotel more difficult* node returned with 70 % likelihood that the hotel was more difficult to book than the flight.
2. The *Check for Airline/Airport strike* and *Check for Train Strike* nodes returned with 50 % likelihood that a strike occurred.
3. The *Check for hotel first* node determines if the *Adapt for Hotel* is invoked first, if the *Adapt for Travel* first, or if only *Adapt for Travel* is invoked (assumes some travel is necessarily involved).
4. The *Adapt for Hotel* node in Fig. 8 invokes the subprocess shown in Fig. 9 and involves the steps of searching, evaluating, presenting, and booking a hotel room. While the workflow was executed, the case study invoked no actual actions.

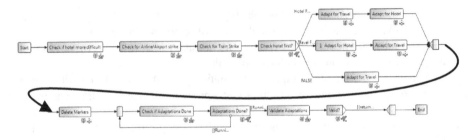

Fig. 8. *Factor-based Adaptation* workflow.

Fig. 9. *Adapt for Hotel* adaptation workflow.

5. The *Adapt for Travel* node in Fig. 8 invokes the subprocess shown in Fig. 10. It determines the appropriate type of travel medium that, in turn, invokes one of the adaptation subprocesses shown in Fig. 11. While these workflows were executed, for the case study no actual actions were invoked. The reason for assuming custom workflows rather than one generic workflow is that realistically each type of transportation may require different types of data and different service interfaces and interactions.

6. After the adaptations are invoked, the *Delete Markers* node in Fig. 8 invokes the *Delete Markers* adaptation workflow shown in Fig. 12 as a subprocess to delete any variation point markers remaining in the target workflow.

7. The *Check if Adaptations Done* and *Adaptations Done* in Fig. 8 is a loop that waits for the requested adaptations to complete before continuing.

8. As an example for a governance and compliance checking capability, the *Validate Adaptations* and *Valid* nodes in Fig. 8 verify that at least one transport type, at least payment, at least one booking exist in the target workflow after all adaptations were applied. While this compliance checking is "pulled-in" here, it could also be placed in a separate workflow, triggered based on some event occurring, e.g., that an adaptation occurred, and thus reactively pushed externally without the target workflow being aware of or including or excluding the compliance check.

Going back to the initial workflow in Fig. 6, the *Charge Credit Card* node is a subprocess (shown in Fig. 13) that attempts to charge the credit card and, if unsuccessful, the *Payment failed* node invokes the *Payment failed* adaptation subprocess (Fig. 14), which uses the replace process fragment pattern that was shown in Fig. 3.

5.1.3 Resulting Travel Booking Workflow

The resulting *travel booking* process instance is shown in Fig. 15 and, because it has already been adapted to its preferences and appropriate context, it exhibits a fairly simplistic workflow that does not show all of the possibilities that do not apply to its current context.

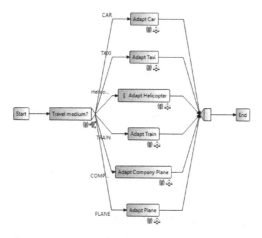

Fig. 10. The *Adapt for Travel* adaptation workflow.

Fig. 11. The a) *Adapt Car* b) *Adapt Taxi* c) *Adapt Helicopter* d) *Adapt Train* e) *Adapt Company Plane* and f) *Adapt Plane* adaptation workflows.

Fig. 12. The *Delete Markers* adaptation workflow.

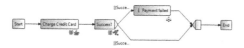

Fig. 13. The *Charge Credit Card* adaptation workflow.

Fig. 14. The *Payment failed* adaptation workflow.

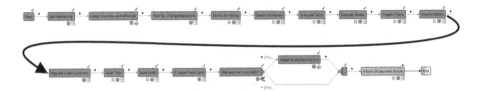

Fig. 15. Resulting travel booking workflow after the adaptations were applied.

This case study demonstrated workflow-driven adaptations of workflows, utilizing adaptation patterns as workflows, aspect-oriented adaptations (transportation vs. payment), variation points were demonstrated with markers being replaced with the actually required workflow activities (based on preferences and environmental context) during enactment, support for proactive (e.g., preferences) and reactive (e.g., payment error) adaptations, pull adaptations, composability in that larger adaptations were composed of smaller adaptation subprocesses, process compliance and governance, and service-oriented adaptation services, in that the adaptations were invoked via REST web services.

5.1.4   Conventional Travel Booking Workflow

We modeled the *travel booking* workflow conventionally without taking any adaptations into account as shown in Fig. 16. Due to space constraints, it is not intended to be readable, but to show a possible process model structure and to determine an estimate of a possible number of nodes required. This workflow consisted of 153 nodes.

In summary, from this business domain case study we see that adaptations can be readily modeled and modularized in workflows, variation points can be incorporated, compliance checks included, and that both proactive and reactive adaptations are feasible. Since during process modelling the actual preferences and contextual information are often unclear, conventional modeling cannot yet utilize these and thus the

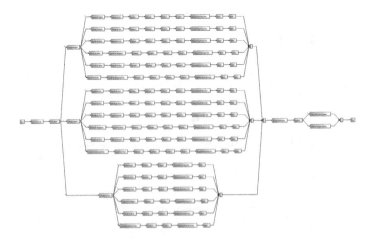

Fig. 16. Conventionally modeled *Travel booking* workflow (assuming no adaptation).

conventional model typically must consider all possible combinations, resulting in unwieldy models. In contrast, with the AProPro approach the adaptations are specified as workflows, which can be modularized, easily maintained, and flexibly triggered and applied, resulting in a relatively simple adapted and thus tailored target workflow.

5.2 Case Study in Software Engineering

In addition to demonstrating the AProPro approach in a different domain, the following case study also involved a remote cloud deployment configuration to demonstrate the capability for cloud-based provisioning of adaptation workflows.

5.2.1 Sequential Waterfall Process

For a representative target for the application of adaptation processes, a sequential workflow was chosen, loosely following a waterfall process (WP) [33] consisting of common SE activities for an approved software change request. It represents any standard process in a fictitious organization. The activity sequence is shown in Fig. 17.

Fig. 17. The initial (unadapted) *Waterfall Process* (WP).

5.2.2 Quality Assurance Adaptation Process

To demonstrate process governance and an Adaptation Process producing process variants, a Quality Assurance Adaptation Process (QAAP) variously adapts a target process based on situational factors.

Assume the SE process for a software change varies depending on its urgency, risk, and the worker's experience. The SE organization's policy normally expects at least a peer review before code is committed. The WP already includes this activity, although the adaptation workflow could also check policy compliance and insert such a missing activity. Three configurable boolean parameters were utilized for this process in Fig. 18: Urgent, High Risk, and Junior Engineer (denoting the worker experience level, with false implying a more senior worker). The 'SetConditions' task allows a user to set workflow values, which is skipped when invoked as a service. The following cases besides the default *Peer Review* (no change) were supported:

Code Review Case: A Code Review is required if the circumstances are 'NOT urgent AND (high risk OR junior engineer).' In this case:

- The node Peer Review is deleted via the Delete Process Fragment
- A node Code Review is inserted via the Insert Process Fragment Pattern

No Review Case: Foregoing a review is only tolerated when the situation is 'urgent AND NOT high risk AND NOT junior engineer.' In this case:

- The Peer Review node is removed via the Delete Process Fragment Pattern.

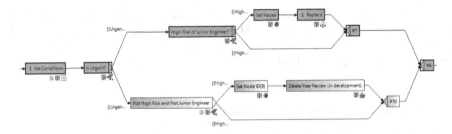

Fig. 18. Quality Assurance Adaptation Process (QAAP).

Fig. 19. WP after application of the QAAP.

Figure 19 shows the result of the application of QAAP to WP for 'not urgent and high risk', resulting in activity *Code Review* replacing *Peer Review*. In a context-aware dBPM environment, such input values could also be automatically determined.

5.2.3 TDD adaptation Process

In test-driven development (TDD) [34], test preparation activities precede corresponding development activities. To support the TDD aspect in the WP, the *Unit Test* is executed before *Implement* and *Integration Test* executed before *Integrate*. Thus, the TDD Adaptation Process (TDDAP) shown in Fig. 20 utilizes the Move Process Fragment Pattern twice.

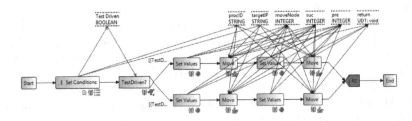

Fig. 20. Test-Driven Development Adaptation Process (TDDAP).

The resulting adaptations are shown in Fig. 21.

Fig. 21. WP after application of the TDDAP.

5.2.4   Aspect-Oriented Adaptations

Multiple separate Adaptation processes can be advantageous for modularity and maintainability. Analogous to aspect-orientation, each aspect and its associated adaptations can be modeled in separate conditionally dependent adaptation processes. In Fig. 22, both QAAP and TDDAP were applied to the target WP, with each adaptation process representing a different aspect (reviews or testing).

Fig. 22. Waterfall Process after application of both Adaptation Processes.

5.2.5   Self-adaptive Processes

Self-adaptive processes support the integrative modeling of possible adaptations into the target processes themselves. As shown in Fig. 23, both the QAAP and TDDAP adaptations were modeled before the WP, with the target process for the adaptations being the enacting process instance itself. This demonstrates the feasibility of adapting adaptation workflows and of recursive adaptations, and in a similar way adaptations could be integrated into process exception handlers.

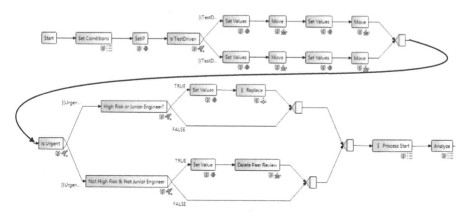

Fig. 23. Self-adaptive Waterfall Process partial screenshot (continues to right as in Fig. 17).

5.3   Measurements

To determine the performance of dBPM adaptation operations by an adaptation process in a geographically distributed cloud scenario, the durations for various basic operations (insert, delete, move) and adaptation processes (QAAP and TDDAP) were measured in a remote cloud configuration.

The test procedure was as follows: On system B, the Apache CXF REST server was started, and then the target workflow was manually started via the AristaFlow client to bring it into a started initialized state. On system A, an adaptation workflow was triggered by a REST client using Postman 2.0 in a Chrome web browser with which the necessary adaptation parameters were entered (e.g., procID, target workflow IP address, etc.). Activities in the adaptation workflow send adaptation requests via REST to system B. All latency and processing times were measured within systems A and B.

For the case that an initial measurement was significantly longer than the ones following (e.g., due to initialization and caching effects), this value was noted separately and not included in the average, since a dormant adaptation process might exhibit such an effect, whereas an active adaptation process would not. Each measurement was repeated in accordance with setup and test procedure described previously. To gather upper bounds, neither optimizations nor performance tuning were attempted.

Operation durations for the execution of the basic adaptations insert (Table 1), delete (Table 2), and move (Table 3) in a local and a remote configuration were measured. The average was calculated from the four measurements that followed the initial measurement. To see if cloud network delays play a significant role, the network latencies and the adaptation times are differentiated, which is also depicted in Fig. 24.

Table 1. Insert operation duration (in seconds).

	Local (B to B)		Remote (A to B)	
	Initial	Average	Initial	Average
Adaptation	4.033	3.468	3.588	3.203
Latency	0.418	0.373	0.686	0.675
Total	4.451	3.842	4.275	3.878

Table 2. Delete operation duration (in seconds).

	Local (B to B)		Remote (A to B)	
	Initial	Average	Initial	Average
Adaptation	3.251	3.295	2.880	3.749
Latency	0.444	0.448	1.013	0.674
Total	3.695	3.743	3.893	4.423

Table 4 shows average of five repeated execution durations for the QAAP and separately for the TDDAP. For a self-adaptive process, Fig. 23 combines the QAAP and TDDAP workflow fragments before the WP fragment. When executed three times in a local configuration, the average duration was 34.321 s. This corresponds closely with the sum of the separate QAAP and TDDAP measured times. Thus, there appears

Table 3. Move operation duration (in seconds).

	Local (B to B)		Remote (A to B)	
	Initial	Average	Initial	Average
Adaptation	6.796	3.311	6.105	4.005
Latency	0.577	0.347	0.772	0.692
Total	7.374	3.658	6.877	4.697

Table 4. Average Adaptation Process duration (seconds).

	Local (B to B)	Remote (A to B)
QAAP (1 replace)	15.748	16.285
TDDAP (2 swaps)	14.971	14.226

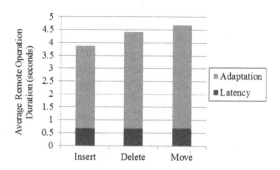

Fig. 24. Average duration (in seconds) for various remote basic adaptation operations.

to be no significant performance benefit to integrating adaptation logic in the target process when using a communication interface. Hence, for the aforementioned benefits of process modularization, separating the adaptation logic from target processes and supporting aspect-oriented processes appears practical.

Performance results show that the adaptation delays are potentially tolerable for non-time-critical situations in dBPM, such as proactive or predictive adaptations. When reactive adaptations to executing processes in the cloud are involved, or when human actors cause adaptations and await responses, the delays may be unsatisfactory. Networking had a relatively minor effect on the overall operation duration. Available RAM limitations likely affected PAIS performance, and different configurations and profiling could provide further performance insights.

In summary, the evaluation demonstrated that the solution concept is technically viable for non-time-critical cloud scenarios and can be practically realized by extending a currently available adaptive PAIS. Furthermore, adaptive process modularization and cloud distribution appears to currently have relatively little performance impact versus the cost of the adaptive workflow operations themselves.

6 Conclusions

AProPro provides a flexible cloud-capable approach for process adaptation. Its feasibility was shown with a realization and case studies in the business domain and engineering domain, involving cloud-based adaptation workflows and measurements. Key adaptation capabilities towards dBPM were shown, including workflow-driven adaptations of workflows, variation points, aspect-oriented adaptations, self-adapting workflows, composability, process governance, and the cloud-based provisioning of adaptation processes with an Adaptations-as-a-Service (AaaS) paradigm. Proactive adaptations were applied in push fashion and pulled via self-adaptation. Measurements show that pursuing cloud-based process distribution and adaptation modularization is likely not detrimental to performance, but that the actual application of process adaptations involves certain latencies.

The advantages of the AProPro adaptations for dBPM could be readily realized and benefit various domains such as healthcare, automotive, etc. For instance, a healthcare process could view allergies as an aspect and utilize an allergy adaptation workflow.

The solution faces issues analogous to those of aspect-oriented approaches, in that it may not be readily clear to process modelers which adaptations or effects may be applied in what order at any given workflow point. Thus, additional PAIS tooling and process simulation should support adaptation management, version and variant management, compatibility checking, and make adaptation effects or conflicts visible to process modelers.

Future work will investigate these issues, and also involves comprehensive adaptation pattern coverage, empirical studies, optimizations, and heterogeneous PAIS testing. To achieve the dBPM vision, further work in the process community includes standardization work on interchangeable concrete process templates, repositories, and AaaS cloud APIs, which could further the provisioning, exchange, and reuse of workflows, especially adaptive workflows such as those of the AProPro approach, thus mitigating hindrances for widely modeling and supporting dBPM adaptation.

Acknowledgments. The author thanks Florian Sorg for his assistance with the implementation and evaluation and Gregor Grambow for his assistance with the concept. This work was supported by AristaFlow and an AWS in Education Grant award.

References

1. Weske, M.: Business Process Management: Concepts, Languages, Architectures. Springer Science & Business Media, Heidelberg (2012)
2. Van Der Aalst, W., Van Hee, K.M.: Workflow Management: Models, Methods, and Systems. MIT press, Massachusetts (2004)
3. Reichert, M., Weber, B.: Enabling Flexibility in Process-aware Information Systems: Challenges, Methods, Technologies. Springer Science & Business Media, Heidelberg (2012)

4. Reichert, M., Dadam, P., Rinderle-Ma, S., Jurisch, M., Kreher, U., Göser, K.: Architecural principles and components of adaptive process management technology. In: PRIMIUM - Process Innovation for Enterprise Software. Lecture Notes in Informatics (LNI) (P-151), pp. 81–97. Koellen-Verlag (2009)
5. Russell, N., ter Hofstede, A.H.M., van der Aalst,W.M.P., Mulyar, N.: Workflow Control-Flow Patterns: A Revised View. BPM Center Report BPM-06-22 (2006)
6. Weber, B., Reichert, M., Rinderle-Ma, S.: Change patterns and change support features– enhancing flexibility in process-aware information systems. Data Knowl. Eng. **66**, 438–466 (2008)
7. Grambow, G., Oberhauser, R., Reichert, M.: Employing semantically driven adaptation for amalgamating software quality assurance with process management. In: Proceedings of the 2nd International Conference on Adaptive and Self-adaptive Systems and Applications, pp. 58–67. IARIA XPS Press (2010)
8. Grambow, G., Oberhauser, R., Reichert, M.: Contextual injection of quality measures into software engineering processes. Int. J. Adv. Softw. **4**(1 & 2), 76–99 (2011)
9. Grambow, G., Oberhauser, R., Reichert, M.: Event-driven exception handling for software engineering processes. In: Daniel, F., Barkaoui, K., Dustdar, S. (eds.) BPM Workshops 2011, Part I. LNBIP, vol. 99, pp. 414–426. Springer, Heidelberg (2012)
10. Grambow, G., Oberhauser, R., Reichert, M.: User-centric abstraction of workflow logic applied to software engineering processes. In: Bajec, M., Eder, J. (eds.) CAiSE Workshops 2012. LNBIP, vol. 112, pp. 307–321. Springer, Heidelberg (2012)
11. Oberhauser, R.: Adapting processes via adaptation processes - a flexible and cloud-capable adaptation approach for dynamic business process management. In: Proceedings of the Fifth International Symposium on Business Modeling and Software Design, pp. 9–18. SCITEPRESS (2015). ISBN 978-989-758-111-3, doi:10.5220/0005885000090018
12. Rinderle, S., Reichert, M., Dadam, P.: Correctness criteria for dynamic changes in workflow systems–a survey. Data Knowl. Eng. **50**(1), 9–34 (2004)
13. Pesic, M., Schonenberg, H., van der Aalst, W.M.P.: Declare: full support for loosely-structured processes. In: Proceedings of the 11th IEEE International Enterprise Distributed Object Computing Conference (EDOC 2007), pp. 287–298. IEEE CPS (2007)
14. Van der Aalst, W.M., Weske, M., Grünbauer, D.: Case handling: a new paradigm for business process support. Data Knowl. Eng. **53**(2), 129–162 (2005)
15. de Man, H.: Case management: A review of modeling approaches. BPTrends (January 2009)
16. Minor, M., Bergmann, R., Görg, S., Walter, K.: Towards case-based adaptation of workflows. In: Bichindaritz, I., Montani, S. (eds.) ICCBR 2010. LNCS, vol. 6176, pp. 421–435. Springer, Heidelberg (2010)
17. Müller, R., Greiner, U., Rahm, E.: Agentwork - a workflow system supporting rule-based workflow adaptation. Data Knowl. Eng. **51**(2), 223–256 (2004)
18. Burmeister, B., Arnold, M., Copaciu, F., Rimassa, G.: BDI-agents for agile goal-oriented business processes. In: Proceedings of the 7th International Joint Conference on Autonomous Agents and Multiagent Systems: Industrial Track, pp. 37–44. International Foundation for Autonomous Agents and Multiagent Systems (2008)
19. Object Management Group: Business Process Model and Notation (BPMN) Version 2.0. Object Management Group (2011)
20. Charfi, A., Mezini, M.: Ao4bpel: An aspect-oriented extension to BPEL. World Wide Web **10**(3), 309–344 (2007)
21. Charfi, A., Müller, H., Mezini, M.: Aspect-oriented business process modeling with AO4BPMN. In: Kühne, T., Selic, B., Gervais, M.-P., Terrier, F. (eds.) ECMFA 2010. LNCS, vol. 6138, pp. 48–61. Springer, Heidelberg (2010)

22. Hallerbach, A., Bauer, T., Reichert, M.: Capturing variability in business process models: the Provop approach. J. Softw. Maint. Evol. Res. Pract. **22**(6–7), 519–546 (2010)

23. Döhring, M., Zimmermann, B.: vBPMN: event-aware workflow variants by weaving BPMN2 and business rules. In: Halpin, T., Nurcan, S., Krogstie, J., Soffer, P., Proper, E., Schmidt, R., Bider, I. (eds.) BPMDS 2011 and EMMSAD 2011. LNBIP, vol. 81, pp. 332–341. Springer, Heidelberg (2011)

24. Milanovic, M., Gasevic, D., Rocha, L.: Modeling flexible business processes with business rule patterns. In: Proceedings of the 15th Enterprise Distributed Object Computing Conference (EDOC 2011), pp. 65–74. IEEE (2011)

25. Marrella, A., Mecella, M., Sardina, S.: SmartPM: an adaptive process management system through situation calculus, indigolog, and classical planning. In: Proceedings of the Fourteenth International Conference on Principles of Knowledge Representation and Reasoning (KR 2014). AAAI Press (2014)

26. La Rosa, M., Wohed, P., Mendling, J., Ter Hofstede, A.H., Reijers, H.A., van der Aalst, W. M.: Managing process model complexity via abstract syntax modifications. IEEE Trans. Indus. Inf. **7**(4), 614–629 (2011)

27. La Rosa, M., Reijers, H.A., Van Der Aalst, W.M., Dijkman, R.M., Mendling, J., Dumas, M., Garcia-Banuelos, L.: APROMORE: an advanced process model repository. Expert Syst. Appl. **38**(6), 7029–7040 (2011)

28. Haisjackl, C., Barba, I., Zugal, S., Soffer, P., Hadar, I., Reichert, M., Pinggera, J., Weber, B.: Understanding declare models: strategies, pitfalls, empirical results. Softw. Syst. Model. **15**, 1–28 (2014)

29. Pichler, P., Weber, B., Zugal, S., Pinggera, J., Mendling, J., Reijers, H.A.: Imperative versus declarative process modeling languages: an empirical investigation. In: Daniel, F., Barkaoui, K., Dustdar, S. (eds.) BPM Workshops 2011, Part I. LNBIP, vol. 99, pp. 383–394. Springer, Heidelberg (2012)

30. Reijers, H.A., Mendling, J., Dijkman, R.M.: Human and automatic modularizations of process models to enhance their comprehension. Inf. Syst. **36**(5), 881–897 (2011)

31. Döhring, M., Reijers, H.A., Smirnov, S.: Configuration vs. adaptation for business process variant maintenance: an empirical study. Inf. Syst. **39**, 108–133 (2014)

32. Object Management Group: BPMN 2.0 by Example. Object Management Group (2010)

33. Royce, W.: Managing the development of large software systems. Proc. IEEE WESCON **26**(8), 328–388 (1970)

34. Beck, K.: Test-Driven Development by Example. Addison-Wesley Professional, Boston (2003)

New Approaches for Automated Process Model Discovery

Christian Glaschke[(✉)] and Norbert Gronau

Chair of Business Information Systems and Electronic Government,
University of Potsdam, Potsdam, Germany
{cglaschke,ngronau}@lswi.de

Abstract. The implementation of business processes through the use of information systems (ERP, CRM, PLM and MES) has become a key success factor for companies. For further development and optimization of processes, many companies havent trusted processes for the analysis. Surveying as-is processes is complex and only possible by manual recording. To perform this task automatically the theory shows us different approaches (process mining, Application Usage Mining and Web Usage Mining). The target of the concepts and tools is to complement the process of continuous improvement in the company with meaningful process models, which can be reconstructed from protocols and user actions in the information systems. This article focuses on the limitations of these concepts and the challenges they present and gives an outlook on how future solutions must work to speed up the process of continuous improvement and to meet the challenges of heterogeneity in IS-architectures.

1 Introduction

For more than 20 years business process management has been the leading paradigm for organizing and restructuring corporations and public entities. Although all kinds of companies use business process management in certain areas, there are some challenges that require further analysis. To name only a few:

1. Improving learning while performing a business process
2. Making better use of person-bound knowledge that is generated in or used during the business process
3. The establishment of PDCA cycles (plan-do-check-act) in process management, that enable the detection and subsequent correction of deviations without interrupting the business process
4. Typically, business processes today are supported by enterprise systems like ERP, CRM or SCM. Normally, there are deviations between the intended process covered, the ERP and the actual process that is run in the company (cf. Gronau, 2015)
5. The human interface is more important than ever in most business processes, despite automation. When the automated business process is interrupted, it is a human that has to decide how to propel the process further. The description of human interfaces is by no-way interoperable now.

© Springer International Publishing Switzerland 2016
B. Shishkov (Ed.): BMSD 2015, LNBIP 257, pp. 23–36, 2016.
DOI: 10.1007/978-3-319-40512-4_2

6. A better real world awareness of the objects of business processes (persons, information, cases, instances and customer materials) currently available, as well as approaches to integrate such information into the process, is more necessary than ever.

With respect to all these new challenges, detailed and purpose-specific modeling is the precondition for a purposeful analysis of the business process necessary for its improvement. The detection of business processes and the investigation into necessary attributes of all objects tends to be very time-consuming and is still incapable of being fully automated. There are some approaches like process mining (cf. Van der Aalst, 2011a) that can help identify process patterns or recurrent instances, but the mere act of modeling itself is one of the most challenging tasks. This process also heavily influences the quality of the results. Incorrect or missing attributes or objects mean that the purpose of analysis and the goal of the improvement cannot be reached.

Therefore, this paper describes ongoing research activities to determine an approach to automatically identify business processes and model them from the information that can be derived from information systems like ERP and CRM.

2 Process Model Discovery in Time from Internet of Things

In this section, the topic of process model discovery in the area of a total digital integration is discussed. Current trends, such as the internet of things, industrial internet and digitalization (cf. Kagermann, 2014) are some of the main drivers for the development of new concepts and technologies in the area of business process modeling. At the center of these approaches lies the question of how it is possible to attain more efficient and transparent business processes. Hence, there is great demand for a current and trustworthy as-is process model (Houy et al., 2011). Such a model is necessary to decide how to optimize or reengineer the process. Inquiries to determine as-is processes are very complex and labor intensive, and are typically carried out by manual forms of observation and data collection.

The main question of the present paper is: How can as-is processes in a corporation or a public entity be determined automatically for further analysis? This question has tackled in the past by using a variety of different viewpoints. For instance, there are techniques that use either certain properties of technologies (Web Usage Mining, cf. Zhong, 2013) or log files from enterprise systems to reconstruct as-is processes. This approach is called Application Usage and Process Mining. These tools and methods have to be integrated into what are today more heterogeneous application landscapes with variable technologies and application systems (cf. Huber, 2015). This trend will be even more intense in the future when more system elements from the Internet of Things are incorporated within the application landscape. Given that this development will occur in the near future, the research question of this contribution can be stated as follows: What kind of information about the environment and the enterprise are necessary in order to be able to discover processes automatically? To answer this question, current research approaches are described and their limitations analyzed. Additionally, solutions that allow for the use and analysis of the available data are outlined, and the existing challenges facing the development of a new method are illustrated. At the end, an outlook for further research is given.

3 Existing Process Discovery Approaches and Their Limitations

Currently, there are different approaches available for the observation and interpretation of already documented process-, user- and object behavior. Among these techniques, we can count the examples of process mining (cf. Van der Aalst, 2012), application Usage Mining (cf. Kassem, 2005), Web Usage Mining (cf. Bhart, 2014) and RFID technologies (cf. Finkenzeller, 2015). Different classification criteria that allow for a differentiation of these technologies are given in Table 1. In this synoptic overview, the 1st row "Subject of analysis" indicates from which source the analyzed events are obtained.

Table 1. Overview of the existing technologies for the collection of event data

Criteria	Process mining	Web usage mining	Application usage mining	RFID
Subject of analysis	Application system	Web-based application	Application system	RFID infrastructure
Data basis configuration	Configuration of applications	Configuration of applications	Configuration of applications	Configuration of the infrastructure
Data source	Event logs	Event logs + traffic evaluation	Event logs + meta data	Event logs
Outcome	Workflow model	User story	Workflow model	Flow diagram

Furthermore, Table 1 illustrates that certain technologies or hardware components are needed as prerequisite for the application of the above-mentioned process discovery approaches (see 2nd row: "Data basis configuration"). However, in all of these approaches, the database generation is configuration dependent. Nevertheless, the respective initial effort to be made differs significantly depending on the individual application (due to a varying complexity of processes, systems and data quality) and therefore is not integrated in the here presented synoptic overview as a separate criterion. As "Data source" (see 3rd row), all approaches presented here use the event logs generated by the respective research subject (i.e. process-, user- or object behavior). In case of RFID, for instance, these event logs are a result of the scanning processes. The respective "Outcome" (see: 4th row) of each approach is also quite different. So, whereas Application Usage Mining and Process Mining generate workflow models, Web Usage Mining is used to produce user stories, which are presented in the form of flowcharts. For both mining approaches, tool support is available. The prototype of Application Mining, on the contrary, has not been further worked on so that no tools have been developed. In case of the RFID systems, we also have to arrange without any tools that might allow for an analysis of the data as processes. For this purpose, we rather have to use the technology and approach offered by Process Mining.

In the following, these four approaches will be briefly introduced and the respective state of the art in research and practice will be outlined.

3.1 Process Mining

A well-known approach for process discovery is the concept of Process Mining, which was developed by Van der Aalst and his research group at the Technical University of Eindhoven (The Netherlands). This approach uses log files from application systems (for instance ERP systems) to reconstruct processes. To be successful in that effort, the application system has to provide the needed information in a specific manner (i.e. as shown in Table 2).

Table 2. Example for a logfile

PID	Activity	Worker	Timestamp
452	Registration	55	2011-12-24, 11:10:21
452	Investigation	56	2011-12-24, 11:15:21
452	Consulting	33	2011-12-24, 12:17:10
452	Dismissal	55	2011-12-24, 12:47:11
453	Registration	55	2011-12-24, 11:16:35
453	Investigation	56	2011-12-24, 11:27:12
453	Consulting	12	2011-12-24, 11:52:37

An important component needed for this listing of process instances is the process identification number (PID). This number is used to create a process diagram based on more than just one process instance (cf. Van der Aalst, 2012). In the background, petri networks are used here (i) to allow for the generation of process diagrams, (ii) to describe the different conditions of the process and (iii) to create a graph for visualization purposes and analysis (cf. Van der Aalst, 2011a and Accorsi, 2012).

In an article from Thiede and Fuerstenau 2016, an extensive literature review on this topic is presented. The respective findings resulting from the authors analysis of publications on Process Mining that have been published in the Top 20 AIS Journals between 2004 and 2015 are illustrated in Fig. 1. As can be deduced from this overview, many research projects concentrate on the field of "digital services" and among these especially on the subtype of single systems. Thiede and Fuerstenau (2016) define the concept of "service" broadly as: "the application of specialized knowledge skills through deeds, processes, and performances for the benefit of customers (Vargo and Lusch, 2004, p. 2). For instance, a customer buying an article in a web shop (digital service) receives it by a dispatching service (non-digital)."

Cross-system observations of the processes, however, have so far only been presented by very few studies and also these works primarily focus on the aspect of PID synchronization. Additionally, there are only few works dealing with the combination of digital and non-digital services (i.e. "real" goods flow). Another insight of this review is that only few papers take up the issue of a cross-system- or cross-organizational application of process mining (cf. Zeng, 2013).

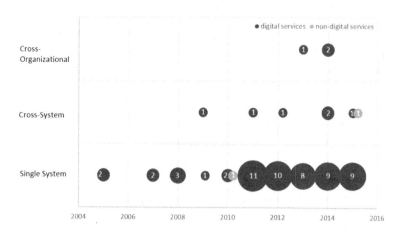

Fig. 1. Research overview over the relevant findings published in the Top 20 IS Journals (cf. Thiede and Fuerstenau, 2016)

3.2 Application Usage Mining

Another approach that uses more than one input source is Application Usage Mining. In this approach, the log files are complemented by additional data from the database of the information system, for instance on the users, workflows and functions of the system. This information is used to further enrich the workflow models. In the background of this approach petri networks are also used to describe the logic of the process and to summarize the possible states of a system (cf. Kassem, 2005).

3.3 Web Usage Mining

Another possibility to record the interactions between user and system are log files of web-based systems. This approach is called Web Usage Mining. Here, the access point for the process recording is the technology used (PHP, HTML, Javascript ...). Just as in case of the Process Mining Approach, the server can here record user requests and results into logs. The session ID is therefore used as process ID (cf. Bhart, 2014). This principle is typically used for analyzing the users behavior and not for reconstructing business processes, but a first adaptation for web-based application systems is presented by Van der Aalst, 2011b.

3.4 RFID

Due to the digitalization process, today, data on numerous business objects are available. So, for instance, the position vectors of an object can nowadays be calculated in real-time due to RFID technologies (cf. Zhang et al. 2012). These data can then be used to analyze the goods flow like, for example, demonstrated in Jakkhupan 2012. For this purpose, the objects involved in the process are first tracked and then the respective data are saved. In a typical RFID infrastructure as shown in Fig. 2, the readers send unprocessed data to an application system. In other architectures, middleware has to be used for this purpose (Abad et al. 2012).

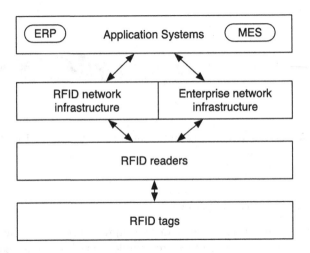

Fig. 2. RFID infrastructure (cf. Krishna 2007)

A combination of both technologies, i.e. of RFID and Process Mining, has already been used by Fernandez et al. (2015) and Zhou (2010) for the reconstruction of Health Care Processes. Thus, it could be evidenced that the log files of RFID infrastructures are also suitable for an application in the context of Process Mining applications and techniques.

3.5 Evaluation

Process Mining relies on the assumption that one system that is able to generate data about the entire business processes and can deliver log files in the necessary quality does exist. This assumption, however, is not valid for enterprises with a huge number of information systems working (cf. Fuerstenau and Glaschke 2015), for instance, with breed solutions, federated ERP systems or combinations of different system classes (PLM, ERP, DMS and MES) that are used together in the business process. Furthermore, customizing the application systems is very time consuming and a very high level of expertise is required for this task. One feature that additionally complicates this approach is that the functions executed by the application system are used as a first hint for classification and instance creation. Hence, the relevant process tasks and functions have to be known before the log files can be customized.

Starting from the preconditions that for a successful execution of business processes more than just one application system and different technologies are used and that some of the tasks are even performed outside the information systems (i.e. non-digitally), new approaches are necessary to be able to automatically discover or record business processes. To sum up, it can be said that existing approaches for data collection either possess specific knowledge about the process or concentrate on just one application system or one single technology. Besides, it has become evident in this context that Real-World Awareness can be significantly improved by means of RFID technologies.

4 Identified Possibilities for Data Capturing

This section shows possibilities to collect data from performed processes without being dependent on specific application systems or technologies. Another aim of this section is to describe which information user and environment can deliver and how this information can be captured.

4.1 Screen Capturing and Optical Character Recognition

A main point of criticism about the approaches presented in Sect. 3 is that a lot of work is necessary to configure the log data, and that meta information for the enrichment of log files in a structured manner has to be available. To obtain this information without any knowledge about the business process, an approach is needed which works independently from application systems. Application systems are ideally closed systems with complex interactions with clients that use different data formats.

There is only one object that shows all the interactions between user and system, the screen. To be able to use this valuable source of information, screen captures can be analyzed by an OCR software (Shekappa et al., 2015). From this information a matrix can then be derived (Table 2). The lines are the clients where the software captures the screen content. The columns are the different points in time when the screen capturing took place. Every cell is the result of an OCR recognition $f(t,c)$ at a certain moment (for instance t for time and c for Client). Available screen capturing software is also able to capture the cursor positions and mouse clicks of the user (cf. Huang et al., 2011 and Johnson et al., 2012). Therefore, it is also possible to analyze table cells in an application system selected by the user.

This approach delivers data about the interactions of the user with a terminal that is sorted by time but unstructured. It is also possible to find out the cursor position, and to analyze which fields were selected by the user and which functions were performed. This information can be used for structuring the data (Table 3).

Table 3. Results table for OCR recording

Client	t1	t2	t3	t4	t5	t6	t7
c1	f(t1,c1)	f(t2,c1)	f(t3,c1)	f(t4,c1)	f(t5,c1)	f(t6,c1)	f(t7,c1)
c2	f(t1,c2)	f(t2,c2)	f(t3,c2)	f(t4,c2)	f(t5,c2)	f(t6,c2)	f(t7,c2)
c3	f(t1,c3)	f(t2,c3)	f(t3,c3)	f(t4,c3)	f(t5,c3)	f(t6,c3)	f(t7,c3)

4.2   Operating System Information

Another point of criticism concerning the approaches presented in Sect. 2 is the exclusive focus on application systems. Other software running on the computer also delivers data that can be used for the reconstruction of processes and the generation of meta information.

Aside from the user entries, the operating system can also deliver other valuable information. This might include log-in credentials, the program used and the data entered. Additionally, the operating system is responsible for file operations and network access (cf. Tanenbaum, 2003). Using this information it is possible to determine which file was opened or processed.

4.3   Process ID in Application Systems

The process ID makes a substantial contribution to the discovery of a process. It makes it possible to distinguish between different process instances. From that structure, in turn, a process model can be reconstructed. In application systems, a huge set of distinct numbers for different kinds of data and levels of detail exist. Execution data exist for the accomplishment of business processes. This data, for instance, reveals the change of storage data when a delivery document changes the stored amount of an item by a booking process. This delivery document has a unique number and also points to its logical predecessors. The offer number can be found in the order; the order number is mentioned on a factory order or on a delivery document. The document flow that can be created from these numbers can be reconstructed or read from the leading application systems supporting this process. Additionally, these numbers are also available when corresponding with a client, for instance ticket numbers or invoice numbers. Master data identifies a business object (product resource, storage facility) uniquely by a number (cf. Schemm, 2009). In some cases, not only are the products identified, but also the object instances. Therefore, a serial number or batch number is used. These numbers are typically printed onto the product and are used for traceability of every single item or batch job in logistics and manufacturing.

4.4 Tracking of Business Objects

As described in Sect. 3.4 (RFID), the tracking of business objects (products, document files, employees, ...) is an important source of data. However, not only RFID can serve this purpose, but there are also other locating procedures like, for example, GPS that can be used for data collection. These technologies can all provide real-time information and are well-suited for recording the objects movements. A combination of the procedures presented in Sect. 3.4 would even be indicative of the interactions between the objects. As an example of this technique we can take the situation when an employee driving a forklift truck to transport products is equipped with RFID or GPS technology. Thus, and based on simple rules, it would be possible to identify specific interactions based on the respective movement profiles.

First research works in this area deal with the forecasting of knowledge distribution through the registration of position- and time vectors (cf. Sultanow, 2015 and Gronau, 2014). More precisely, Sultanow described and developed an approach to visualize the distribution of knowledge and knowledge objects. Another result of this kind of research projects is the representation of knowledge distribution in the form of a process model using the Knowledge Modeling and Description Language (KMDL) (Gronau, 2005).

4.5 Summary

The here presented approaches have revealed essential and partially unused data sources for Process Model Discovery. Hence, the great challenge consists, on the one hand, in overcoming the system limits in a cross organizational approach and, on the other hand, in generating and fostering Real World Awareness in order to also take into account traditional, i.e. non-digital services.

Furthermore, it could be observed that currently there is a trend of further enriching process models by collecting the respective necessary information that results from the execution of processes. This means that more detailed process models should be designed that are able to map the IT system as well as the staff and other business objects.

To conclude, it can be underlined that the mere generation of flow diagrams and workflow models does not yet fulfill the objective of actual business process modeling. For this purpose, more work will have to be done in order to aggregate the respective data at this level.

5 Challenges During the Development of a Method

Combining the information from the different approaches in Sect. 4 leads to different challenges for further research. In this section, the problems are elaborated with the help of an exemplary scenario. This scenario is described at first to depict the challenges. A special emphasis is put on the aspects of the existing approaches Process Mining, Application Usage Mining and Web Usage Mining that constitute weaknesses.

5.1   The Example of the Data Entry Process

To be able to describe the challenges a scenario was developed, in which a product entry process is performed. In Fig. 3, the process is illustrated in the KMDL process view (Gronau, 2005).

The process goes as follows: after a successful order from the procurement process (process interface), the goods are delivered. The delivery is accepted and driven through a scan gate. The information system "scan gate control" shows the warehouse employee (role) the listing of the delivered parts on a client computer and shows the serial, order and supplier numbers from the RFID tags of the packages. After checking that information, the warehouse employee approves the delivery document for the delivery man and in the scan gate control Software the parts list. The data from the scan gate control system is entered into the ERP system as a quality control system. In the ERP system, a new bill of delivery is generated that contains the articles and their amounts. The warehouse employee unpacks the goods and gets the bill of delivery in the ERP system in order to check the quantities. After confirming the amount, the ERP bill of delivery is handed over for inspection to the Quality Control System, which creates a test order, which includes the different properties of the articles. The Quality employee checks the properties per serial number and deposited a test result. Some parts are identified as unsuitable. This has to be entered into the quality control system. Most articles pass the amount check successfully. Acknowledging that the ERP system has been checked automatically produces the results of the quality assurance task and generates a storage location for every serial number of the delivered goods in the bill of delivery. Good parts are now transported to the manufacturing storage, bad parts into a reclaim storage yard. Articles marked as consumables are stored in the warehousing process. In process step book delivery note the articles in different charge carrier / transport units are separated. Then, the delivery will be booked. The ERP system generates from a transfer order, which is processed by the logistics department. Hence, the goods are stored in different locations.

5.2   Challenges of Automated Process Model Discovery

The first challenge for the approaches from Sect. 3 is to recognize that the procurement process is the trigger for the warehouse entry process. In the process

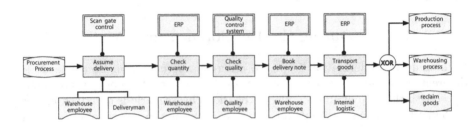

Fig. 3. Product entry process

"assume delivery", the order number is the only connection between these two processes. This connection has to be recognized and assigned to the order process. This is the main result to expect from the method to be developed. Therefore, the recognition mechanism has to find out that the same order number is now used during the delivery, and has to interpret this as a unique number.

Using the statements above we can formulate some requirements for the necessary recognition mechanism.

The method has to reliably find out the unique identifiers by screen capturing and OCR.

A second challenge can be derived from the "assume delivery" process. Here it is necessary to find out that the serial numbers indicate the different flows of goods. To achieve this, the products that are equipped with RFID tags at different locations (storage, quality control, ...) show the serial numbers and the current location belonging to that serial number. Of course, the information about the locations of the RFID reader stations must be known. Second challenge: The method must combine information from the screen capturing with the determined location of the goods.

Another challenge is the assignment of roles and information systems to the steps of the process. The warehouse employee logs himself into the system with his mobile device and connects himself to the scan gate control system. The operating system then captures the user group or the log-in name. With other information systems the process is performed in a similar manner. The operating system registers the usage of the scan gate control software and allocates this software to the process. The only role in the exemplary process that cannot be captured in this manner is the delivery man. Third challenge: The method must be able to recognize the external and internal roles involved in the process.

The next challenge is it to differentiate between the different process steps. In the example, the differentiation between the process steps "assume delivery" and "check quantity" can be performed by different information systems. When the process transfers from "check quantity" to "check quality", different roles and different systems allow one to find out that different process steps are performed. A differentiation on that level is at any rate impossible. An example of this can be seen in the work of a sourcing employee who works with an ERP system and does everything in the sourcing process, from ordering to invoice checks, on his or her own. Fourth challenge: The method must discover the different process steps and be able to see the limit of one process step and the beginning of another one. The fifth challenge is to find out the description of the process. To that end, a lot of information is collected from OCR or screen capturing, but their interpretation is difficult. An example is the "check quantity" process, and the question: how can we derive that term? One approach would be to assign the function to the location; another approach would be to use the window title of the ERP system "delivery note". Sometimes this task can be done by manual configuration, or by screen capturing. The fifth challenge is, therefore, that the method must be able to determine the name of a process step.

The sixth challenge is to recognize different target locations (storage locations in the logistic process) from logistics and from the transport of goods. Therefore, these different locations have to be distinguished in the process by using different process interfaces. To meet this challenge, the master data of the storage in the warehouse management system could be used to help understand the structure of the storage groups and their functionality in the process. Another possibility is to assign this information to the different locations. When this information is available for differentiation, the process interfaces into the storage area can be reconstructed. The sixth challenge is: The method must have knowledge that specifies the environment.

6   Conclusion and Outlook

The contribution has shown that an automated discovery of process models is possible when some new approaches are applied. The investigation of current approaches showed that systems and technologies deliver valuable information about the process flow, but a configuration for a case of specific use is necessary. The main gap in the research is the lack of consideration of human tasks and environmental data. For the research task to develop a new integrated approach, a couple of challenges must be dealt with. One of the most important requirements of a new method is to see the corporation and its data sources in an integrated manner. Another important topic is the collection of data according to location, time and their connection to the process model. No satisfactory answer could be given to the research question concerning which information about the user and the environment has to be collected in order to be able to sufficiently discover process models. On one hand, information about location must be available (for instance which task is performed where), while on the other hand, the master data that holds that information has to be investigated. In any case, the demand for and benefit of that kind of input can be shown. Finally, there remains the question of how the recognition mechanism uses semantic techniques. Here it might be possible that the user has to assist the recognition mechanism to describe the process models. An open issue after creating process models is to interpret these semi-formal models. To reach an understanding about a process solely by using a model is very difficult. The authors thinks that human beings, too, will have to participate in that process in the future.

References

Abad, I., Cerrada, C., Cerrada, J.A., Heradio, R., Valero, E.: Managing RFID sensors networks with a general purpose RFID middleware. Sensors **12**(6), 7719–7737 (2012)

Accorsi, R., Stocker, T.: On the exploitation of process mining for security audits: the conformance checking case. In: ACM Symposium on Applied Computing (2012). doi:10.1145/2245276.2232051

Bhart, P.: Prediction model using web usage mining techniques. IJCATR **3**(12), 827–830 (2014). doi:10.7753/IJCATR0312.1015

Fernandez-Latas, C., Lizondo, A., Monton, E., Benedi, J.M., Traver, V.: Process mining methodology for health process tracking using real-time indoor location systems. Sensors **15**(12), 29821–29840 (2015)

Finkenzeller, K.: RFID Handbook: Fundamentals and practical applications of transponders, contactless smart cards and NFC, vol. 7. Carl Hanser Verlag, Munich (2015). (in German)

Fuerstenau, D., Glaschke, C.: Weighting of integration qualities in is architectures: a production case. Paper presented at the ECIS 2015, Germany (2015)

Gronau, N.: Trends and future research in enterprise systems. In: Sedera, D., Gronau, N., Sumner, M. (eds.) Pre-ICIS 2010-2012. LNBIP, vol. 198, pp. 271–280. Springer, Heidelberg (2015)

Gronau, N., Mueller, C., Korf, R.: KMDL-capturing, analysing and improving knowledge-intensive business processes. J. Univ. Comput. Sci. **11**(4), 452–472 (2005)

Gronau, N., Sultanow, E.: Real-time reporting and analysis about knowledge events. In: IM+io Fachzeitschrift fuer Innovation, Organisation und. Management, pp. 80–87 (2014) (in German)

Houy, C., Fettke, P., Loos, P., Van der Aalst, W.M.P., Krogstie, J.: Business process management in the large. Bus. Inf. Syst. Eng. **3**, 385–388 (2011). doi:10.1007/s12599-011-0181-5

Huang, J., White, R.W., Dumais, S.: No clicks, no problem: using cursor movements to understand and improve search. In: Proceeding CHI 2011 Proceedings of the SIGCHI Conference on Human Factors in Computing Systems, pp. 1225–1234 (2011). doi:10.1145/1978942.1979125

Huber, S.: Information Integration in Dynamic Business Networks: Architectures, Methods and Applications. Springer, Heidelberg (2015). doi:10.1007/978-3-658-07748-8. (in German)

Jakkhupan, W., Archint, S., Li, Y.: Business process analysis and simulation for the RFID and EPCglobal network enabled supply chain: a proof-of-concept approach. Netw. Comput. Appl. **34**(3), 949–957 (2012)

Johnson, A., Mulder, B., Sijbinga, A., Hulsebos, L.: Action as a window to perception: measuring attention with mouse movements. Appl. Cogn. Psychol. **26**, 802–809 (2012). doi:10.1002/acp.2862

Kagermann, H.: Take advantage of opportunities on industry 4.0. In: Bauernhansl, T., ten Hompel, M., Vogel-Heuser, B. (eds.) Industrie 4.0 in Produktion, Automatisierung und Logistik, pp. 603–613. Springer, Heidelberg (2014). doi:10.1007/978-3-658-04682-8. (in German)

Kassem, G., Rautenstrauch, C.: Application usage mining to improve enterprise workflows: ERP systems SAP R/3 as example. In: Proceedings of the 2005 Information Resources Management Association International Conference. IDEA group Publishing (2005)

Krishna, P., Husalc, D.: RFID infrastructure. IEEE Commun. Mag. **45**(9), 4–10 (2007)

Krogstie, J.: Capturing enterprise data integration challenges using a semiotic data quality framework. BISE **57**(1), 27–36 (2015)

Schemm, J.W.: Inter-Enterprise Master Data Management. Springer, Heidelberg (2009). (in German)

Shekappa, B., Mallikarjun, A., Shivarama, J.: Best practices in digitization: planning and workflow processes. In: International Conference on the theme Emerging Technologies and Future of Libraries: Issues and Challenges, pp. 332–340 (2015)

Sultanow, E., Cox, S., Brockmann, C., Gronau, N.: Real world awareness via the knowledge modeling and description language. In: Khosrow-Pour, M. (ed.) Encyclopedia of Information Science and Technology, 3rd edn, pp. 5224–5234 (2015). doi:10.4018/978-1-4666-5888-2.ch516

Tanenbaum, A.S.: Modern Operations Systems, 2nd edn. Pearson Studium, Munich (2003)

Thiede, M., Fuerstenau, D.: The Technological Maturity of Process Mining: An Exploration of the Status Quo in Top IS Journals. Paper presented at the MKWI 2016, Germany (2016)

Tiwari, A., Turner, C.J., Majeed, B.: A review of business process mining: state of the art and future trends. Bus. Process Manag. J. 14(1), 5–22 (2008)

Van der Aalst, W., Accorsi, R., Ullrich, M.: Process mining (2012). http://www.gi.de/nc/service/informatiklexikon/detailansicht/article/process-mining.htm. Accessed 24 Feb 2016. (in German)

Van der Aalst, W.: Process Mining: Discovery, Conformance and Enhancement of Business Processes. Springer, Heidelberg (2011)

Van der Aalst, W.: Service mining: using process mining to discover, check, and improve service behavior. IEEE Trans. Serv. Comput. 6(4), 525–535 (2011)

Vargo, S., Lusch, R.: Evolving to a new dominant logic for marketing. J. Mark. 68(1), 1–17 (2004)

Zhang, Y., Jiang, P., Huang, G., Qu, T., Zhou, G., Hong, J.: RFID-enabled real-time manufacturing information tracking infrastructure for extended enterprises. J. Intell. Manuf. 23, 2357–2366 (2012)

Lu, Z., Yao, Y., Zhong, N.: Web log mining. In: Zhong, N., Liu, J., Yao, Y. (eds.) Web Intelligence, pp. 173–194. Springer, Heidelberg (2003)

Zhou, W., Piramuthu, S.: Framework, strategy and evaluation of health care processes with RFID. Decis. Support Sys. 50(1), 222–233 (2010)

A Business Process Meta-Model for Knowledge Identification Based on a Core Ontology

Mariam Ben Hassen[(⊠)], Mohamed Turki, and Faïez Gargouri

ISIMS, MIRACL Laboratory, University of Sfax,
P.O. Box 242, 3021 Sfax, Tunisia
mariembenhassen@yahoo.fr, mohamed_turki@yahoo.fr,
faiez.gargouri@isims.rnu.tn

Abstract. Business process modeling (BPM) has become primary concern for any successful organization to improve the management of their individual and collective crucial knowledge. In this paper, we propose a new multi-perspective meta-model of business processes modeling for knowledge management (KM), called BPM4KI (Business Process Meta-Model for Knowledge Identification). This meta-model is semantically rich and well founded on COOP, a core ontology of organization's processes. It covers all aspects of BPM and KM: the functional, organizational, behavioral, informational, intentional and knowledge perspectives. The aim of BPM4KI is to develop a rich and expressive graphical representation of BPs, especially, the sensitive business processes (SBPs) in order to identify and localize the crucial knowledge that is mobilized and created by these processes. Besides, it is evaluated through a real SBP scenario from medical domain in the context of the organization of protection of the motor disabled people of Sfax-Tunisia (ASHMS).

Keywords: Knowledge management · Knowledge identification · Sensitive process · Core ontology of organization's processes · Business process modeling

1 Introduction

Currently, organizations are increasingly aware of the importance of tacit and explicit knowledge owned by their members which corresponds to their experience, skills and accumulated knowledge about the firm activities. In order to improve their performance, such organizations have become conscious of the necessity to effectively identify, acquire, store, distribute, and reuse all individual and organizational knowledge mobilized and created by their business processes[1] (BPs). This knowledge represents a competitive, decisive and lasting advantage and a source of wealth to be valorized.

---

[1] Several definitions were proposed in the literature for the notion of a BP, among them we cite the two following: According to [1] "A business process is a collection of activities that takes one or more kinds of inputs and creates outputs that is of value for the customer. A business process has a goal and is affected by events occurring in the external world or other processes". According to [2] "A business process is a set of logically related tasks performed to achieve a defined business outcome". BP may be represented by a BP model (and its corresponding diagram in a graphical notation), which usually comprises the control flow of well-structured activities that an organization performs to achieve its objectives.

© Springer International Publishing Switzerland 2016
B. Shishkov (Ed.): BMSD 2015, LNBIP 257, pp. 37–61, 2016.
DOI: 10.1007/978-3-319-40512-4_3

In fact, according to the literature review, in term of the process view several researchers and practitioners have been focusing on the management of the BPs. Particularly in the information systems engineering, many works have been developed [3–6] and aim to model, improve and optimize the BPs. In accordance with the KM view, few methods focusing on BP analysis for knowledge identification have been proposed by researchers on KM [7–11].

BPM has become an effective way of managing organization's knowledge which needs to be capitalized. The integration of KM into BPs was identified as the most pressing as well as the most promising practical and theoretical task in KM [12]. Therefore, several attempts have already been made to integrate the domain of KM and BPM, which consist in introducing the process dimension into KM or knowledge dimension into BP models. Generally, different research approaches can be segregated into two different categories: (1) process oriented Knowledge Management approaches [13–16] and (2) knowledge oriented BPM approaches [17–25].

However, considering existing research, the integration of KM and BP orientation has not yet received sufficient attention. In fact, the knowledge dimension (i.e. the knowledge required to perform activities, the knowledge created as a result of BP activities, the sources of knowledge, the explicit knowledge, the tacit knowledge, individual and collective dimension of knowledge/activities, the knowledge flows between sources and activities, the different opportunities of knowledge conversion, etc.) needed for BPM is not explicitly represented, integrated and implemented in BP meta-models.

In this paper, we try to bridge the gap between KM and BPM, addressing an important issue that is not often raised in KM methodology: the problem of identification and localization of crucial knowledge[2] that is mobilized by the sensitive business processes (SBPs) [7, 9, 10]. In fact, the more organization's BPs are sensitive, the more they can mobilize crucial knowledge (i.e., specific knowledge on which it is necessary to capitalize).

To address this research gap, the current paper proposes a new multi-dimensional meta-model of BPs for KM, entitled BPM4KI (Business Process Meta-Model for Knowledge Identification). This meta-model aims to enrich the graphical representation of BPs in order to improve the localization and identification of crucial knowledge mobilized and created by these processes.

BPM4KI highlights the concepts and relationships needed to completely and adequately address all SBP essential characteristics from several perspectives. It covers all aspects of BPM and KM: the functional, organizational, behavioral, informational, intentional and knowledge perspectives. The first five perspectives are inherited from [26] as typically oriented towards business modeling and enriched by some new

---

[2] The first facet of knowledge capitalization process concerns problems bound to the identification and localization of crucial knowledge, that is knowledge (explicit knowledge) and knowhow (tacit knowledge) which are necessary for decision-making processes and for the progress of the essential processes which constitute the heart of the activities of the company: it is necessary to identify them, to localize them, to characterize them, to make cartographies of them, to estimate their economic value and to organize them into a hierarchy [7].

concepts defined by the core ontology of organization's processes (COOP) proposed by [11], which is useful for the characterization and conceptualization of SBPs. We extend the above-mentioned perspectives with the "knowledge perspective" in order to address all relevant issues related to KM (and deeply bridge the gap between KM and BP models).

Furthermore, we intend to integrate and implement the proposed BPM4KI meta-model in the most suitable notations for BPM, namely, the Business Process Modeling Notation (BPMN 2.0) [27]. In practice, this BPMN extension will enable us to have a rich and expressive representation of SBPs which are likely to mobilize crucial knowledge.

The rest of the paper is structured as follows: Sect. 2 briefly presents related works relevant to the research problem to analyze the existing work on BPM for KM. Section 3 presents background information on the core ontology COOP to explain and justify its usefulness to deepen the characterization of concepts relating to SBP notion. Section 4 presents fundamental characteristics regarding SBP and related work about modeling SBP. Section 5 presents the proposed BPM4KI meta-model. Section 6 illustrates the application of BPM4KI concepts in medical practical scenario. Section 7 concludes the paper and underlines some future research.

2   Related Works

Following a literature survey in the KM domain, we have found very few works addressing the analysis and modeling of BPs for knowledge identification. In this section, we analyze the main methodologies relevant to the research problem. We consider the Global Analysis METHodology [7], the identifying crucial knowledge methodology [9] and the Sensitive Organization's Process Identification Methodology [10].

The Global Analysis Methodology (GAMETH) proposed by [7] comprises three main phases gathering the following steps: (i) "Identifying the sensitive processes" specifies the project context, defines the domain and limits of the intervention and determines the processes targeted to be deeply analyzed. According to this author, "*A sensitive process is a process, which represents the important issues which are collectively acknowledged: weakness of the process which risks not attaining its objectives, obstacles to overcome; (iii) difficult challenge to take in charge; (iv) produced goods or services which are strategic in regard to the organization's orientations*". (ii) "Identifying the determining problems" aims at distinguishing the problems which weaken the critical activities, (i.e. the activities that could endanger the sensitive processes due to dysfunctions and constraints which affect it and generate determining problems). (iii) "Identifying the Crucial Knowledge" is intended to define, localize and characterize the knowledge to be capitalized.

The methodology for identifying the crucial knowledge proposed by [9] is based on the GAMETH framework and was validated in an automotive French company. It aims at capitalizing the knowledge mobilized and created in the course of a project. It is composed of three phases: (i) Determining "Reference Knowledge"; (ii) Constructing Preference model; (iii) Classifying "Potential Crucial Knowledge".

The authors [10, 11] have in depth dealt with the issue of identifying "Sensitive organization's processes". They have proposed a new multi-criteria methodology entitled SOPIM (Sensitive Organization's Process Identification Methodology) and a Core Ontology of Organization's Processes (COOP) to help evaluate and identify the SBPs. SOPIM is composed of two main phases: (i) Construction of the preference model, and (ii) Exploitation of the preference model (decision rules) to classify the "Potential Sensitive organization's processes". This methodology was conducted and consolidated in the association of protection of the motor-disabled people of Sfax – Tunisia (ASHMS).

The above-mentioned approaches intend to identify, characterize, model and analyze the SBPs, in order to localize the crucial knowledge. However, the crucial BPM phase has not been studied in depth. Four major limitations can be emphasized. In particular, we have noted the absence of: (i) a rigorous scientific approach of BPM for knowledge identification, (ii) a rigorous conceptual specification for the SBP notion and clarity in the representation of important SBP features, (iii) expressiveness of BPM approaches and BP models to represent SBPs, that explicitly integrate all relevant aspects related to knowledge perspective and other aspects which cover the BPM and (iv) a rigorous scientific approach helping in the evaluation and choice of a better formalism for representing SBPs.

So, in order to remedy for this lack, this paper aims to extend and consolidate previous work [9, 10], mainly to reduce the gap between BPM and KM and address an important problem that is not often dealt with by KM methodologies. Exactly, our mission aims to enrich and optimize the operation of "modeling and representation of identified SBPs" in order to increase the probability of localizing and identifying the crucial knowledge that requires capitalization. This reduces the cost of the operation of capitalizing on knowledge.

The first step to address existing limitations and reach this objective is the specification of consistent conceptualization with associated representation notation, that is able to explicit the rich semantics embedded into a SBP representation, precisely describing all SBP essential characteristics (such as complexity, flexibility, intensive acquisition, sharing, storage and (re)use of knowledge in challenging activities; diversity of information and knowledge sources; socialization; assistance of many experts (who carry out actions with high levels of expertise, creativity and innovation); distal intention that plans and controls the action; high degree of collaboration and interaction among agents/experts; the knowledge conversion; the dynamic aspects; etc.) is very relevant. In fact, this is not a trivial task, since SBP involve many subjective and complex concepts that are subject to different interpretations. Later, we briefly describe the most important specific particularities for SBPs modeling, highlighting its key features.

In this work, we rely on COOP, a core ontology of organization's processes proposed by [11] in order to deepen the characterization of concepts related to SBP notion to localize the knowledge mobilized and created by these processes, which may be crucial. In fact, this ontology provides a referential of semantically rich concepts relating to the BPs domain that are defined in a rigorous and consensual way to characterize the concepts useful for the analysis and identification of SBPs.

In the following section, we present some background needed to explain and justify the choice of the core ontology of organization's processes.

3 Background: A Core Ontology of Organization's Processes

This section presents the Core Ontology of Organization's Processes [11], which encompasses a clear and semantically rich definition of BPs.

For building the COOP ontology, the authors have adopted a multi-layer and multi-component approach already used to structure the ontological resources of the OntoSpec method [28]. The set of all these resources constitutes a global and consistent ontology (named by the same name of the method). This multi-level of abstraction approach amounts to apply a same set of generic principles for the conceptualization of the various domains covered by an application ontology. The main motivation is to facilitate the development and maintenance of the domain ontologies and to ensure a high degree of cross-domain consistency.

To carry out the BP analysis, the authors adopt a basic ontological principle, which can be summarized as follows: the *object* and the *process* are two complementary sides of any reality. According to this principle, corresponding to a view widely shared in Formal ontology, this complimentarily of the objects and processes is explained by a strong mutual dependence, as stated by Galton and Mizoguchi [29]: "(a) *matter and objects by nature presuppose the participation in processes or events*, and (b) *processes and events by nature presuppose the existence of matter or objects.*". This principle is already firmly anchored in most upper-level ontologies, including BFO and DOLCE.

To establish the ontological foundations of business processes, COOP is structured according to three levels of abstraction (foundational, collective, and organizational) which are organized around a minimum set of central concepts: (1) at the foundational level (DOLCE[3] [30]), the distinction between Endurants and Perdurants anchors the complementarities of the object and process views for the analysis of any reality; (2) at the collective level, Collectives are defined as Agentive Entity and the foundations for the intentional behaviors of these plural entities are laid; (3) at the organizational level, Organizations - as Collectives intentionally built and endowed with a formal structure - are introduced and their Processes - as deliberate, and structured actions culminating in a result bringing added value to a client - are defined. Originality of the core ontology of business processes in the field of formal ontologies of organizations (especially vis-à-vis the work of Bottazzi and Ferrario [31]) is the account of actions and business processes. This ontological framework constitutes a solid basis for the analysis of the BPs.

Formally, the authors adopt the following characterization for the notion of *BP:*

- A `Business Process` is a `Collective Action` which *hasForAgent* an `Organization`. It is therefore an `Action` of `Organization`.
- Each `Business Process` must provide a result which have a value. It is therefore a `Culminated Process`.

---

[3] http://www.loa-cnr.it/DOLCE.html.

- The Business Process meets an Organizational Objective; it is *controlledBy* a Distal Intention. Then the Business Process is a Deliberate Action.
- Each Business Process *hasForproperPart* at least one Organizational Action (Organizational Activity) which *hasForAgent*, either a Human or an Organization Unit.
- A Business Process is a set of activities which need some coordination to be performed. These activities are more or less ordered according possibly to a pre-defined order.

Furthermore, Several features have been defined in the literature and retained by COOP to classify Business Processes according some dimensions (see Fig. 1) as follow: the *granularity, affiliation of operant agents, perceptible value, strategic* and *repetition* dimension.

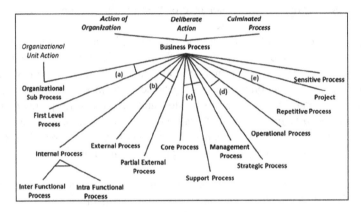

Fig. 1. Business Processes are classified according to several dimensions: (a) *granularity*, (b) *affiliation*, (c) *value*, (d) *strategic*, (e) *repetition*.

In addition, COOP is used to construct the criteria for the characterization and identification of the SBPs in order to locate the crucial knowledge. Indeed, COOP is a very effective tool used by the decision makers in order to share a set of concepts that relates to the field of organization's processes. These concepts are defined with a rigorous and consensual way and represent a referential which can be shared by the decision makers to enhance and optimize the organizational activities.

In this paper, we reuse and integrate a set of generic and central concepts of COOP, that we judge crucial to explicit and organize the concepts and relationships that characterize a SBP to improve their modeling.

4 Sensitive Business Processes Specification

4.1 SBP Characterization

A SBP is a particular type of BP. It has its own characteristics that distinguish it from classical BPs (see [11]). Thus, taking into account, on the one hand, the elements in the definitions proposed in the literature review [7, 9–11], and on the other hand, the emergence of new forms of modern organization, we deduce and adopt for our notion of SBP the following characterization. A BP is described as "sensitive", if at least one of the following requirements is fulfilled:

- It mobilizes "crucial knowledge", i.e. the risk of their loss and the cost of their (re) creation is considered to be important. Thus, their contribution to reach the firm objectives is very important and their use duration is long [32].
- It contains activities that valorize the acquisition, storage, dissemination, sharing, and creation and (re) use of organizational knowledge. It presents a large diversity of information and knowledge sources.
- It is heavily dependent on the tacit knowledge embedded in the stakeholders' minds (experts, specialists, etc.). In fact, this knowledge is mainly implicit, rarely explicit and disseminated the by experts who hold it, and will therefore be difficult to identify, exploit and valorize by other collaborators.
- It includes a high number of critical activities [7, 9, 10] mobilizing crucial knowledge. In our context, a critical activity mobilizes different types of knowledge: (i) imperfect individual and collective knowledge (tacit and/or explicit) (i.e. missing, poorly mastered, incomplete, uncertain, etc.) which are necessary for solving critical determining problems; (ii) a great amount of heterogeneous knowledge recorded (documented) on multiple knowledge sources (dispersed and sometimes lacking accessibility); (iii) expertise and/or rare knowledge held by a very small number of experts (who carry out actions with high levels of experience, expertise, creativity and innovation); (iv) very important tacit organizational knowledge, often linked to competences, abilities and practical experiences of their holders (This activity is based on several experimentations).
- It is very complex and dynamic and has a high number of activities (individual and/or collective) which are flexible. It can be semi-structured, structured and unstructured (depending on your abstraction), in the sense that it presents a very dynamic and unpredictable control-flow, comprising highly complex activities that may change over time or at design-and run-time.
- It mobilizes a large number of business domains/skills (in terms of internal and external organization unit operating in the BP). Its execution involves many participants and the assistance of many experts, with heterogeneous skills, experience and expertise levels.
- It involves a large number of external agents who are not affiliated to the organization. It is then known as a collaborative inter-organizational process.
- It has a high number of collaborative activities that mobilize, exchange, share and generate new organizational knowledge (tacit and explicit) created during the interaction among agents. Also, it depends on knowledge flows and transfer of data,

information and knowledge objects between communicating process participants. So that, it focus on the dynamic conversion of knowledge[4] [8].

- It possesses a high degree of dynamism in the objectives' change associated to it, essentially, in decision making context. The change of organizational objective leads to a new organizational distal intention which is necessary to control the SBP.
- Its contribution to reach strategic objectives of the organization is very important. Thus, it represents the essential process which constitutes the heart of the organization's activities.
- Their realization duration and cost are important.

According to the above mentioned characteristics of SBP, we find that risk-sensitivity, crucial knowledge, critical activities (individual and collective) belonging to it (which lead to the knowledge identification), high degree of tacit knowledge mobilized and exchanged among experts, diversity of information and knowledge sources (input and output), collaborative activities, distal intention that plans and controls the action, inter-organizational collaborations, flexibility, dynamic aspects and the high degree of its contribution to reach the organization's strategic objectives are the key requirements for specifying SBP that cannot be effectively served by classical BPs.

Due to those characteristics, organizing the knowledge in SBPs or building a SBP model is not an easy task. The selection and adoption of a suitable BPM formalism for SBPs modeling is critical. In this context, several BPM approaches have been proposed in BP engineering as likely to represent SBP.

4.2 SBP Modeling Approaches

Several approaches/formalisms for BPs have been proposed in BP engineering, with fundamental differences regarding aspects related to expressiveness, flexibility, adaptability, dynamism and complexity.

Some traditional workflows/BPM formalisms that are largely used in current research and practice scenarios in organizations, including Event Driven Process Chain (EPC) [34], UML 2.0 Activity Diagrams (AD) [35], Process Specification Language (PSL) [36], Business Process Modeling Notation (BPMN 2.0) [27] and many more have been adapted to allow the representation of the intrinsic elements of knowledge within BPs.

In fact, this category of formalisms is suitable for process perspective representation (that display a defined, well structured, highly stable and (low) complex sequence of activities). Moreover, they support data and information inclusion into BP models. They can be used to implicitly identify certain issues related to knowledge flows, such as the information sources that are required, generated, or modified by an activity.

---

[4] Internalization – generation of new knowledge, when new tacit knowledge is generated from explicit knowledge. Externalization – materialization of knowledge, when tacit knowledge is transformed into explicit knowledge. Combination – use of existing explicit knowledge to create new explicit knowledge. Socialization – sharing knowledge, when existing tacit knowledge is used for the generation of new tacit knowledge.

However, certain limitations can be observed. One the one hand, they are not suited to deal with the ad-hoc effects, frequent exceptions, and common changes in SBP activities. On the other hand, they are less appropriate (i.e. not powerful enough) for BPM that involve the cooperation of multiple actors. Additionally, conventional formalisms do not distinguish between definitions of data, information, and knowledge and do not provide specific symbols for their representation in BP. These concepts are not being represented separately and accurately in the BP models and are often represented by the same modeling constructs. However, this distinction is useful and essential for our modeling context.

Additionally to BPM formalisms, some authors have attempted to develop approaches for the representation of knowledge intensive processes [14] where basic phenomenon is knowledge. In these processes, the principal success factor is adequate modeling of knowledge conversions. Usually knowledge is modeled using specific knowledge modeling approaches and notations, such as Business Process Knowledge Method (BPKM) [37], Oliveira's methodology [38], Knowledge Modeling Description Language (KMDL 2.2) [14], Knowledge Transfer Agent (KTA) [39], DECOR [40], CommonKADS [41], PROMOTE [18], GPO-WM [15], the work of Donadel [42], Notation for Knowledge-Intensive Processes (NKIP) [25], etc. These BP oriented KM approaches have not been widely adopted by organizations and are very incipient, comprising only a subset of all KIP characteristics, as discussed in [43]. Most of these approaches focus on storing and sharing knowledge and are convenient for knowledge conversion. At the same time they have limited capabilities. In particular, they lack the ability to model in an adequate manner the process perspectives as a whole (the structural, behavioral, organizational and informational dimensions). Moreover, some proposals do not address the representation of artifacts and dynamic aspects of BP and modeling agents [44], while others do not explicitly differentiate between tacit and explicit knowledge [37, 39, 41, 42], which is relevant in SBPs due to, for instance, the high degree of tacit knowledge developed and exchanged among agents through inter-organizational collaboration.

Furthermore, following the study of the available BPs meta-models and ontologies associated with the main BPM formalisms, we notice that the defined concepts-actions specification (Process, Activity, Sub-process, Task, function, action) do not take into account the individual/collective dimension of the actions. However, taking into consideration such a dimension is very important in our research context, given that we are interested in the localization of knowledge mobilized to realize the BP. This knowledge taken in the action may be either individual or collective/organizational (tacit or explicit). These actions of organization (collective and individual) are taken into consideration in the core ontology COOP [11].

Despite it mobilizes crucial knowledge within an organization and their key role for organizational KM, existing BPM approaches have shortcomings concerning their ability to explicitly incorporate the knowledge dimension within BPs models and represent SBPs. None of those proposals adequately includes or addresses all or at least most of the SBPs important characteristics presented previously (knowledge aspects, flexibility, collaboration and interaction among agents, dynamics aspect, intentions behind each action, etc.) as well as relevant issues at the intersection of KM and BPM. This leads to ambiguity and misunderstanding of the developed SBPs models.

Based on this analysis, the SBPs representation is a lot more difficult. So, such formalism should take into account all semantic dimensions and criteria enabling to characterize in depth the notion of process, while covering the functional, organizational, behavioral, informational, intentional and knowledge aspects. Therefore, there is a need to precisely define the specification of a SBP, including the concepts and relationships between them that adequately address the knowledge within their actions and all SBP essential aspects. To address this research gap, we propose a semantically rich conceptualization of a SBP organized in a meta-model, the Business Process Meta-model for Knowledge Identification. BPM4KI explicit and organize the key concepts and relationships to completely characterize a SBP from different perspectives, giving an expressive representation of SBPs, integrating all aspects of BPM and KM.

5   A Meta-Model of the Business Process Modeling for Knowledge Identification

In order to improve the SBP representation and localize and identify in depth the crucial knowledge, we propose a new Business Process Meta-model for Knowledge Identification (BPM4KI) addressing the requirements of the SBP seen before. In fact, based on some related work done in the fields of workflows/BP meta-models and ontology engineering (in various contexts) [11, 26, 27, 34, 37, 43, 45–53], we have shown some limitations addressing the SBP modeling. BPM4KI covers all aspects of BPM and KM. It comprises concepts from several and complimentary perspectives that are crucial for a complete understanding and representation of a SBP, namely the functional perspective, the organizational perspective, the behavioral perspective, the informational perspective, the intentional perspective and the knowledge perspective. The generic meta-model we have developed is based on the core ontology COOP [11] and categorized according to the framework developed by [26]. As a reminder, COOP provides taxonomy of semantically rich concepts for conceptualizing BPs in various contexts (such as Action, Action of Organization, Individual Action, Action of Collective, Collective, Organization, Distal Intention, Deliberate Action, Sensitive Process, Critical Activity, etc.). While Nurcan's framework consists of five perspectives, each one of them focuses on a BP aspect: functional, organizational, behavioral, informational and intentional. As these perspectives do not capture all relevant aspects related to knowledge dimension, we have extended the above-mentioned framework with a further perspective, namely the "knowledge perspective" to address all relevant issues related to KM and bridge the gap between KM and BPM. It should be noted that Knowledge is crucial concern for a successful business, and might be considered as one of the BP dimensions, because knowledge is related to action, it is implemented in the action, and is essential to its development [7]. Knowledge is used to perform a process, it is created as a result of process execution, and it is distributed among process participants [15].

Figure 2 presents BPM4KI in terms of classes and relationships between classes. The defined concepts that make up the COOP ontology are marked in gray in the meta-model. In the following, we describe the six perspectives making up the BPM4KI meta-model.

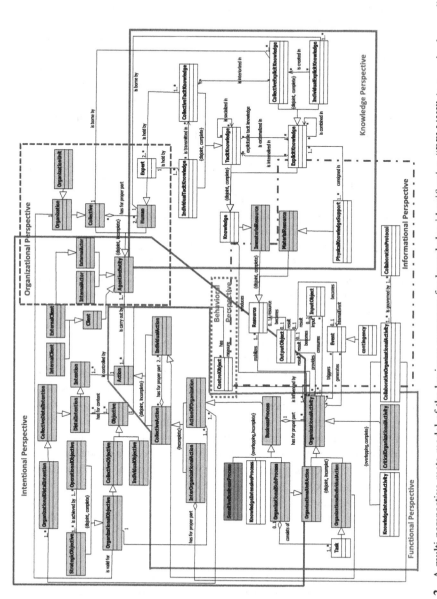

Fig. 2. A multi-perspective meta-model of the business processes for knowledge identification "BPM4KI" (categorized according to six perspectives)

The *Functional Perspective* represents the BP elements which are being performed (*i.e.*, activity, sub-process (composite activity) and tasks (atomic action). Hence, as illustrated in Fig. 2, the BPM4KI meta-model part that can be used to model this perspective is inspired by COOP. It regroups generic classes related to (inheriting from) the Action[5] meta-class. An Action can be individual or collective. An Individual Action *is carried out* (performed) by a single individual (it *hasForAgent* a Human). While a Collective Action (Action of Collective) is a group of several individual actions combining their effects [54]. It *is carried out by* (*hasForAgent*) a Collective, *controlledBy* a Collective Intention and *hasForProperPart* at least two Individual Actions contributing to it [11]. It should be noted that a Collective Action is not only reduced to the sum of individual actions performed by each individual belonging to the collective but concerns also actions that can be carried out collectively by the individuals making up the collective. A Collective Action can be either an Action of Organization, or an Inter-organizational Action. The latter has for agents at least two Organizations. A Business Process is a Collective Action which *hasForAgent* an Organization. It is therefore an Action of Organization carried out by a group of individuals affiliated with the organization. Any Business Process *hasForproperPart* (is composed of) a set of Organizational Actions (or Organizational Activities) coordinated and undertaken according to an intentionally defined objective. An Organizational Activity is an Action which is a *proper part of* an Action of Organization. It can be either an Organizational Individual Action (which is an Individual Action) or an Organizational Unit Action (which is an Action of Organization). In the first case, it is carried out by (*hasForAgent*) a Human affiliated to the Organization. An example is a commercial agent who makes an invoice. While in the second case, it is carried out by an Organization Unit.

An Organizational Sub-Process is an Organizational Unit Action which *is a proper part of* a Business Process. Let's consider the example of a treatment of a customer order. This Business Process *hasForProperPart* four organizational sub-process, namely: (i) Checking of the availability of the ordered products (made by the service); (ii) Preparation of a delivery order (made by the sales department); (iii) Preparation of the invoice (made by the sales department); (iv) The invoice payment (managed by the financial department). Furthermore, an Organizational Activity can either be qualified as a Critical Organizational Activity, or as a Knowledge Intensive Activity[6] [43] or Collaborative Organizational Activity. They can also be described as critical.

---

[5] With respect to our notation, the informal labels on BPM4KI concepts appear in the text in the Courrier new font with First Capital Letters for the concepts and a javaLikeNotation for relations. The same conventions apply for the COOP ontology [11] presented in the paper.

[6] A special type of process activity that is not enough specified to be systematically executed. Its execution is based on previous experiences and tacit knowledge from its executor, may require specialty, may comprise innovation, or may involve making decisions. This activity is unpredictable and defined at runtime [43].

The *Organizational Perspective* represents the different participants (the organizational resources) invoked in the execution of process elements as well as their affiliation. The meta-model elements of this perspective are inspired by COOP. The basic element of this perspective is Agentive Entity. An Agentive Entity (or Intentional Agent) is an entity which has a capacity to carry out (and therefore to repeat) Actions (in particular deliberate actions). It can be specified in the form of a Human, an Informal Group, or an Organization, internal or external to an Organization. An Organization is a Collective (structured and formal) which can carry out an Action of Organization. A Collective is a group of humans unified by a joint intention to form a group capable of acting [54] (Any Collective Action *hasForAgent* a Collective). An Organization Unit is an Organization (in its own right) managed by (and depending on) an encompassing Organization. We recall that a Business Process *hasForAgent* an Organization. Each Business Process *hasForproperPart* at least one Organizational Activity, in turn, may *hasForAgent*, either a Human or an Organization Unit.

The *Behavioural Perspective* basically describes the control flow and the logical sequence of elements to be executed in a process. It includes synchronization, sequence, iterations, decision-making conditions, entry and exit criteria, etc. The basic element of this perspective is Control Object (such as constraints, pre-conditions, post-conditions, triggers, performance indicators, etc.).

The *Informational Perspective* describes the informational entities which are generated, consumed, or exchanged within a process or an activity. It also includes both their structure and the relationships among them. This perspective contains mainly the generic class Resource with its derived class Material Resource (and the specialization class Physical Knowledge Support), Event, InputObject, OutputObject and Collaboration Protocol. In fact, for its accomplishment, an Organizational Activity uses Input Objects (such as materials, data or information), mobilizes Material Resources (or tangible resources) (such as documentary, informational, material and software resources, etc.) and/or immaterial (intangibles) to produce Output Objects (like data, information, services, results, outputs) and under the influence of Control Objects. It can be triggered by Events (which may take various forms), which can in turn produce Events. A Contingency is an external and unpredictable event that influences the process execution (the elements produced or handled and decisions made). This type of events is responsible for determining the execution of unforeseen activities [43]. It should be emphasized that the output or the result of an activity may be an input, an event, a resource for the successor activity or another activity. It can also be a terminal output standing for the achievement of a product awaited by an internal or external client to the organization. Moreover, information object and data object form the basis for knowledge distribution and generation. The creation of new knowledge is done by externalization or combination [33]. It is stored by electronic media or written down in documents.

The *Intentional Perspective* provides an overview perspective of the process and captures important BP context information [26,34]. This perspective (also called BP context perspective [34]) describes major BP characteristics (such as goals and their measures, strategies, the deliverables, the process type and the customer), in order to ensure the BP flexibility. The meta-model elements of this perspective are inspired by COOP. It comprises mainly the generic classes `Distal Intention`, `Collective Distal Intention`, `Objective`, `Organizational Objective`, `Sensitive Business Process` and `Knowledge Intensive Process` (which are some process types), `Output Object` (deliverables), `Control Object` (performance measures) and `Client`. Each `Business Process` meets an `Organizational Objective` (which is an `Objective`) intentionally defined. An `Objective` is an intentional description of the results to be achieved by the completion of the process [54]. From an ontological viewpoint, an `Objective` is defined as a `Proposition` representing the conceptual content of a `Distal Intention`[7]. (A `Distal Intention` *hasForContent* an `Objective` [11] (see Fig. 2)). So, this process *isControlledBy* a `Distal Intention`, in particular an `Organizational Distal Intention` which is a `Collective Distal Intention`. (Then the `Business Process` is a `Deliberate Action` [11]). Every `Organizational Distal Intention` *hasForContent* an `Organizational Objective`. Depending on whether the content of a `Collective Distal Intention` or an `Individual Distal Intention`, an `Objective` can be either an `Individual Objective` or a `Collective Objective`. In the case where a `Collective Objective` *isValidFor* an `Organization`, then it is an `Organizational Objective` which can be either a `Strategic Objective` or an `Operational Objective`. `Strategic Objectives` are long-term objectives that express the organization's strategy. While `Operational Objectives` contribute to the achievement of `Strategic Objectives` (thus, to achieve a strategic objective, we must achieve the operational objectives that compose it). Concrete *Measures* describe the achievement of goals (objectives). Indeed, various performance indicators can be identified, according to the objectives assigned to the process, each focusing on a different aspect (cost, time, quality, capacity, etc.). In this case, `Control Object` may be located in the behavioral perspective as well as in intentional perspective. Each `Business Process` must provide a result which has a value to the organization's clients. The result represents the outputs (deliverables) which are either services or products carried out following the BP execution. Then, `Output Object` can be located in the behavioral perspective as well as in intentional perspective. A `Business Process` satisfies one or more `Clients`. A `Client` is an `Agentive Entity` which uses the service of another `Agentive Entity` (the provider) (the client represents the agent benefiting from the result of the process). It can be either internal or external to the `Organization`. Therefore, a `Business Process` is more precisely a `Culminated Process` which, when successfully carried out, culminates in a `Result` which is useful for a `Client` [11]. Besides, a `Business Process` has a certain process type. In COOP, the authors [11] distinguish different categories of BPs classified according to several dimensions: *granularity*, *value*,

---

[7] According to [55], an intention is a complex process whose content includes a representation of action, thus allowing an agent to be directed to that action. A distal intention plans the action (before its initiation) and then rationally controls to guide it and determine its success. This is a process whose content has an objective and a plan [54].

affiliation, repetition and *piloting* (see Fig. 1). For instance, according to the level of process granularity, we distinguish between First Level Process and Organizational Sub Process. Depending on the affiliation dimension of the agents operating in the process, the authors [11] specify three process classes[8]: *Internal Process, External Process* and *Partial ExternalProcess*. Additionally, we propose to distinguish two other categories of BP according to the *complexity* dimension: Sensitive Business Process and Knowledge Intensive Process [14].

The **Knowledge perspective** provides an overview perspective of the organizational and individual knowledge mobilized by an organization as well as the knowledge flow proceeding within and between organizations. It aims to describe all relevant aspects related to KM. Then, it emphasizes knowledge collection, organization, storage, transfer, sharing, creation and reuse among process participants. Therefore, it specifies the different opportunities of knowledge conversion This perspective distinguishes also between knowledge used to perform (BP) and knowledge created as a result of BP activities. It identifies the different types of knowledge (tacit/explicit dimension) mobilized and created by each type of activity, the different sources of knowledge (where tacit and explicit knowledge is captured), their localization (where they are created or stored and where they are used), inexplicit tacit knowledge and persons holding them, their nature and their organizational coverage (individual/collective dimension). The Knowledge aspects of the meta-model are shown in Fig 2. This perspective contains mainly the generic classes Immaterial Resource, Knowledge, Tacit Knowledge, Explicit Knowledge, Expert and Physical Knowledge Support. In fact, An Organizational Activity mobilizes and produces different types of Knowledge. Knowledge is seen as an Immaterial Resource (or Intangible Resource) of an organization. It is a fluid mix of framed experiences, values, contextual information, and expert insights that provides a framework for evaluating and incorporating new experiences and information. Knowledge can be further refined in explicit (formalized) and tacit (or implicit) knowledge (resided in humans). Tacit knowledge is a Knowledge rooted in action and proper to a specific context, which makes it highly personalized. This form of "personal" knowledge derives from capabilities, experience, mental models and perspectives of process participants and is embedded in their work practices and decision choices. It cannot be easily formalized or shared through an externalization process. It represents the "know-how of an organization". While Explicit knowledge is easy to communicate, share and store, as can be formalized and systematized in a common representation format (e.g., databases, documents, etc.),

---

[8] - An **Internal process** is a Business Process all partsOf which *haveForAgent* either Humans which *areAffiliatedTo* the Business Organization or Organization Units which *areAUnitsOf* the Business Organization. - An **External process** is a Business Process all *partsOf* which *haveForAgent* Agentive Entities which are not *AffiliatedTo* nor *UnitsOf* the Business Organization. - A **partial external** process is a Business Process which has at least one Part which *hasForAgent* an Agentive Entity which is not *AffiliatedTo* the Business Organization and which has at least one Part which *hasForAgent* an Agentive entity which *isAffiliatedTo* the Business Organization.

available, usable and reusable by the organization stakeholders. Explicit knowledge may exist unrelated to their original holder and the achievement of an activity. In organizations, it often becomes embedded and represented, not only in documents or knowledge repositories (data and knowledge bases), but also in organizational routines, processes, practices, norms, etc.

Each kind of Knowledge can be held individually or collectively and is localized in different knowledge sources. The main difference between human knowledge and collective/organizational knowledge is that individual knowledge is combination of individual's own knowledge, experience and skills, but organizational knowledge is a sum of individuals' knowledge which integrates a company's experiences and company-specific knowledge, and already existing in organizational systems, decision-making procedures, processes, products, rules, and culture. Tacit Knowledge is owned by one or more experts. An Expert is a Human who has knowledge, represented, for instance, by his skills, experience, capacities in performing an activity. He carries out Actions with high levels of expertise, creativity and innovation. An Individual Tacit Knowledge is a personal implicit knowledge, which *is held by* one Expert. It is linked to the mental models, talents, innate or acquired experiences and skills, abilities, individual tricks, trades secrets, etc. A Collective Tacit Knowledge *is held by* at least two Experts (which constitute a Collective) and mobilized through a Collective Action. It manifests itself in routines which may be shared and exchanged through direct communication with others. An Individual Explicit Knowledge *is born by* a Human. Its dissemination depends on the person who owns the document. A Collective Explicit Knowledge *is born by* a Collective (i.e. an Organization). It is a formalized knowledge, easily shared, usable and reusable at the collective level of the organization. Its coverage can be global (e.g. the enterprise culture) or partial (i.e. related to structure). Explicit Knowledge is often stored in one or more Physical Knowledge Support (i.e. media, as documents, computer system, etc.) enabling their capitalization, representation, dissemination and sharing among stakeholders of the organization. It is a way for formalizing and storing explicit knowledge. A Physical Knowledge Support is a Material Resource (informational resource), having source of knowledge information interpreted and mobilized by the agents (operating in the BP) during the execution of their activities (these supports transmit not only information, but also significance). From this viewpoint, knowledge is useful for interpreting information (giving meaning) while information is useful for transferring knowledge.

Thus, the concept Physical Knowledge Support belongs to the knowledge and informational perspectives. Besides, a Collaborative Organizational Activity mobilizes and produces new Collective Knowledge (tacit and/or explicit) by a set of interactions (between individuals). A Critical Organizational Activity mobilizes different types of knowledge: Individual Knowledge or Collective Knowledge (tacit and/or explicit) poorly mastered to solve critical determining problems; expertise; rare knowledge held by a very small number of experts; tacit knowledge which is not explainable, very important organizational tacit knowledge, etc. Besides, this activity may threaten Sensitive Business Processes. It should be noted that some classes are shared by different perspectives. For instance, the `Collaborative Organizational Activity` class belongs to all perspectives.

Once modeled, the SBPs can be graphically represented, using the most popular standard for BPM, BPMN 2.0, in order to localize the knowledge that is mobilized and created by these processes. We selected BPMN as the notation for BPM, because it incorporates requirements for SBP modeling better than other formalisms[9], presenting the broadest coverage of the set of BPM4KI concepts. However, despite its strength representation, this notation does not support the key concepts of BPM4KI (as `Sensitive Business Process`, `Collective Action`, `Tacit Knowledge`, `Critical Organizational Activity`, `Expert`, etc.). In order to overcoming the shortcomings of BPMN 2.0 to represent explicitly the relevant SBP aspects, it should be necessary to extend this notation with several additional concepts. This extension must take into consideration, on the one hand, the knowledge dimension, and on the other hand, integrate the new concepts of BPM4KI to represents issues relevant at the intersection of KM and BPM. So, to achieve this goal and reach a rich and expressive representation of SBPs, we start by defining and integrating some specific graphical icons relating to each new proposed concept (see Table 1). In this paper we use these new icons in Sect. 5 to highlight the proposed extension.

Table 1. Graphical representation of the different extended elements

Concept	Sensitive Business Process	Critical Organizational Activity	Collaborative Activity	Expert	Knowledge	Individual Tacit Knowledge	Collective Tacit Knowledge	Individual Explicit Knowledge	Collective Explicit Knowledge
Notation									

6 Evaluation of BPM4KI: Case Study

In this section, we describe a case study carried out to verify usefulness and applicability of the proposed meta-model. Precisely, we aim to evaluate the potential of BPM4KI in providing an adequate understanding and representation of a SBP, as well as in improving the knowledge identification.

---

[9] Since in practice, Process-oriented knowledge modeling approaches are very incipient and used less often than BPM formalisms, we are particularly interested in adapting and extending the widely applicable modeling notations that can represent KM issues in BP models clearly and with a sufficient level of details. In brief, the best characteristics of BPMN are: (i) BPMN is the de facto standard for BPM; (ii) BPMN is very expressive and rich of concepts for modeling process logic, decision points, control flows, various processes and event types, offering a very complex expressive model of BPs; (iii) BPMN is a simple notation, easy to use and readily understandable by all business stakeholders; (iv) BPMN is one of the most recent BPMLs, so it is grounded on the experience of earlier BPMLs, which ontologically makes it one of the most complete BPMLs; (v) BPMN is supported by almost all popular BPM tools; (vi) BPMN is extensible, etc.

6.1   Case Study Description

The case study was conducted in a real practical scenario in the context of the Association of Protection of the Motor-disabled of Sfax-Tunisia (ASHMS). This organization is characterized by highly dynamic, unpredictable, complex and highly intensive
knowledge actions. We are particularly interested in the early care of the disabled
children with cerebral palsy (CP). A depth analysis of the care has been made by [32].
In fact, the amount of medical knowledge mobilized and produced during this medical
care process is very important, heterogeneous and recorded on various scattered
sources. One part of this knowledge is embodied in the mind of health professionals.
Another part, is preserved in the organizational memory as (Reports, Medical Records,
Data Bases, Therapeutic Protocols and Clinical Practice Guidelines). The created
knowledge stems from the interaction of a large number of multidisciplinary healthcare
professionals with heterogeneous skills, expertise and specialties (such as neonatology,
neuro-pediatrics, physical therapy, orthopedics, psychiatry, physiotherapy, speech
therapy, and occupational therapy) and located on geographically remote sites (see
Fig. 3) [32].

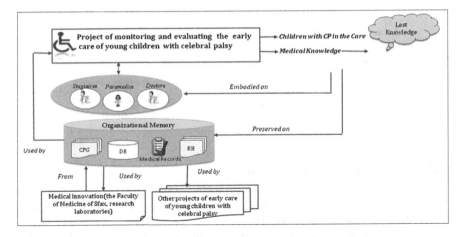

Fig. 3.   General synoptic flow of knowledge

The raised problem concerns on the one hand, the insufficiency and the difficulty to
localize and understand the medical knowledge that is necessary for decision-making,
and on the other hand, the loss of knowledge held by these experts during their
scattering or their departure at the end of the treatment. Thus, the ASHMS risks losing
the acquired know-how for good and transferring this knowledge to new novices if ever
no capitalization action is considered. Capitalizing on all the ASHMS's knowledge
requires important human and financial investments. Furthermore, the resources that
dispose this organization are limited. That's why the ASHMS should focus on only the
so called "crucial knowledge", that is the most valuable/important knowledge. This
permits particularly to save time and money. As presented in [9], "*Identifying crucial*

knowledge can reduce the costs of capitalization operation because it restricts the scope of knowledge to preserve. It is the same for their availability to users and for updating them".

Our main objective consists in improving the localization, identification and sharing of different types and modalities of crucial medical knowledge necessary for performing the medical care process of children with CP. In fact, this SBP is made up of several sub-processes. It consists of a succession of many actions in the form of medical and paramedical examinations and evaluations. As an example, we mention: Process related to neonatology care, process related to neuro-pediatric care, process related to physiotherapy, etc. These processes require taking into consideration certain medical information contained in the medical records as well as certain medical knowledge (results of para-clinical exams, hospitalization reports, medical records, practice guidelines, etc.). A rich and expressive representation of the SBP modeled according to BPM4KI improves the localization and identification of the crucial knowledge that is mobilized by the critical activities. Moreover, it allows the various stakeholders involved in the medical processes to preserve, share and transfer the tacit knowledge as well as to evaluate the amount of lost knowledge if a expert leaves the organization (in order to identify which tacit knowledge in this case should be trans-formed into explicit knowledge).

6.2   The SBP Modeling

In this study, we take into consideration the results of experimentation of the methodology SOPIM proposed by [10] for the early care of children with CP. We recall that the proposed multi-criteria methodology was conducted and validated in the ASHMS organization and aims at evaluating and identifying SBPs for knowledge localization.

We have opted for the SBP "Process related to the neuropediatric care of a child with CP" to illustrate and evaluate the potential of the BPM4KI with regard to its applicability and capability of making all relevant knowledge embedded in a SBP explicit. Indeed, this BP is very complex in terms of business domains/skills (internal and external organizational units involved in the BP), agents and experts operating in the BP, neuro-pediatric fields, number of collaborative organizational activities, number of critical organizational activities, mass of knowledge mobilized by each type of activity, large amount of knowledge produced by each type of activity, number of material/informational resources (e.g. physical knowledge supports) mobilized by each type of activity, etc. Some of its activities are very dependent on the participants experience, expertise and creativity.

Furthermore, in order to observe the practical applicability of the proposed for-malism, we illustrate, in Fig. 4, a SBP model extract of the neuro-pediatric care process using BPMN 2.0, enriched with the knowledge dimension (modeled according to BPM4KI). We have opted for the open source modeling tool Aris Express 2.4 [56]. As stated above, BPMN 2.0 specification does not, however, provide primitives to explicitly represent all relevant aspects related to knowledge dimension in BP models. To remedy for the shortcomings, we have integrated some specific graphical icons in

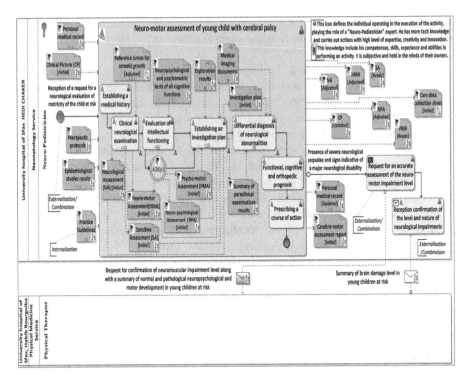

Fig. 4. An extract of the graphical representation model of the process of neuropediatric care of a child with CP carried out with ARIS Express 2.4 tool

the form of BPMN modeling elements (see Table 1). The BPMN SBP model is evaluated and validated by two Neuro-Pediatricians, that were interviewed individually.

During our experimentation, we have identified different types of medical knowledge mobilized and created by each critical activity related to the SBP of neuro-pediatric care. We have distinguished missing or poorly mastered knowledge (individual or collective) necessary to resolve critical problems, expertise, unexplainable tacit knowledge and mastered knowledge necessary and relevant to the proper functioning and development of the activity or produced by the activity. We have also identified the different sources of knowledge, their localization, actors who hold the knowledge, the places where they are usable or used, their nature (like experience, basic knowledge, general knowledge), their degree of formalization (tacit/explicit dimension), their organizational coverage (individual/collective dimension), as well as their quality (perfect or imperfect).

For instance, the knowledge A_3K_{p1} related to "Synthesis assessment of neuro-and psycho-cognitive, neurosensory and praxo-gnosic development of young children at risk and its disorders" is produced by the critical activity A_3 "Qualitative and quantitative evaluation of the intellectual functioning". Note that this materialized/externalized knowledge is created as a result of the activity execution by the Neuro-pediatrician, during which he interacts with information (i.e. source of knowledge information) related to the child at risk (based on his previous experiences and tacit knowledge) to generate and communicate his own knowledge. A_3K_{p1} is stored in the following physical media: the neurological assessment sheet, neuropsychological assessment, the sensitive assessment sheet and the neuro-motor assessment. These physical media of knowledge are located internally within the Neonatology service in the University Hospital Hedi Chaker, precisely in the various archives drawers or patients' directories. A_3K_{p1} is of a scientific, technical and measure nature which is related to patients. It represents a collective explicit knowledge, part of which can be represented in the form of an individual explicit knowledge recorded on the care data collection sheet of the Neuro-pediatrician. This knowledge is imperfect (general, incomplete and uncertain). A_3K_{p1} is mobilized by the activity A_4 "Establishing an investigation plan".

Therefore, the relevance of extending BP models with the knowledge dimension is manifold:

1. Enhance the localization and identification of the crucial knowledge mobilized and produced by the critical activities:

   - Illustrating the knowledge and its sources that are necessary for the execution of BP activities and are generated, created and/or modified as a results of activities.
   - Illustrating the knowledge localization (where knowledge can be obtained and clearly stated) as well as experts who hold the (tacit) knowledge.
   - Illustrating the way in which specific knowledge flows among the activities, or how a specific source is used and modified through the activities.
   - Illustrating transfers of knowledge between sources, and among activities as well as the different opportunities of knowledge conversion (such as internalization, externalization, combination and socialization).
   - Defining the knowledge that is being captured or obtained from specific sources.
   - Possibility to evaluate the amount of lost knowledge if a person-owner of knowledge- leaves the organization.

2. A deeply characterizing of the identified knowledge to determine which ones are more crucial to be exploited:

   - Illustrating the nature and degree of formalization of knowledge
   - Illustrating the organizational coverage of knowledge, their quality, etc.

7   Conclusion and Future Work

This work presented BPM4KI, a BP meta-model to improve the localization and the identification of crucial knowledge, that covers all relevant perspectives for a complete an precise conceptualization of any Sensitive Business Processes (SBP): the knowledge, functional, organizational, behavioral, informational and intentional dimension. The proposed meta-model is semantically rich and well founded on the core ontology COOP [11]. It was evaluated through a case study from medical domain that explored the conceptualization and graphical representation of a SBP.

Various research lines will be performed to complete and deepen the so-called problematic of knowledge identification mobilized by SBPs. Firstly, we consider guiding and justifying the choice of the most suitable formalism for SBPs representation (i.e. the BPMN 2.0 notation) to characterize and improve the knowledge localization. One way of evaluation is to use the conceptualization defined by BPM4KI as a basis for a deeper comparative analysis of the adequacy of both specific BPM formalisms and supporting tools that are able to cover all or at least most relevant elements of a SBP. A further evaluation considering the use of a multi-criteria decision making approach [57] is another direction for future work. In this context, BPM4KI should help to construct a coherent family of criteria for the evaluation of the expressiveness of BPM formalisms/approaches.

Secondly, we consider improving the extended "knowledge perspective" of BPM4KI, relying on core ontology, such as COOK, a core ontology of know-how and knowing-that proposed by [58] in order to take into consideration issues relevant at the intersection of KM and BPM as well as reduce the gap between them.

Thirdly, BPM4KI may be adopted as a basis to enhance existing BPM formalisms as it already provides the main concepts of mainstream BPM formalisms. To achieve this goal, we consider proposing an extension of the BPMN 2.0 specification for KM. Precisely, we intend to integrate and implement the proposed BPM4KI meta-model in the BPMN 2.0 meta-model. This extension must take into consideration, on the one hand, the knowledge dimension, and on the other hand, integrate the new concepts of BPM4KI (and represents issues relevant at the intersection of KM and BPM). In practice, the specification of the BPMN extension will be integrated into a more general framework supporting the SBPs modeling. This framework advocates a MDA (Model Driven Architecture) approach [59] considering (i) at the CIM level, a specific meta-model, the BPM4KI meta-model for modeling SBPs, (ii) at the PIM level, an extension of the BPMN meta-model for visualizing and user validating the modeled SBPs to identify the knowledge, and finally, (iii) at the PSM level, several meta-models for implementing the different extensions (e.g. XPDL and BPEL meta-models). A full and rich representation of BPs (modeled according to BPM4KI) shall allow a better localization and identification of crucial knowledge on which we must capitalize.

References

1. Hammer, M., Champy, J.: Reengineering the corporation: a manifesto for business revolution. Harper Business, New York (1993)
2. Davenport, T.H.: Process Innovation: Reengineering Work Through Information Technology. Harvard Business Press, Boston (1993)
3. Curtis, B., Kellner, M.I., Over, J.: Process modelling. Commun. ACM **35**(9), 75–90 (1992)
4. Melao, N., Pidd, M.: A conceptual framework for understanding business processes and business process modelling. Int. J. Info. Syst. **10**, 105–129 (2000)
5. Nurcan, S., Etien, A., Kaabi, R., Zoukar, I., Rolland, C.: A strategy driven business process modelling approach. Int. J. Business. Proc. Manag. **11**(6), 628–649 (2005)

6. Mili, H., Tremblay, G., Boujaoude, G., Lefebvre, E., Elabed L., Boussaidi, G.El.: Business process modeling languages: sorting through the alphabet soup. ACM. Comput. Surv. **43**(1), 4:1–4:50 (2010)
7. Grundstein, M.: From capitalizing on company knowledge to knowledge management. In: Morey, D., Maybury, M. (eds.): Knowledge Management, Classic and Contemporary Works, Chapt. 12, pp. 261–287. The MIT Press, Cambridge (2000)
8. Tseng, B., Huang, C.: Capitalizing on knowledge: a novel approach to crucial knowledge determination. IEEE Trans. Syst., Man, Cybernetics: Syst. Humans **35**, 919–931 (2005)
9. Saad, I., Grundstein, M., Sabroux, C.: Une méthode d'aide à l'identification des connaissances cruciales pour l'entreprise. Revue SIM **14**(3), 43–79 (2009)
10. Turki, M., Saad, I., Gargouri, F., Kassel, G.: A Business Process Evaluation Methodology for Knowledge Management based on multi-criteria decision making approach. In: Saad, I., Sabroux, C.R., Gargouri, F. (eds.) Information Systems for Knowledge Management. Wiley-ISTE, Chichester (2014a). ISBN: 978-1-84821-664-8
11. Turki, M., Kassel, G., Saad, I., Gargouri, F.: COOP: A Core Ontology of Organization's Processes for group decision making. J. Decis. Syst. **23**(1), 55–68 (2014)
12. Scholl, W., Konig, C., Meyer, B., Heisig, P.: The Future of Knowledge Management. An international Delphi Study. J. Knowl. Manage. **8**(2), 19–35 (2004)
13. Suyeon, K., Hyunseok, H., Euiho, S.: A process-based approach to knowledge flow analysis: a case study of a manufacturing firm. Knowl. Process Manage. **10**(4), 260–276 (2003)
14. Gronau, N., Korf, R., Müller, C.: KMDL-capturing, analyzing and improving knowledge-intensive business processes. J. Univ. Comput. Sci. **11**, 452–472 (2005)
15. Heisig, P.: The GPO-WM® method for the integration of knowledge management into business processes. In: International Conference on Knowledge Management, Graz, Austria, pp. 331–337 (2006)
16. Zhaoli, Z., Zongkai, Y.: Modeling Knowledge Flow using Petri net. In: IEEE International Symposium on Knowledge Acquisition and Modeling Workshop, China, pp. 142–146 (2008)
17. Zhang, X., Li, M.: Workflow-based knowledge flow modeling and control. Chin. J. Softw. **16**(2), 184–193 (2005)
18. Woitsch, R., Karagiannis, D.: Process oriented knowledge management: a service based approach. J. Univ. Comput. Sci. **11**(4), 565–588 (2005)
19. Weidong, Z., Weihui, D.: Integrated Modeling of Business Processes and Knowledge Flow Based on RAD. In: IEEE International Symposium on Knowledge Acquisition and Modeling, China, pp. 49–53 (2008)
20. Supulniece, I., Businska, L., Kirikova, M.: Towards extending BPMN with the knowledge dimension. In: Bider, I., Halpin, T., Krogstie, J., Nurcan, S., Proper, E., Schmidt, R., Ukor, R. (eds.) BPMDS 2010 and EMMSAD 2010. LNBIP, vol. 50, pp. 69–81. Springer, Heidelberg (2010)
21. Businska, L., Kirikova, M.: Knowledge dimension in business process modeling. In: Nurcan, S. (ed.) CAiSE Forum 2011. LNBIP, vol. 107, pp. 186–201. Springer, Heidelberg (2012)
22. Businska, L., Supulniece, I., Kirikova, M.: On data, information, and knowledge representation in business process models. In: The 20th International Conference on Information Systems Development (ISD 2011), pp. 24–26. Springer, Edinburgh, Scotland (2011)
23. Sultanow, E., Zhou, X., Gronau, N., Cox, S.: Modeling of processes, systems and knowledge: a multi-dimensional comparison of 13 chosen methods. Int. Rev. Comput. Softw. **7**(6), 3309–3319 (2012)

24. Liu, D.R., Lai, D.R., Liu, C.H., Chih-Wei, L.: Modeling the knowledge-flow view for collaborative knowledge support. J. Know. Based. Syst. **31**, 41–54 (2012)
25. Netto, J.M, Franca, J.B.S., Baião, F.A., Santoro, F.M.: A notation for Knowledge-Intensive Processes. In: IEEE 17th International Conference on Computer Supported Cooperative Work in Design (CSCWD 2013), vol. 1, pp. 1–6 (2013)
26. Nurcan, S.: A survey on the flexibility requirements related to business processes and modeling artifact. In: Proceedings of the 41st Hawaii International Conference on System Sciences. IEE, Hawaii, USA, pp. 7–10, 378 (2008)
27. OMG: Business Process Modeling and Notation (BPMN). Version 2.0 (2011b). http://www.bpmn.org/
28. Kassel, G.: Integration of the DOLCE top-level ontology into the OntoSpec methodology (2005). CoRR abs/cs/0510050
29. Galton, A., Mizoguchi, R.: The water falls but the waterfall does not fall: New perspectives on objects, processes and events. Appl. Ontology **4**(2), 71–107 (2009)
30. Masolo, C., Borgo, S., Gangemi, A., Guarino, N., Oltramari, A.: WonderWeb Deliverable D18: Ontology Library (final). Technical report, LOA-ISTC, CNR (2003)
31. Bottazzi, E., Ferrario, R.: Preliminaries to a DOLCE ontology of organizations. Int. J. Bus. Proc. Integr. Manag. **4**(4), 225–238 (2009). C. Atkinson et al. (eds.). Special Issue on Vocabularies, Ontologies and Business Rules for Enterprise Modeling
32. Turki, M., Saad, I., Gargouri, F., Kassel, G.: Towards identifying sensitive processes for knowledge localization. In: International Conference on Collaboration Technologies and Systems (CTS 2011), pp. 224–232 (2011)
33. Nonaka, I., Takeuchi, H.: Knowledge-Creating Company: How Japanese Companies Create the Dynamics of Innovation. Oxford University Press, New York (1995)
34. List, B., Korherr, B.: An evaluation of conceptual business process modelling languages. In: ACM Symposium on Applied Computing (SAC 2006). ACM Press, France (2006)
35. OMG: unified modeling language (UML), version 2.0 (2011a). http://www.uml.org/
36. Schlenoff, C., Gruninger, M., Tissot, F., Valois, J.: The process specification language (PSL) overview and version 1.0 specification (2000). http://www.mel.nist.gov/psl/
37. Papavassiliou, G., Mentzas, G.: Knowledge modelling in weakly-structured business processes. J. Know. Manag. **7**(2), 18–33 (2003)
38. Oliveira, F.F.: Ontology Collaboration and its Applications. MSc Dissertation. Programa de Pós-Graduação em Informática, Universidade Federal do Espírito Santo, Vitória, Brazil (2009)
39. Strohmaier, M., Yu, E., Horkoff, J., Aranda, J., Easterbook, S.: Analyzing knowledge transfer effectiveness—an agent-oriented modeling approach. In: Proceedings of the 40th Hawaii International Conference on System Sciences, USA (2007)
40. Abecker, A.: DECORConsortium:DECOR—Delivery of Context- Sensitive Organizational Knowledge, E-Work and E-Commerce. IOS Press, Amsterdam (2001)
41. Schreiber, G., Akkermans, H., Anjewierden, A., Hoog, R., Shadbolt, N., De Velde, W.V., Wielinga, B.: Knowledge Engineering and Management: The Common KADS Methedology. MIT Press, Cambridge (2002)
42. Donadel, A.C.: A method for representing knowledge-intensive processes. M.Sc. dissertation. Programa de Pós-Graduação em Engenharia e Gestão do Conhecimento, Universidade Federal de Santa Catarina, Brazil (2007)
43. França, J.B.S., Santoro, F.M., Baião, F.A.: Towards Characterizing Knowledge-Intensive Processes. In: IEEE International Conference on Computer-Supported Cooperative Work in Design (CSCWD 2012), Wuhan, China (2012)

44. Gronau, N., Weber, E.: Management of knowledge intensive business processes. In: Desel, J., Pernici, B., Weske, M. (eds.) BPM 2004. LNCS, vol. 3080, pp. 163–178. Springer, Heidelberg (2004)
45. Wand, Y., Weber, R.: An ontology model for an information system. IEEE Trans. Softw. Eng. **16**(11), 1282–1292 (1990)
46. Tove ontology project: University of Toronto Enterprise Integration Laboratory (2002). http://www.eil.utoronto.ca/enterprise-modelling/tove/index.html
47. Morley, C., Berthier, D., Maurice-Demourioux M.: Un modèle de processus métier pour les nouvelles formes d'organisation des activités. Actes du 11ème colloque de l'Association Information & Management, "Systèmes d'Information et Collaboration: Etat de l'Art et Perspectives", Luxembourg, pp. 7–9 (2006)
48. Pedrinaci, C., Domingue, J., Alves de Medeiros, A.K.: A core ontology for business process analysis. In: Bechhofer, S., Hauswirth, M., Hoffmann, J., Koubarakis, M. (eds.) ESWC 2008. LNCS, vol. 5021, pp. 49–64. Springer, Heidelberg (2008)
49. Saidani, O., Nurcan, S.: Business process modeling: a multi-perspective approach integrating variability. In: Bider, I., Gaaloul, K., Krogstie, J., Nurcan, S., Proper, H.A., Schmidt, R., Soffer, P. (eds.) BPMDS 2014 and EMMSAD 2014. LNBIP, vol. 175, pp. 169–183. Springer, Heidelberg (2014)
50. Cabral, L., Norton, B., Domingue, J.: The business process modelling ontology. In: 4th International Workshop on Semantic Business Process Management (SBPM 2009), Workshop at ESWC 2009, Crete, Greece (2009)
51. Aldin, L., De Cesare, S.: Semantic reuse of business process models via generalisation. In: MCIS, vol. Paper 48 (2011)
52. Farideh, H., Pericles, L., Frances, B., Joseph, B.: A Unified View of Business Process Modelling Languages. In: CAiSE (2014)
53. Oscar, M.R.-E., Martínez-García, A.I., Vizcaíno, A., Favela, J., Piattini, M.: Modeling and analysis of knowledge flows in software processes through the extension of the software process engineering metamodel. Int. J. Softw. Eng. Knowl. Eng. **19**(02), 185–211 (2009)
54. Kassel, G., Turki, M., Saad, I., Gargouri, F.: From collective actions to actions of organizations: an ontological analysis. In: Symposium Understanding and Modelling Collective Phenomena (UMoCop), University of Birmingham, Birmingham, England (2012)
55. Pacherie, E.: The phenomenology of action: A conceptual framework, In: Gallagher, S. (eds.) Elseiver Journal, pp. 179–217 (2007)
56. The IDS-Scheer website (2013). http://www.ids-scheer.com/
57. Roy, B., Bouyssou D. Aide multicritère à la décision: méthodes et cas, Economica Paris (1993)
58. Ghrab, S., Saad, I., Kassel, G., Gargouri, F.: An ontological framework for improving the model of contribution degree of knowledge. In: International Conference on Knowledge Management, Information and Knowledge Systems (KMIKS 2015), Tunisia, pp. 45–58 (2015)
59. OMG. MDA Guide Version 1.0.1 (2003). http://www.omg.org/cgi-bin/doc?omg/03-06-01

Semantic Technologies for the Integration of Methods into an Enterprise Architecture

Peter Rosina[✉] and Bernhard Bauer

Software Methodologies for Distributed Systems, Institute of Computer Science,
University of Augsburg, Universitätsstr. 6a, 86135 Augsburg, Germany
{peter.rosina,bernhard.bauer}@ds-lab.org

Abstract. In order to face today's challenges in product development, like product complexity, variability and a shortening of development cycles, for instance, in the automotive domain, the Product Development Process (PDP) tends to entail more and more virtual tasks instead of physical, conventional ones, for example, implemented by Computer Aided x (CAx) technologies. The introduced novel approach promotes this transformation by supporting the appropriate stakeholders in formalizing, analyzing, assessing, comparing and hence selecting the most suitable methods, like physical and virtual design methods or CAx methods, that are utilized to execute these tasks.

The separation of knowledge types by applying Semantic Technologies, like ontologies, rules and queries, enables the appropriate roles to manage this knowledge independently and in their own way, because (conceptual) domain knowledge, (operational) business rules and an implemented data model have different lifecycles, scopes and owners. Furthermore, this particular domain and business knowledge features interdependencies with remaining enterprise knowledge, including business processes, organizational aspects and the IT architecture, which is usually modeled in an Enterprise Architecture (EA). Therefore, we showcase the implementation and integration of a method meta model, method contexts, like metrics and product knowledge, and an EA using Semantic Technologies to promote the transparency, interchange, interconnection, synchronization, sharing, reusability, re-deployment, up-to-dateness and maintenance of this particular knowledge and consequently analyses and assessments based on it.

Keywords: Methods · Modeling · Ontologies · SPARQL · Semantic web · Enterprise architecture

1 Introduction

Newly emerging and changing markets and their diverse demands lead to an increased product variability, increasing functional complexity and regulatory requirements in the product development. Simultaneously, however, costs and development times shall be reduced and qualities increased which causes conflicting goals. One contribution to cope with these challenges is the introduction

© Springer International Publishing Switzerland 2016
B. Shishkov (Ed.): BMSD 2015, LNBIP 257, pp. 62–79, 2016.
DOI: 10.1007/978-3-319-40512-4_4

and promotion of virtual product development which promises to overcome these defiances by substituting conventional, physical tasks with virtual ones. Thereby, the considered tasks can usually be repeated more often and performed faster at lower costs. Besides, Knowledge Management is simplified which increases process flexibility, because the regarded resources exist as data that can be managed and reused, supported by IT solutions, for instance, Computer Aided x (CAx) technologies. These tasks in a process are usually supported by numerous methods, for instance, design methods, which in turn are conducted by utilizing tools which implicates that one goal is to supersede conventional methods and the connected tools with virtual or digital ones. Naturally, a multitude of different disciplines and departments, for instance, physical crash tests and virtual simulations, have to collaborate, cooperate and interact during a product development process which entails the application of a large number of various technologies and working methods (*cf.* Sect. 3).

Our goal is to create an integrated meta model that depicts this domain of methods, technologies and tools in order to support stakeholders in their daily work. This approach has already been introduced in [1] and the work in hand features an extended implementation section, especially focusing on the queries and analyses based on integrated method and EA knowledge bases (KBs). Nowadays, a method selection for a defined purpose, an analysis of the entirety of methods in a company and the method monitoring are mainly manual tasks, ever and anon assisted by basic IT documents, like spreadsheets. Formalizing this knowledge allow the involved roles to analyze methods along the product development process, for instance, for finding virtual replacements for physical tests. This meta model and the resulting ontology are introduced and explained in Sect. 4.

We realize our meta model, resulting ontologies and a prototypical application, following the ONTORULE approach [2], a methodology for creating and managing knowledge and logic based on ontologies and rules. This approach tackles challenges and provides solutions for the required knowledge acquisition, management and execution phases, related to various stakeholder roles. Using Semantic Web technologies (*cf.* Sect. 2.1) bears many advantages: on the one hand, it enables a clear separation of domain and business knowledge, that can be extended and modified by domain and business experts. On the other hand, this knowledge can be implemented and managed independently from the applications that process it.

Finally, in order to benefit mutually from the additional knowledge available in an enterprise, we illustrate how to combine our method meta model with an EA meta model in Sect. 5. The basics about EA are introduced earlier in Sect. 2.2. The implementation and evaluation is exemplified in Sect. 6 with selected queries and a brief introduction to a prototypical demonstrator showcasing the method meta ontology and its application. Furthermore, we discuss the opportunities that emerge by combining method and EA meta models. The final Sect. 7 then concludes this paper.

2   Basics

2.1   Semantic Web Technologies

Bringing the Semantic Web to fruition is an collaborative endeavor of various research groups, industrial partners and organizations pursuing the common goal to enrich the WWW with semantic data, thus transforming the web from an un- or semi-structured document based technology to a knowledge-centered one. [3] developed the vision of the Semantic Web in order to make the web's meaning machine-readable and -interpretable and hence integrate heterogeneous data and infer new information from existing KBs automatically. The according technologies and architecture are depicted in the prominent Semantic Web Stack in Fig. 1. However, we do not apply these technologies for the WWW, but for the enhancement and realization of enterprise models and their applications, which are usually non-public. The lower layers provide the technological basement for the subsequent upper layers. The highlighted layers' containing formats, i.e., RDFS, OWL [5], RIF [6] and SPARQL [7], serve as our technological foundation. This paper represents an excerpt of our ongoing work. Therefore, we focus on modeling ontologies with the knowledge representation language OWL and the query language SPARQL. OWL ontologies separate a terminological box (TBox), representing the ontological concepts, and the modeled individuals in the assertional box (ABox).

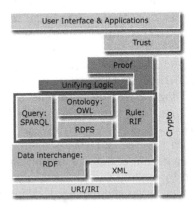

Fig. 1. Semantic Web layercake (after [4]).

2.2   Enterprise Architecture Management

Many enterprises' IT landscapes have reached a degree of complexity that is only hard to understand and manage [8]. Additionally, the IT needs to be aligned to business services and processes for an optimal and efficient support. For this purpose, many organizations have established an EA Management (EAM), motivated by the circumstance, that business is changing faster and faster due to shorter development cycles, adaptation and reorientation of business models and an overall need for improving the business and IT alignment. EAM helps companies to reduce costs for maintenance and developments when confronted with an increasing number of systems by analyzing "areas of common activity within or between organizations, where information and other resources are exchanged to guide future states from an integrated viewpoint of strategy, business and technology" [9]. Success factors are a goal-oriented adaption towards changing market and boundary conditions, the detection of redundancies and the definition, determination and an ongoing assessment of the various EAM Key Performance Indicators (KPIs) [10].

An EA's centerpiece is its meta model. It represents the diverse required aspects of a company's IT and business structures. These are, for instance, elements such as processes, services, organizational structures, data, applications and technologies. They are connected and organized via various relations and clusters which form the EA. The IT architecture can be further subdivided into architectures covering software and technology. Every company is unique, with diverging requirements, goals and focus areas. For this reason, a suitable, customized meta model is more important when introducing an EAM in a company than a tool which comes along with an inflexible standard meta model. An EA Framework (EAF) describes a methodology for developing an EA and its use during operation. It points out the relevant aspects and focuses that an enterprise should consider when creating information systems. Some examples for EAFs are *The Open Group Architecture Framework (TOGAF)* [11], *ISO 19439:2006* or the *US Federal EAF*, to name just a few [12].

TOGAF, together with ArchiMate [13], serves as the foundation for our EA meta model. It provides a methodology for the design, planning, development, implementation and maintenance of an EA [11]. It does not feature a specific model the companies can use, but offers meta models and guidelines that should be applied autonomously. TOGAF partitions an EA into four main architecture tiers: the *Business, Data, Application* and *Technology architecture*. The *Data* and *Application Architecture* are part of the *Information Systems Architecture*. In this paper, we mainly focus on the business level and its relations to the information systems, for instance by dealing with business strategy, processes, organizational structure and business capabilities and the applications relevant for the execution of the business processes. The meta model along with suitable tools and an EAF allows the enterprise to document and monitor the business and IT architecture in a holistic way which enables the architects and managers to react faster to occurring changes in an agile enterprise. Furthermore, modeling the business and IT architecture leads to an increased transparency which in return drives the use of a common vocabulary in the company and hence reduces misunderstandings. Other benefits are the advancement of standardization, an improvement and assurance of quality, a reduction of IT costs and consequently an improved coping with risks.

Generally speaking, the above listed advantages should provide a fillip for any organization. However, introducing an EAM is especially worthwhile for big enterprises. Such an enterprise can even be an "extended enterprise", that "nowadays frequently includes partners, suppliers and customers", as well as internal business units [11]. On the one hand, small organizations shun the undertaking, because it is wedded to a lot of effort – time- and resource-wise. On the other hand, a big enterprise, with an historically evolved IT landscape and complex business processes, will see the most benefits from such an endeavor. In our work, we mainly focus on the business level and its relations to the information systems, for instance by dealing with business strategy, processes, organizational structure and the applications relevant for the execution of the tasks.

3   Related Work

Our model has been mostly influenced by the domain of CAx methods, in particular, our primary goal was to model and analyze CAD, CAE and CAT methods. However, we soon discovered, that a method meta model covering not only CAx, but a much bigger selection of working and design methods is of even greater value. Depending on the department or company, even of the same domain, e.g., automotive engineering, a method can be synonymous to a *tool*, a *process*, a kind of technique for solving or analyzing problems or a combination thereof. In software engineering, the term is usually associated with a *procedure*, i.e., a segment of a framework, of a software development methodology, e.g., the waterfall model or an agile development framework. This ambiguity impedes the communication between people with a different background and leads to unnecessary misunderstandings and coordination phases. Thus, a standardization of the semantics would be worthwhile.

Methods have been used for decades in the domain of Design Theory and Methodology – an approach for the methodical development of products by using "effective methods to support particular development steps and [guide users] to efficiently solve development tasks" [14]. However, according to [15], the industry only reluctantly adapts design methodological models and methods. By definition, a method is a systematic *procedure* for the *attainment* of something, for instance, for the attainment of [scientific] insights or practical results [16]. Because our running example originates from the automotive domain, we also incorporate domain specific method definitions and are inspired by existing method frameworks, e.g., from systems engineering and method development (*cf.* [17]). A method consists of one or many *procedures* that are interconnected by logical rules (*alternative, predecessor, successor*, etc.) [18,19]. Methods are prescriptive which means they are perceived as some kind of instruction or plan [20] and they cannot be applied universally, but *every method has a particular stage in the development process* where its execution offers the best outcome (*cf.* [21]). More precise, methods are used in development processes for supporting a systematic and *aimed execution of tasks* [20]. Additionally, plans and methods must be adapted to the specific situation they are used in which means that a method can produce entirely different results and qualities depending on its environment. Among others, this includes the user itself. They have different knowledge, experiences, skills, tendencies and their form on the day is variable as well. Furthermore, the quality *depends on the tools* that are used to execute a method, the type of *business process* a method supports and of course the *quality of its input parameters*. According to [22], methodical support should be coordinated with its respective boundary conditions. In particular, it should be differentiated between the boundary conditions of the *organizational and operational layers* [17]. Boundary conditions of the organizational kind include *role descriptions*, the mapping to *business processes, organizational structures* etc. The operational layer comprises information about the *tools* used to conduct the method, its *qualities, time consumption* and *costs*. [23] define the relations between the different method concepts in even more detail by defining the relations between them: methods can be vertically linked, thus creating *method chains* – the outcome of the previous method is the input for the next method. A *method alliance* on the other hand, is a horizontal composition of methods, i.e., a family of similar, alternative methods. Another important concept is the *perspective*, i.e., how methods are perceived and what level of detail and focus is presented to the user. Another significant aspect for the definition of methods, more precise for the framework of methods [23], is the *methods' structure*. According to [20], it is not a simple task to clearly classify methods and put them in some hierarchical structure. A kind of network or graph, e.g., an ontology, is best suited for this task, because single methods and their partial procedures can be applied in other methods as modules as well which "supports a flexible selection, adaption and combination of methods" [20].

A method typically consists of the five bullet points listed below [20]:

Purpose / Goal: A task in the development process which is supported by the method.

Situation: The scope, problem descriptions and boundary conditions the method is usually appropriate for.

Effect: Effects and side effects, that are attained by executing the method, i.e., the method's output.

Procedure: The performed steps when executing the method.

Tools: Form sheets, check lists, software, test beds, etc.

[24] have analyzed the selection, adaption and application of product development methods for the impersonal transfer of method know-how, which resulted in the Munich Model of Methods (MMM). It acts as the foundation for a method model which consists of method building blocks that are linked by method attributes. Furthermore, the model supports the implementation of *superior tasks* and *resources* and *support* (*cf.* Fig. 2) can be related to a procedure.

The MMM comprises various steps for applying a method. The diagram depicted in Fig. 2 is horizontally split into four phases. It juxtapositions method attributes and the method implementation during the *process action*. The first lane deals with the clarification of the method's use case scenario. The following lanes represent the method selection, its customization and its application. Vertically, the model is divided into different process building blocks, i.e., the requirements phase, boundary conditions and concerns concerning the method

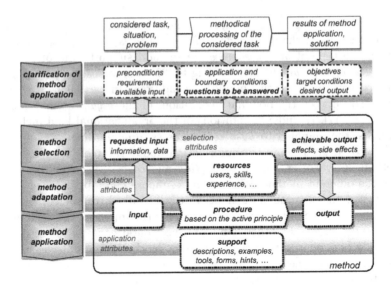

Fig. 2. The *Munich Model of Methods* from [20, 24].

application and of course the method's *goal* and *output* in the third vertical lane [25]. The single phases are supported by various *tools*. The majority of the depicted blocks are also covered by our method ontology, because the concepts concerning a method definition, like *input, output, goal, procedure* etc., necessarily have to be implemented in a meta model when dealing with design methods.

4   Method Meta Model

Our method meta model allows to semantically express the relations of tools and methods in combination with their tasks and processes on an abstract layer but also offers the possibility to describe concrete methods and their boundary conditions, e.g., the available time or budget.

Furthermore, our model allows to annotate the quality of their interactions, based on a maturity scale.

To achieve a common understanding, we created a method meta model that has been implemented with OWL later on, by working closely together with industrial partners and regarding state-of-the-art definitions and models. Further necessary knowledge that has been derived from our gathered requirements, i.e., to answer requested information, has been implemented in the form of queries and rules.

4.1   Method Ontology

The resulting method ontology's core structure is depicted in Fig. 3. We use the attribute "core", because this ontology can and should be extended with further ontologies. The ellipses in the figure represent ontology classes and the directed edges stand for properties, whereas their beginning is the property's domain and the arrowhead represents its range. Multiple properties between the same classes are consolidated into a single edge for a better overview; they are separated by commas between the edges' labels, though.

When talking about a method's maturity, quality or other concerns, we have to take into account, that a method can be applied at several points in a company's processes. Usually, the quality of data or resources rises over time, when the product itself is becoming more and more ready for series production. Assuming that we have a method A in our method KB which can be applied at two different points of time in the product development process, it is conceivable that this method is conducted using input resources of a differing quality. Vice versa, the method's application is resulting in similar, but of differing quality, resources which have to be available at a specific point of time in the process, e.g., a milestone. Nonetheless, it is still the same method, supported by the same tools and performed by similar procedures. Independently, a method can also be applied with the same, or at least the same quality and kind of, resources multiple times in a process. In order to distinguish between these (concrete) instances of a method and the general (abstract) method they have been derived from, we have introduced the concepts Concrete Method and Abstract Method. An abstract method M_a is a concept that defines a class of process-independent methods. A concrete method M_c is a concept that defines a class of methods, linked to a process action and derived from an abstract method M_a.

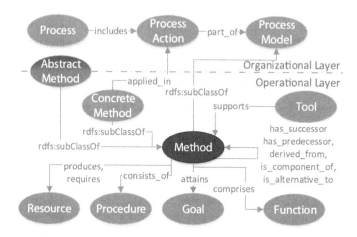

Fig. 3. Structure of the core method ontology.

In Fig. 3, both, the Abstract Method and the Concrete Method, are specializations of the concept Method. The Method is a specialized type of a Process model. Methods offer suggestions for specific tasks' sequences and the fashion on how these tasks are to be conducted [20]. Following the example of [26], a `Process Action` is equivalent to a task and hence, a `Concrete Method` is `applied_in` a specific task that is again related to a `Process`. Because both method types inherit the object properties of `Method`, we can model inter-relationships between `Concrete Methods` and respectively `Abstract Methods`, and can also state that some arbitrary `Concrete Method` is `derived_from` a specific `Abstract Method`. The remaining object properties allow us to model classes of methods such as method chains and alliances (`has_successor`, `has_predecessor`, `is_alternative_to`).

The three concepts at the bottom right of Fig. 3, namely `Procedure`, `Goal` and `Function`, are used to formally describe the methods' contexts, resp. its comprised procedures (*cf.* Sect. 3).

An instance of the class `Procedure` can either describe this method's procedure in textual form with the given RDFS properties (*rdfs:comment*, *rdfs:seeAlso*, *rdfs:label*, ...) or can be linked to more complex constructs, like a class `Document` (not part of the figure) which again may link to a document in the file system. Otherwise, if a method makes use of another method, object properties, like `is_component_of` shall be used.

Taking into account, that a method is always purposeful and therefore always focused on a solution of a problem or task [20], a `Method attains` the concept `Goal`. The method's `Goal` is the class that can describe the method's contribution to the enterprise's strategy or overall value creation. For example, we can create the classes `ProductAssurance` or `VehiclePropertyAssurance` as a `Goal`'s subclasses. When a specific method assures an arbitrary business product, the respective instance can be linked to the `Product` of a product ontology.

Usually, a `Method` is `supported` by a number of `Tools` that are to make its application more effective and efficient [20]. The term and therefore the respective class `Tool` covers a wide range of different auxiliaries or assistive equipment. In the domain of CAx, this can be all kind of testing equipment, physical implements, simulation or modeling software, but also arbitrary business software, statistical analyses or something totally different. Besides, the term also comprises simple assistive things, like forms, checklists etc.

4.2 Extending the Method Ontology

Up to now, the introduced method meta model allows to observe and compare methods based on their semantic context information, assumed the appropriate SPARQL queries have been implemented, for instance, the application of methods and tools during a specific process can be queried. Example queries can be found in Sect. 6. Additionally, we further extend the method ontology with other ontologies, covering metrics, resources, descriptions, enterprise vocabulary etc., in order to model and be able to analyze a company's method landscape in a holistic way.

Therefore, our core method ontology acts as an upper ontology that can be mapped to extending ontologies, like a process, resource and metrics ontology [1]. Independent from the chosen mapping paradigm between the ontologies, a company wants to model its own KB, covering their use cases. This domain ontology shall import the introduced method upper ontology. It specializes the concepts of the upper ontologies with domain specific ones and provides the TBox for our specialized assertions (ABox), i.e., *Concrete Method Instances* M_{c_u} and *Abstract Method Instances* M_{a_v}.

For instance, it can be used to provide a necessary taxonomy for the domain of CAx methods by introducing new concepts, e.g., `CAE Method`, `CAD Method` and `CAT Method` or a more general method, like *dc:MethodOfInstruction* from Dublin Core. Along with new kinds of methods, apposite, more specialized metrics or other arbitrary parameters can be introduced in the same way.

The knowledge for creating an own domain-specific ontology can either be acquired from existing company sources, like documents, or from experience, by interviewing experts as described in the ONTORULE methodology [2].

Besides, one of the big advantages of using Semantic Web technologies is having this vast amount of publicly available community ontologies, for instance, FOAF [27] or SKOS [28], that can be used as extensions, geared to the company's needs.

In order to compare methods based on their KPIs, for instance, the method's cost, input and output quality, maturity or duration, we developed a metrics ontology, covering the required quality attributes. Next to selection criteria, the metrics can act as indicator for strengths and weaknesses in the company's method framework and allows to detect gaps, e.g., processes that are scarcely supported by methods. This information is valuable for the strategic method development. The model can also be extended with arbitrary execution or evolution quality attributes (the so called "ilities"), like usability, reliability, manageability etc. Which kind of non-functional requirements to choose is facultative and up to the company's knowledge and methods engineers.

In accordance with the distinction between concrete and abstract methods (Sect. 4.1), we also distinguish between `Concrete Resources` and `Abstract Resources` in the developed resource ontology. This model covers the required inputs and produced outputs of our methods. When modeling an `Abstract Method`, the knowledge engineer can define the type of resources that are required or produced by this method, for instance, a general placeholder parameter for an abstract CAD model name. But not until the `Concrete Method` instance is modeled and assigned to a process action, the `Concrete Resources` can be named, for example, a particular drawing. Following current best practices, like the example of the W3C Product Modelling Incubator Group [29], our resource ontology, is influenced by a standard product model, namely STEP (AP 214/242) [30]. We decided not to model a product's inner structure, like PDM systems do, but to confine ourselves with more abstract concepts, because our method ontology's purpose is still to model only the meta level of the method landscape, i.e., analogous to the method concept, we treat the products as a black box.

Furthermore, we have used SKOS to manage the heterogeneity of the enterprise's vocabulary, i.e., methods and policies, like regulations [31]. This way, multiple labels can be annotated to all the ontology's entities which makes them generally intelligible, e.g., by enabling a multilingual use or making the semantics more comprehensible for people with differing professional backgrounds.

5   Enterprise Integration

Combining the knowledge about methods that are used in the enterprise with an EA in a product development division is mutually beneficial, because this way, the strategic, business and technical domains, represented in the EA, and their relationships on methods and vice versa can be inferred and analyzed. The mapping of these domains is performed using a mapping ontology while keeping both KBs separated. Consequently, the knowledge is exchanged and shared, but can be maintained independently.

Integrating our method meta model into an EAF bears many advantages. First of all, the combined meta models allow stakeholders to perform novel kinds of analyses, like impact analyses or discovering business, IT and method relations which in turn leads to a higher transparency. For example, the responsibility of the modeled actors and roles can be identified or the concern "Which system/application supports which methods?", as exemplified in Listing 2. This SPARQL query returns all results of the modeled methods that are supported by tools which again are implemented on a technology component, hence this query harnesses both ontologies and integrated knowledge in order to respond.

Furthermore, a company benefits from such a mapping approach through a concerted and defined meaning of the modeled concepts and vocabulary. OWL, especially the extension SKOS, supports the use of various labels, hence different vocabularies can be attached to the concepts, if required [31].

As a prerequisite for the integration of our method meta model into an EA meta model, we first need to obtain a formalized model. We have decided to use TOGAF and ArchiMate as a foundation for our EA because of their popularity and maturity. However, the Open Group does not provide a formalized model of their framework but considers TOGAF as an approach that should be further refined and implemented. Nevertheless, using ontologies and other Semantic Web technologies for the realization of EAs has been done for years now (cf. [32]). As a consequence and inspired by the above mentioned EA frameworks and meta models, we also created our own hybrid EA ontology using OWL. The developed meta model is depicted in Fig. 4, representing the known concepts from TOGAF and ArchiMate.

An important requirement for this EA ontology has been a suitable coverage of the concepts known from our core method meta ontology, together with the extended method ontologies. Thereby, we want to make use of newly generated relations, for instance, from methods to business objects or capabilities. The TOGAF Core Content Metamodel, combined with the Archimate Design approach fulfill this requirement and can be extended when specialized concepts are needed. We use the same generic concepts (OWL meta model) and extend the EA concepts with a more specific domain meta model.

After selecting the EA model, we need to establish mappings from our method ontologies' concepts and entities to the already existing elements in the EA.

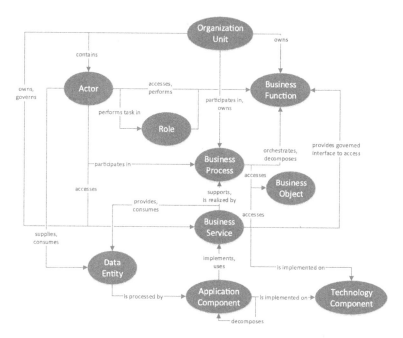

Fig. 4. Enterprise Architecture ontology based on TOGAF and ArchiMate meta models.

Technically, we could pursue different mapping techniques for combining our ontologies: we could use the other ontology's concept URIs directly, which is the standard way in Semantic Web. For example, by importing the ontology into ours, we can use *eam:Business_Process* as a replacement for our *method:Process* in the method ontology. However, a fundamental idea behind our integration is the retained separation of both KBs, because each domain – the method knowledge and the EA knowledge – is the particular responsibility of a dedicated organizational unit and hence, changes in the other ontology can be opaque. An alternative option would be to use an upper ontology, like UMBEL [33], which is certainly a reasonable choice when combining lots of domains. We do not need such an explosion of our domain for the scenario at hand, though. Another technique is to use feature models in order to select appropriate ontologies for a project [34]. These feature models contain the information about the possible, required and prohibited mappings between the single ontologies. Depending on the domains, a knowledge engineer wants to cover in his KB, various conceivable combinations are feasible, particularly if different ontology versions or even competing ontologies are at our disposal. The technique we have chosen to map the TBoxes is the use of an own mapping ontology for combining the various concepts, for instance, by using *owl:equivalentClass* or *rdfs:subClassOf*. This option can be implemented very fast, the mappings are traceable in one ontology, and it offers a good overview for a manageable amount of concepts, which is sufficient for the prototypical introduction presented in this paper.

Furthermore, next to matching the ontologies' TBoxes, we make statements about the individuals in the ABoxes that represent our model. The respective individuals, e.g., the modeled processes, are usually matched using OWL notation, as in *owl:sameIndividual*.

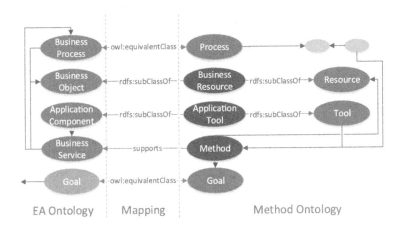

Fig. 5. Mapping of EA and method ontology.

When comparing our core method ontology's with our EA ontology's concept names, we encounter some obvious similarities which are candidates for concepts intersections. An equal or similar name, however, does not automatically infer synonymous semantics. The considered key concept `Process` from our method ontology and the concept `Business Process` from the EA ontology are identical, though, especially when regarding the TOGAF "Process Modeling Extension". The conceptual mapping between both ontologies is depicted in Fig. 5. We state that both concepts are equal, as illustrated in Listing 1, even though the different processes can vary in their granularity.

```
<rdf:Description
    rdf:about="http://ds-lab.org/EAM#Business_Process">
<owl:equivalentClass
    rdf:resource="http://ds-lab.org/Method#Process"/>
</rdf:Description>
```

Listing 1. Excerpt from the mapping ontology.

Our intentions for the methods' input and output `Resources` are semantically covered by the concept `Business Object`, known from the ArchiMate Business Layer Metamodel. This concept "represents a business entity (e.g. an invoice) that is used during the execution of a business process" [35]. Processes can perform all kind of create, read, update and delete (CRUD) operations on a business object, which either represents a virtual or physical object (or both) [13]. This applies to our methods' relations and the corresponding resources, as well. Nevertheless, only a subset of the modeled EA business objects are pertinent for the analysis of our meta method ontology and vice versa. Therefore, both concepts share the common subclass **Business Resource** (*cf.* Fig. 5). This subclass is modeled in a domain ontology, importing the upper method ontology.

The same reasoning applies to the concepts **Tool** and **Application Component**. A lot of business software is of no interest for the method domain and tools of the method domain can also include physical devices and implements. Consequently, we introduce the concept **Application Tool**. The various individuals in the ontologies' ABoxes are then mapped to their counterpart using properties that express the appropriate similarity.

Additionally, **Methods** represent a link between **Business Services**, process actions and tools. They express, how and when a business service can be applied to a specific process.

The final depicted mapping between both ontologies deals with the motivation extension, since the utilization of methods as well as stakeholders in EA intend to achieve a **Goal**. Albeit, we have to take into account that these goals may represent a different level of granularity.

The remaining concepts of the core meta method model feature no counterpart in the EA ontology, even though both models feature a concept named **Function**. A function in TOGAF "delivers business capabilities closely aligned to an organization [...]. Also referred to as 'business function"' [11], whereas a function in our meta method model represents an appropriated behavior of a technical system [17].

6   Implementation and Evaluation

The combination of an enterprise architecture with our method ontologies and the respective domain models enable methods engineers, enterprise architects, domain experts and other stakeholders to conduct novel kind of analyses. For example, we can compare and hence select the most suitable methods, based on the modeled KPIs, at specific process phases in the product development. Furthermore, a purposeful development and shutdown of methods is made possible by performing analyses based on the baseline and target architectures. The new concepts and contributions, namely the use of standard Semantic Web technologies, the EA integration, the evolved method meta model, along with the extending ontologies and the corresponding queries and rules, have been modeled, formalized and executed with a chosen set of test scenarios that showcase the proof of concept.

For this purpose, we formalized the ontologies depicted in Figs. 3 and 4 and aligned them as described in Sect. 5. Therefore, we have used the ontology editor Protégé [36]. An Apache Jena Fuseki server[1] is used as our store for the datasets and provides services for SPARQL queries and updates. For example, the query depicted in Listing 2 uses the integrated model in order to

---

[1] https://jena.apache.org/documentation/fuseki2/; retrieved 01/12/2016.

return methods, tools and the technology components they are implemented on. Thereby, this query makes use of the mapping between `method:Tool` and `eam:ApplicationComponent`, as explained in the former section.

```
   prefix  method:  <http://ds-lab.org/Method#>
2  prefix  eam:  <http://ds-lab.org/EAM#>
   prefix  :  <http://ds-lab.org/MethodIntegration#>
4
   SELECT ?m ?aC ?tC
6  WHERE {
     ?m a method:Method.
8    ?aC method:supports ?m.
     ?aC a eam:ApplicationComponent.
10   ?aC eam:isImplementedOn ?tC.
     ?tC a eam:TechnologyComponent.
12 }
```

Listing 2. SPARQL query for receiving methods, tools and their corresponding technology components.

Furthermore, we control our data quality with implemented queries. These constraints can either be specified as SPARQL ASK or SELECT statements and support the domain and knowledge engineers by detecting orphaned, missing or unutilized entities in our KBs, for instance, methods that are not used in any process can be detected with the query from Listing 3. These methods can either be **Abstract Methods** or **Concrete Methods**. First, we select all available methods, then we use negations, provided by the MINUS arguments, to calculate and remove the incompatible solution sets of methods that are either directly or indirectly connected to a **Process Action**.

```
   prefix  method:  <http://ds-lab.org/Method#>
2  prefix  :  <http://ds-lab.org/MethodIntegration#>

4  SELECT ?m
   WHERE {
6    ?m a method:Method.
     MINUS { ?cM method:derived_from ?m.
8       ?cM method:applied_in ?pA. }
     MINUS { ?m method:derived_from ?aM.
10      ?m method:applied_in ?pA. }
   }
```

Listing 3. SPARQL query for data quality control. Lists all unused methods.

An earlier, specialized version of the introduced method meta model, together with a prototypical implementation has been developed and published during the FP7 ONTORULE project [37]. It utilizes various method KPIs, like quality, costs and time consumption and plots these methods and metrics, based on their attribute values and their relation to the product development process which allows domain engineers to compare and assess their expected application results. This demonstrator proofs the feasibility and illustrates the benefits of our approach. The evaluation has been conducted at a large automobile manufacturer. It has been implemented using an alternative knowledge representation and rule language (ObjectLogic), though, covering a tailored meta model that realizes a particular automotive use case.

7 Conclusion

In this paper, we have shown how domain and business knowledge in the product development, especially method and EA knowledge, can be formalized and integrated using Semantic Technologies which leads to more transparency and awareness and hence enables analyses and the assessment of concerted knowledge in order to support decision-making in an enterprise. These decisions can be based on a method's context information, for instance, references to the processes they are used in, quality attributes, the methods' in- and outputs and the tools that support those methods. The defined method meta model is based on industrial insights as well as an elaborated literature research. As a consequence, it is on an abstract level and implemented as an upper ontology in order to be able to harmonize numerous method classifications from diverse backgrounds, for instance, from the CAx domain.

We developed, implemented and integrated an EA ontology with our method ontology, which bears many mutual benefits. Thereby, we can exploit relationships and dependencies between methods, processes, such as a PDP, IT, business objects and the enterprise strategy which increases their flexibility, quality and efficiency. For example, it allows predicating even more complex statements on expected qualities, costs, time consumption or other metrics and ensuing KPIs which is a strong motive for domain experts when comparing and hence selecting an appropriate method or even method-mixes best suited for the task at hand in the product development. In addition, it enables stakeholders to conduct further novel kinds of analyses, like the analysis of relationships on a strategic level, promoting a targeted method development and shutdown; on the business level, e.g., between roles, processes and methods; for rising data quality by finding blank spots, lacunae or duplicates; and also on a business to IT level, for instance, by providing an overview of the applied method software tools.

Using Semantic Technologies for this approach is very valuable, because the modeled knowledge can be verified, new knowledge can be inferred and external knowledge, like public Semantic Web ontologies, can be harnessed in the enterprise scenario. However, the primary reason has been the separation of domain knowledge, business knowledge and logic in order to support different lifecycles, scopes and knowledge owners which is beneficial for diversely evolving knowledge and variable innovation and maintenance cycles.

References

1. Rosina, P., Bauer, B.: Enterprise methods management using semantic web technologies. In: Shishkov, B. (ed.) Fifth International Symposium on Business Modeling and Software Design (BMSD). Scitepress, Milan (2015)
2. de Sainte Marie, C., Iglesias Escudero, M., Rosina, P.: The ONTORULE project : where ontology meets business rules. In: Rudolph, S., Gutierrez, C. (eds.) RR 2011. LNCS, vol. 6902, pp. 24–29. Springer, Heidelberg (2011)
3. Berners-Lee, T., Hendler, J., Lassila, O.: The semantic web. Sci. Am. **284**(5), 34–43 (2001)
4. W3C: Semantic Web layercake diagram. (2007). http://www.w3.org/2007/03/layerCake.png. Accessed 20 April 2015
5. W3C OWL Working Group: OWL 2 web ontology language document overview (2012). http://www.w3.org/TR/owl2-overview/. Accessed 20 April 2015
6. Kifer, M., Boley, H.: RIF Overview, 2nd edn. W3C, New York (2013). http://www.w3.org/TR/rif-overview/. Accessed 20 April 2015
7. Harris, S., Seaborne, A.: SPARQL 1.1 Query Language (2013). http://www.w3.org/TR/sparql11-query/. Accessed 20 April 2015
8. Hanschke, I.: Strategisches Management der IT-Landschaft. Carl Hanser Verlag München, Munich (2013)
9. EABOK Consortium: Enterprise Architecture Body of Knowledge (2015). http://www2.mitre.org/public/eabok/index.html. Accessed 20 April 2015
10. Auer, G., Basten, D., Berneaus, M., Däberitz, D., Freitag, A., Haas, H., Kröber, G., Schmidtmann, V., Schweikert, R., Stettiner, E., Thielscher, J., Triebel, T., Weber, M., Weisbecker, A.: Enterprise Architecture Management neue Disziplin für die ganzheitliche Unternehmensentwicklung. Bundesverband Informationswirtschaft Telekommunikation und neue Medien e. V., Berlin (2011)
11. The Open Group: TOGAF Version 9.1. Van Haren Publishing, Zaltbommel (2011)
12. Matthes, D.: Enterprise Architecture Frameworks Kompendium. Springer, Berlin, Heidelberg (2011)
13. The Open Group: ArchiMate 2.1 Specification. The Open Group, Berkshire (2013)
14. Birkhofer, H. (ed.): The Future of Design Methodology. Springer-Verlag London Limited, London (2011)
15. Pahl, G., Beitz, W., Feldhusen, J., Grote, K.H.: Pahl/Beitz Konstruktionslehre: Grundlagen erfolgreicher Produktentwicklung. Methoden und Anwendung, 7th edn. Springer, Berlin, Heidelberg (2007)
16. Duden: 'methode' (2015). http://www.duden.de/rechtschreibung/Methode. Accessed 20 April 2015
17. Weigt, M.: Systemtechnische Methodenentwicklung. Ph.D. thesis, Universität Karlsruhe (TH) (2008)
18. Hesse, W., Merbeth, G., Frölich, R.: Software-Entwicklung - Vorgehensmodelle, Projektführung und Produktverwaltung. In: Handbuch der Informatik, vol. 5.3. Oldenbourg-Verlag, Munich (1992)
19. Chroust, G.: Modelle der Software-Entwicklung - Aufbau und Interpretation von Vorgehensmodellen. Oldenbourg-Verlag, Munich, Germany (1992)
20. Lindemann, U.: Vorgehensmodelle, Grundprinzipien und Methoden. In: Methodische Entwicklung technischer Produkte. Springer, Heidelberg, Garching (2009)
21. Meerkamm, H.: Methodology and Computer-aided tools - a powerful interaction for product development. In: Birkhofer, H. (ed.) The Future of Design Methodology, pp. 55–65. Springer-Verlag London Limited, London (2011)

22. Müller, J.: Arbeitsmethoden der Technikwissenschaften: Systematik, Heuristik, Kreativität. Springer, Heidelberg (1990)
23. Cronholm, S., Ågerfalk, P.: On the concept of method in information systems development. In: Käkölä, T. (ed.) 22nd Information Systems Research in Scandinavia (IRIS 22), Keuruu, Finland (1999)
24. Braun, T., Lindemann, U.: Supporting the selection, adaptation and application of methods in product development. In: International Conference on Engineering Design, ICED 2003. Design Society (2003)
25. Braun, T.: Methodische Unterstützung der strategischen Produktplanung in einem mittelständisch geprägten Umfeld. Ph.D. thesis, TU Munich, Munich, Germany (2005)
26. Eisenbarth, T.: Semantic Process models - transformation, adaption, resource consideration. Ph.D. thesis, University of Augsburg, Augsburg, Germany (2013)
27. Brickley, D., Miller, L.: FOAF Vocabulary Specification (2014). http://xmlns.com/foaf/spec/. Accessed 20 April 2015
28. Isaac, A., Summers, E.: SKOS simple knowledge organization system primer (2009). http://www.w3.org/TR/skos-primer/. Accessed 20 April 2015
29. W3PM: Product modelling using semantic web technologies (2009). http://www.w3.org/2005/Incubator/w3pm/XGR-w3pm/. Accessed 20 April 2015
30. ISO: ISO 10303–242: 2014 - Industrial automation systems and integration - Product data representation and exchange - Part 242: Application protocol: Managed model-based 3D engineering (2014)
31. Omrane, N., Nazarenko, A., Rosina, P., Szulman, S., Westphal, C.: Lexicalized ontology for a business rules management platform: an automotive use case. In: Palmirani, M. (ed.) RuleML - America 2011. LNCS, vol. 7018, pp. 179–192. Springer, Heidelberg (2011)
32. Ortmann, J., Diefenthaler, P., Lautenbacher, F., Hess, C., Chen, W.: Unternehmensarchitekturen mit Semantischen Technologien. HMD Praxis der Wirtschaftsinformatik **51**, 616–626 (2014)
33. Giasson, F., Bergman, M.: Upper Mapping and Binding Exchange Layer (UMBEL) Specification (2015). http://techwiki.umbel.org/index.php/UMBEL_Specification. Accessed 20 April 2015
34. Langermeier, M., Driessen, T., Rosina, P., Bauer, B.: Change and version management in variability models for modular ontologies. In: 16th International Conference on Enterprise Information Systems (ICEIS), Lisbon, Portugal (2014)
35. Buckl, S., Ernst, A., Lankes, J., Matthes, F.: Enterprise architecture management pattern catalog. Technical report, Software Engineering for Business Information Systems (sebis), Munich, Germany (2008)
36. Stanford Center for Biomedical Informatics Research (BMIR): Protégé (2015). http://protege.stanford.edu/
37. Rosina, P., Kiss, E.M.: D4.3 - AUDI R&D Business Orchestration System. ONTORULE Project (2011)

Supporting the Security Certification and Privacy Level Agreements in the Context of Clouds

Amir Shayan Ahmadian[1], Fabian Coerschulte[1], and Jan Jürjens[1,2(✉)]

[1] Institute for Software Technology, University of Koblenz-Landau,
Koblenz, Germany
`ahmadian@uni-koblenz.de`, `fabian.coerschulte@tu-dortmund.de`
[2] Fraunhofer Institute for Software and Systems Engineering ISST,
Dortmund, Germany
`jan@jurjens.de`
`http://jan.jurjens.de`

Abstract. Outsourcing services into the cloud is a worthwhile alternative to classic service models from both a customers and providers point of view. Therefore many new cloud providers surface, offering their cloud solutions. The trust and acceptance for cloud solutions are however still not given for many customers since a lot of security incidents related to cloud computing were reported. One possibility for companies to raise the trust in the own products is to gain a certification for them based on ISO27001. The certification is however a large hurdle, especially for small and medium enterprises since they lack resources and know-how. In this paper we present an overview of the ClouDAT framework. It represents a tool based approach to help in the certification process for cloud services specifically tailored to SMEs.

Keywords: Cloud computing · Certifying cloud providers · Risk analysis methods · Risk treatment methods · Privacy level agreements

1 Introduction

Cloud computing is a business model that kept gaining importance in the recent years. The National Institute of Standards and Technology describes cloud computing as "ubiquitous, convenient, on-demand network access to a shared pool of configurable computing resources (e.g., networks, servers, storage, applications, and services) that can be rapidly provisioned and released with minimal management effort or service provider interaction" [25]. Cloud computing provides a very interesting opportunity for IT enterprises to service a large amount of customers by offering dynamic scalability, elasticity, and a cost model that is based on pay-as-you-go model.

This research was partially supported by the research project Visual Privacy Management in User Centric Open Environments (supported by the EU's Horizon 2020 programme, Proposal number: 653642).

© Springer International Publishing Switzerland 2016
B. Shishkov (Ed.): BMSD 2015, LNBIP 257, pp. 80–95, 2016.
DOI: 10.1007/978-3-319-40512-4_5

The utilization of cloud computing services has been ever growing in the past years and the growth of this business model is expected to continue in the near future [2]. However, the acceptance of cloud computing is growing slowly, due to the fact that cloud computing introduces new threats and vulnerabilities. Therefore, besides all the advantages of cloud computing, cloud providers need to convince the cloud customers of security.

A possible way to encounter scepticism and raise acceptance is the certification of cloud providers according to standards like ISO27001 [16]. However, for small and medium-sized enterprises (SMEs), offering cloud solutions is a rather complex task, due to the lack of know-how and resources to conduct an ISO27001 compliant risk assessment and generate the appropriate documentation to reach the certification. The ClouDAT project [9] offers a framework helping SMEs handling the certification process. It contains a cloud-specific risk assessment process and allows the automatic generation of ISO27001 compliant documentation based on the outcomings of the risk assessments.

In Sect. 2 we present a high-level overview of ClouDAT and introduce the risk analysis process. In Sect. 3 we deliver an in-depth insight into the underlying metamodel to introduce the key concepts of ClouDATs risk analysis. Based on this insight, Sect. 4 gives a detailed introduction into the methodology associated with the metamodel to point out the benefits that ClouDAT offers SMEs. Moreover, in Sect. 5, we introduce UMLsec [21], an extension of UML for secure system development, along with the CARiSMA [4] tool that supports UMLsec models. Section 6 provides an introduction to the use of formalized privacy level agreements in conjunction with ClouDAT framework. in Sect. 7 a conclusion is provided.

2   The Security Certification Approach

In the first step we introduce the structure of the ClouDAT framework and outline its risk analysis process.

2.1   The ClouDAT Framework

The result of the ClouDAT project [9] is the ClouDAT framework. This framework is available as open source and supports SMEs by providing a means for certifying cloud services. Generally, the ClouDAT framework establishes an Information Security Management System (ISMS) based on the ISO 27001 [16] standard. The development of an ISMS allows organizations to implement a framework for managing the security of their information assets such as financial information, employee and customer information. The framework contains different parts:

- A metamodel for the risk analysis process complying with ISO 27001 standard.
- A metamodel for the risk treatment process complying with ISO 27001 standard.

- A catalog of security requirements.
- A catalog of cloud-specific threats.
- A catalog of security controls.
- Different editors to model cloud environment and use cases, security requirements, and security controls.

In the rest of this section, the above mentioned parts are described along with the ClouDAT risk analysis process. The metamodels are introduced in the respective sections.

2.2   The Overview of the ClouDAT Risk Analysis Process

Figure 1 [1] presents an overview of the our risk analysis process, which complies with ISO 27001 standard. In the following, we summarize the different phases of the process.

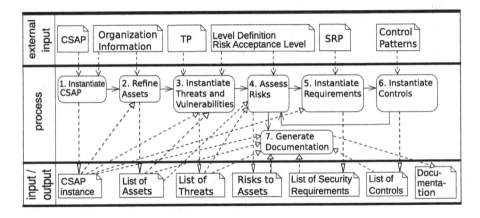

Fig. 1. Risk analysis process

Cloud Elements Identification. In this phase, the scope and the boundaries of the ISMS is defined. To this end, we employ the Cloud System Analysis Pattern (CSAP) [3]. CSAP provides a structured approach to describe cloud environments. It provides a framework to model their elements, such as data elements, physical objects, and stakeholders. Moreover, it describes the relations between the cloud elements.

The process of the asset identification starts with instantiating the CSAP. In the first step, the cloud customers and the required cloud services are identified. Then the cloud is instantiated, which consists of different types of cloud elements.

Refine Cloud Elements. This phase complies with Sect. 4.2.1 d of the ISO 27001 standard. The main goal of this phase is to determine the cloud elements that are important to the risk analysis. Later, for these cloud elements, the risk analysis is performed. The results of this phase are collected in a table, which is called *cloud element list*. This table contains all mandatory cloud elements for the risk analysis.

The cloud elements refinement is performed in two steps [1]:

- Refine cloud elements and their location: In this step the abstract mandatory cloud elements are refined into more concrete and detailed cloud elements. Moreover, the location of the cloud elements are identified.
- Assign responsibilities and relationships: In this step the responsibilities of the cloud elements are identified and the relations between the cloud elements are determined.

Instantiate Threats and Vulnerabilities. In this phase, for all the cloud elements that were specified in the previous phase a threat analysis is performed. Generally, in the threat analysis, it is investigated whether a cloud element is endangered. Moreover, it is examined if a cloud element has vulnerabilities that can be exploited by a threat. In the ClouDAT framework a catalog of predefined threats and vulnerabilities for cloud elements is provided. This catalog is based on previous works, for instance [5,11,14]. Additionally, the list of cloud computing top threats [6] from Cloud Security Alliance (CSA) is considered. The provided catalog is a starting point for the threat analysis and should not be considered as complete.

Assess Risks. This phase complies to sect. 4.2.1 of the ISO 27001 standard. The results of this phase declare the existing risk to the cloud elements, and specify whether a cloud element requires risk treatment. Before starting the risk analysis, the risk approach and the risk acceptance level must be specified. Generally, the risk assessment is based on the business impact, and the security failures. Business impacts express the consequences that affect the failure of the security goals. Furthermore, considering the threats and the vulnerabilities that are identified in the last phase, we need to determine the likelihood of potential security failures for all menaced cloud elements.

The multiplication of the likelihoods for the security failures and the values that are assigned to the business impacts estimates the risk levels of the cloud elements. By comparing the estimated risk levels of cloud elements and the defined risk acceptance level, the cloud elements that require risk treatment are identified.

Instantiate Security Requirements. In this phase we consider all the cloud elements with an unaccepted risk level. We need to define a risk treatment method to reduce the risks. We comply with ISO 27001 Sect. 6.1.3 by defining and applying an information security risk treatment process. The ISO 27001 specifies the following treatments:

– Applying appropriate controls.
– Accepting risks.
– Avoiding risks.
– Transferring the associated business risks to other parties.

In Sect. 4 we describe our risk treatment method completely. In this section, we only summarize our method. Generally, if a cloud element has an unacceptable risk level, security requirements have to be defined. To this end, security requirement patterns (SRP) are defined (Sect. 3). In a concrete certification process, security requirement patterns are instantiated, and for each cloud element with an unaccepted risk level, a security requirement will be defined. ClouDAT framework provides a catalog of predefined SRPs.

Instantiate Controls. Our risk treatment process complies with ISO 27001, and mainly contains applying appropriate security controls considering the security controls provided in Annex A of the ISO 27001. Generally, the selection of the controls is based on the cloud elements with unaccepted risk level, which are identified during risk assessment. Similar to security requirement patterns, the representation of the security controls is specified by control patterns (CP), and a catalog of predefined security controls is provided. As we mentioned above, we describe our risk treatment method in more details in Sect. 4.3.

Generate Documentation. In the final phase of our risk analysis process, a document is generated. This document contains the list of refined cloud elements, the list of threats and corresponding vulnerabilities, the list of cloud elements with unaccepted risk level, the list of security requirements, and finally the list of selected controls to reduce the identified risks. The resulting documentation is used as a reference for the certification. In the following sections, we describe the underlying concepts of the risk analysis process in more details together with the basic metamodels.

3 Risk Analysis Metamodel

This section describes the foundations of the risk analysis process in detail. Therefore, it takes a closer look at a simplified version of the risk analysis metamodel defined by the ClouDAT process.

Figure 2 shows an excerpt of the full risk analysis metamodel class diagram. Since we only want to discuss the key concepts, this illustration hides several classes and additional implementation detail.

The goal of the risk analysis phase is to identify the risks affecting the cloud elements that were found during the "Cloud Elements Identification" phase (see Sect. 2.2 and [1]). The central element for this step of the ClouDAT approach is the CloudElement. This can basically be anything of value to the company; from documentation to real physical systems. A cloud element is identified by a

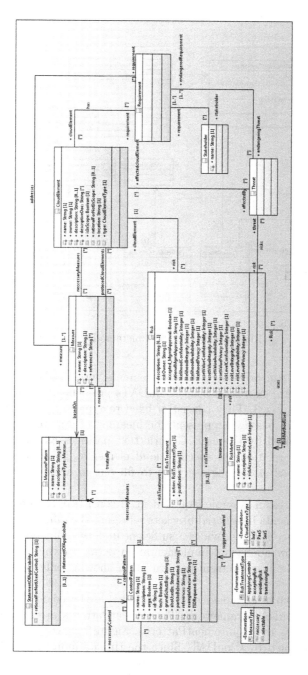

Fig. 2. Risk analysis metamodel excerpt

unique name und contains additional information such as type, owner, descriptions and a location. Additionally it can be excluded from the scope of the risk analysis once a convincing explanatory statement (rational) for this case is given.

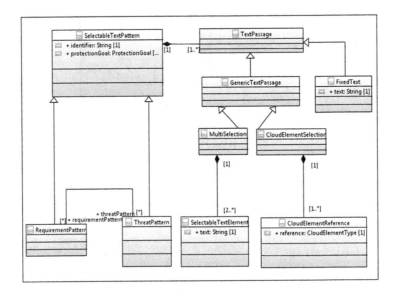

Fig. 3. Selectable text metamodel.

CloudElements can be subject to requirements verbalized by stakeholders. The requirements are expressed using ClouDATs pre-defined RequirementPatterns illustrated in Fig. 3. They consist of fixed text passages and generic text passages. Fixed text passages represent the meaning of a security requirement and can not be edited by the user. Generic text passages can for example be multi selections or relations to specific cloud elements. The requirement patterns can be seen as clozes the user has to fill out in order to instantiate a certain requirement.

Figure 4 illustrates an example requirement. It consists of fixed text and multi selections. The elements in squared brackets represent the different options for a multi selection. Since Fig. 3 provides a sufficient understanding of the concepts, Fig. 2 does not show additional implementation detail for the instantiation of requirements based on requirement patterns, thus showing only the requirement class.

Requirements can be endangered by threats that are based on ThreatPatterns defined by the ClouDAT framework. The ThreatPatterns are shown in Fig. 3 and are very similar to RequirementPatterns. Figure 5 shows an example for a threat pattern defined by ClouDAT. Since the threats indirectly endanger the CloudElements, there is also an association to it.

The presence of threats entails risks. While threats are very abstract and by themselves propose no danger to a company, risks do. A risk represents the

The cloud computing system shall ensure that a

[cloud customer, end customer, administrator]

only has the permissions of the assigned roles for

[cloud service]

Fig. 4. An example of security requirement pattern.

Disclosure of communication between the

[cloud service] and the

[cloud customer, end customer, administrator]

for example by network sniffing or gaining access to relevant areas.

Fig. 5. An example of threat pattern.

"potential that a given threat will exploit vulnerabilities of an asset or group of assets and thereby cause harm to the organization" [15]. The risk class contains a description, which serves as unique identifier for a risk and a risk owner, which is the person responsible for a given risk. It is also possible, that a risk is accepted by the management without further treatment (acceptedMgmtApproval). This case however demands for a convincing explanatory statement (rationalMgmtApproval). Furthermore a risk consists of likelihoods, business impacts (assetValue) and the resulting risk levels for the protection goals confidentiality, integrity, availability and privacy. Since a certification requires every risk to be handled or accepted, it is mandatory to deliver an acceptance rule for every risk. The acceptance rule is called RiskMethod in ClouDAT, and contains a name, description and riskAcceptanceLevel. The acceptance level can be seen as a threshold not to be exceeded by risks using the RiskMethod.

The risks exceeding the acceptance level have to be treated by the user. Therefore ClouDAT allows the definition of RiskTreatments that consist of a treatment action and a justification that explains, why a certain action has been taken. ClouDAT allows to treat a risk by applying controls, accepting the risk, avoiding the risk or transfering the risk. In case a risk is treated by applying controls, the user has to specify the measures that were used to reduce the risk.

ClouDAT distinguishes between controls and measures. A control describes an action that can be taken to reduce a risk but is defined on a very abstract level, while a measure is a concrete implementation of a control. A control for example is "Asymmetric encryption" and a possible measure based on this control could be the implementation of a specific encryption protocol like RSA.

The class ControlPattern allows the definition of controls and consists of an id, name, description and indicators whether it is required by ISO27001 or it is an organizational or a technical control. Furthermore it is possible to provide example measures or an example for the control based on the IT-Grundschutz. Controls can also suggest the use of other controls or require the implementation of other controls. For example, the control "Password management system" requires the implementation of a "User registration and de-registration" system and suggests the "Use of secret authentication information". CloudDAT provides an extensive list of possible controls based on the ISO27001 (see Sect. 4).

A control can provide MeasurePatterns which can be seen as implementation possibilities for the given control. A MeasurePattern consists of a name, description and an indication whether the Measure is neccessary to implement the control or just a selectable implementation method. The concrete instantiation of a MeasurePattern is a Measure, that is associated with requirements and CloudElements.

4   Risk Treatment Method

As we mentioned in Sect. 2.2, our risk treatment method complies with the ISO 27001 and is specified with four different treatment methods, applying appropriate controls, accepting risks, avoiding risks, and transferring the associated business risks to other parties.

According to the ISO 27001 Sect. 6.1.3, considering the risk assessment results, an appropriate security risk treatment option must be selected. To this end, all the security controls that are necessary to the risk treatment must be determined. Afterwards, a comparison of the determined controls with those in the ISO 27001 must be performed, verifying that no mandatory controls have been excluded. Subsequently, a statement of applicability that incorporates the mandatory controls and explanations for inclusions and exclusions of the controls must be provided. In the following sections, we describe these steps in more details.

4.1   Security Controls

In order to apply appropriate controls, we need to specify a list of security controls, from which the proper security controls are selected to reduce the risks of the organization. "Controls include any process, policy, device, practice, or other action which modify risks" [17]. The Annex A of the ISO 27001 standard provides the normative controls of the standard. Different international organizations have provided governance documents such as the NIST-SP800-53 [26], the DISA Secure Application Security Technical Implementation Guide (STIG) [10], and the Cloud Security Alliance Cloud Control Matrix (CCM) [8]. In such documents, a set of security controls are collected. Likewise, in the course of ClouDAT project, we provide a control list. The control list contains:

- Security controls of ISO 27001 standard.
- Self-defined security controls: Security requirements have to be fulfilled by controls, hence to cover all security requirements we have defined a few security controls additionally.
- Security patterns: A security pattern, using some security mechanism, describes a solution to the problem of controlling a set of threats. We consider some of the security patterns, which are provided in [12], as security controls.

4.2 The Structure of the Control List

Figure 6 presents a snapshot of the control list. Due to the lack of space, we do not show the whole table. The control list is simply a table which contains all above mentioned security controls. For each control a set of aspects are defined. In the following, we describe these aspects.

ID (ISO 27002)	Control/Measure —Text (ISO 27002)	Dependencies	Req (Ausarbeitung)	Protected Cloud Element
A.5.1.2	Review of the information security policy.	5.1.1 necessary	- referenced indirectly from Security Management and others	generic
A.6.1.1	Information security roles and responsibilities	A.9.2.3 necessary A.5.1.1 necessary	- referenced indirectly from Security Management and others	generic
A.6.1.2	Segregation of duties	5.1.1 necessary	Security Management 7 Security Management 15	generic
A.6.1.3	Contact with authorities	Necessary: A.6.1.3	Security Management 18	generic
A.6.1.4	Contact with special interest groups	-	- referenced indirectly from Security Management	generic
A.6.1.5	Information security in project management	Necessary: 25.4		generic

Fig. 6. A snapshot from the control list.

- ID: The documented controls presented in control list are generally based on the security controls provided in annex A of ISO 27001, and Sects. 5 to 18 of ISO 27002 respectively. These controls are identified by the same ID as in the ISO documents. In the cases, which the standards do not provide appropriate controls, self-defined controls are provided, with the IDs beginning at 19.1 in order to avoid conflicts with the ISO controls.
- Control Text: A short title for the control. For ISO controls, the title matches the one in the original document. Self-defined controls are labeled similarly.
- Dependencies: This entry gives a list of other controls. Mainly two kinds of dependencies are defined:
  - Necessary: The other control should be implemented as well in the most cases. If the user chooses not to apply the necessary control, the reason must be justified.

- Suggested: The other control might be useful to support the current control or its measure. The tool offers these controls as an option to the user.
- ISO 27001 - 2005 reference: The controls are based on the ISO revision of 2013. For the controls that have equivalent controls in the version 2005, the ID is given respectively.
- Security Requirement: List of relevant security requirements.
- Refinement of (ID): A reference to the control, which is refined by the provided control.
- Refined by (ID): A reference to the control, which refines the provided control.
- Protected Asset: List of the assets, which are protected by the provided control.
- Instance Type: The instance type of the control, when it is possible.
- Asset necessary to perform control with relevant security aspect: The implementation of a control can lead to the creation of additional assets, that need to be protected accordingly.
- BSI References: The related entries from the BSI Grundschutz catalogues.
- Also used in: List of similar controls from CCM (Cloud Control Matrix).
- Technology/Organization: Each control is classified whether it is primarily (+) or supportively (∼) technical or organizational.
- Description of control: A textual description of the control.

4.3 Risk Treatment Process

In Sect. 2.2, we described that after risk assessment, for the cloud elements with unaccepted risk level, appropriate security requirements are elicited. In the control list for each control a set of security requirements are specified. This mapping between controls and requirements simply indicates, which control fulfills which security requirement. Consequently, according to the elicited requirements, we can determine the necessary controls to reduce the risks. In this process the dependencies between the controls are considered.

After the selection of the controls, we need to verify whether the risk levels of the cloud elements are reduced. To this end, we need to perform the risk assessment for particular cloud elements to check whether the controls reduce the risk levels or a modification of the controls or other controls are required. This process is iterated until there exists no cloud elements with an unaccepted risk level. However, sometimes we need to avoid or ignore the risk. Or alternatively, we need to transfer the risk to other parties. These decisions are manually made by the security analyzer and must be reasoned.

Furthermore, we need to provide a statement of applicability (compliant with Sect. 6.1.3 c-d of the ISO 27001). To this end, we have provided a template. This template is simply a table, in which for each selected control either must be justified why the control is excluded, or the overview of the implementation is provided, i.e. the necessary and suggested controls to perform the control are listed.

As an example for the risk treatment process, consider the case, in which the confidentiality of the personal data in a organization, for which we have

have performed the risk analysis, is threaten. In Sect. 3, we have introduced the security requirement patterns. In our SRP catalog such a pattern exists:

"Confidentiality of personal data of [cloud customer, end customer] shall be achieved."

As we have already mentioned, a SRP has variable and fixed text passages. To instantiate the security requirement pattern, from the list of identified and refined cloud elements, an element as a representation of the cloud customer or end customer must be inserted into the variable text passage. Assume that the name of the Organization is *Organization A*, then the instantiated requirement is:

"Confidentiality of personal data of Organization A shall be achieved."

Using the provided mappings between security requirements and security controls in the control list, we select the relevant control:

"To address the security requirement, we apply the controls of the ISO 27001, e.g. access control policy (A.9.1.1), working in secure areas (A.11.1.5), network controls (A.13.1.1), including the controls that are specified as necessary to perform along with mentioned controls."

5   CARISMA, An External Security Analysis Tool

Along the risk assessment process, which is provided by the ClouDAT framework to certify cloud providers and generate documentation, the ClouDAT framework offers the functionality to analyze different cloud services and softwares with the help of external security analysis tools. For instance, consider the case, in which the cloud provider uses self developed cryptographic protocols instead of the standard protocols. In this case, an external tool for analyzing the protocols is needed. An appropriate external tool with different functionalities for security analysis is the CARiSMA tool framework. It offers different automatic verification plugins of UML diagrams for critical requirements. Generally, it provides automated analysis of UMLsec [21] models for security requirements.

UMLsec is an extension of UML in form of an UML profile that provides model-driven development for secure information systems [13]. It can be used to express security requirements within UML diagrams (such as secure information flow [19]). Tags and stereotypes are used to express security requirements and assumptions on system environments. Moreover, constraints are used to determine whether requirements are satisfied by the system design UMLsec [21].

The UMLsec approach has been used in a number of applications [20,23,24].

System security analysis using UMLsec requires an architectural analysis of the software system. To this end, all the components, objects, cloud elements, and the dependencies between them are needed.

In the case of a legacy system, these can be extracted from the code base using techniques for program comprehension such as [27].

In a certification process, it is possible to use different CARiSMA plugins as external tools for security analysis. For instance, we consider Control A.9.1.1 from ISO 27001 standard. It states, that an access control policy based on business and information security requirements must be established, documented, and reviewed [17]. There exists different approaches to establish access controls. Generally, an access control method restricts the access to information and information processing facilities. If a cloud provider requires an external tool to control the access to information, the RABAC analyzer plugin of the CARiSMA can be used [4]. This plugin is based on the concept of Role Attribute Based Access Control (RABAC) [18], and is implemented and integrated to the ClouDAT framework for the access control analysis in cloud environments.

Above, we mentioned that a cloud provider may need an external tool to analyze cryptographic protocols. CARiSMA offers Sequence Diagram Crypto FOL-Analyzer [22] for security analysis of cryptographic protocols. This plugin as an input receives a protocol, which is expressed as an UML sequence diagram, and performs the analysis.

The CARiSMA website [4] provides more information about the different plugins for the security analysis.

6   Privacy Level Agreement

In this section, we describe how Privacy Level Agreements (PLAs) in conjunction with ClouDAT framework can be used to assist the small and medium cloud providers to ensure security and privacy levels in their services. In the course of VisiOn[1] project and our current research, we develop a visual privacy management platform, which allows the citizens, who communicate with public administration authorities, to achieve desired levels of privacy by creating and monitoring a personal privacy level agreement. A PLA as an appendix to a service level agreement (SLA) describes the level of privacy protection that a service provider will maintain. Cloud Security Alliance (CSA) provides a PLA outline for cloud service providers, in which information privacy and personal data protection practices are addressed. PLA outline intends to provide a possibility to determine a guideline of essential personal data protection legal requirements, to achieve a baseline of compliance with mandatory personal data protection legislation across the EU. Moreover, in a structured way, verify the level of personal data protection offered by different CSPs [7].

In each document generated by the ClouDAT framework to assist the SMEs in the process of certifying their services, valuable information on threats, vulnerabilities, risks and security measures are provided. According to the PLA outline, such information are also needed to create PLAs. Thus, the document generated by ClouDAT can be used as an input to create PLAs. To this end, a formal description of PLA outline is required. Therefore, in our current research we intend to provide a metamodel based on the metamodel provided in Fig. 2. In this way, in a structured way first we specify the PLA outline (in XML format), and afterwards we can automatically generate some parts of the PLA regarding the relevant information provided by ClouDAT framework.

---

[1] http://www.visioneuproject.eu/.

The overall approach, how a PLA can be generated formally is provided in Fig. 7. According to this figure, in addition to the ClouDAT framework, a questionnaire is used to generate the other parts of the PLA such as the cloud provider information, the data protection inquiries, the data processing methods, and personal data location. This questionnaire is a simple application, for which a set of predefined questions are provided. Different other external tools such as security analysis or threat analysis tools may be also used to generate different sections of the PLA. After generating the PLA, a textual format of the PLA will be provided.

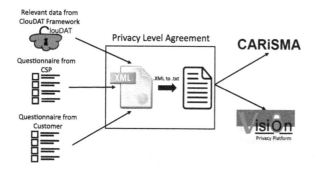

Fig. 7. Overall approach to generate a formalized PLA

The generated PLA can be used for different purposes. In our research, we plan to use the PLA as an input to CARiSMA to perform different security and privacy checks. To this end, currently we are developing new concepts and security checks, for which the infomration provided in the PLA are used as inputs.

7 Conclusions

The certification of cloud computing infrastructures is a very complex task for small and medium-sized enterprises. It requires a lot of effort to be taken because it is mandatory to do a detailed risk assessment and analysis and create detailed documentation of the efforts taken. ClouDAT provides a full fledged framework to support small and medium-sized enterprises in the cloud system certification process based on ISO27001. It consists of a detailed workflow on how to conduct the risk analysis and contains detailed lists of assets, requirements, threats, risks and controls to support the user during assesment phases. ClouDAT allows the user to analyse a modeled scenario both using integrated analysis methods and external analysis tools, thus exposing potential certification problems during analysis. Furthermore ClouDAT allows the automatic generation of ISO27001 compliant certification document, which helps the user in the certification process.

References

1. Alebrahim, A., Hatebur, D., Goeke, L.: Pattern-based and ISO 27001 compliant risk analysis for cloud systems. In: 2014 IEEE 1st Workshop on Evolving Security and Privacy Requirements Engineering (ESPRE), pp. 42–47, August 2014
2. Armbrust, M., Fox, A., Griffith, R., Joseph, A.D., Katz, R.H., Konwinski, A., Lee, G., Patterson, D.A., Rabkin, A., Stoica, I., Zaharia, M.: Above the clouds: a berkeley view of cloud computing. Technical report UCB/EECS-2009-28, EECS Department, University of California, Berkeley. http://www.eecs.berkeley.edu/Pubs/TechRpts/2009/EECS-2009-28.html
3. Beckers, K., Schmidt, H., Kuster, J., Fassbender, S.: Pattern-based support for context establishment and asset identification of the ISO 27000 in the field of cloud computing. In: 2011 Sixth International Conference on Availability, Reliability and Security (ARES), pp. 327–333, August 2011
4. CARiSMA: Carisma framework, May 2015. https://www-secse.cs.tu-dortmund.de/carisma/
5. Cloud Security Alliance: Security guidance for critical areas of focus in cloud computing v3.0 (2011). https://downloads.cloudsecurityalliance.org/initiatives/guidance/csaguide.v3.0.pdf
6. Cloud Security Alliance: The notorious nine cloud computing top threats in 2013, February 2013. https://cloudsecurityalliance.org/download/the-notorious-nine-cloud-computing-top-threats-in-2013/
7. Cloud Security Alliance: Privacy level agreement: A compliance tool for providing cloud services in the European union, February 2013. https://cloudsecurityalliance.org/download/thenotorious-nine-cloud-computing-top-threats-in-2013/
8. Cloud Security Alliance: Cloud Control Matrix (2014). https://downloads.cloudsecurityalliance.org/initiatives/ccm/ccm-v3.0.1.zip
9. ClouDAT: Cloudat project, May 2015. http://ti.uni-due.de/ti/clouddat/de/
10. DISA: Application Security and Development STIG V3 R10 (2015). http://iase.disa.mil/stigs/Documents/U_Application_Security_and_Development_V3R4_STIG.zip
11. European Network and Information Security Agency: Cloud computing - benefits, risks and recommendations for information security (2009). https://resilience.enisa.europa.eu/cloud-security-and-resilience/publications/cloud-computing-benefits-risks-and-recommendations-for-information-security
12. Fernandez-Buglioni, E.: Security Patterns in Practice: Designing Secure Architectures Using Software Patterns, 1st edn. Wiley, New York (2013)
13. Fernández-Medina, E., Jürjens, J., Trujillo, J., Jajodia, S.: Model-driven development for secure information systems. Inf. Softw. Technol. **51**(5), 809–814 (2009)
14. Heiser, J., Nicolett, M.: Assessing the security risks of cloud computing, June 2008. https://www.gartner.com/doc/685308/assessing-security-risks-cloud-computing
15. ISO: ISO/IEC 27005 Information technology - Security techniques - Information security risk management. ISO 27005: 2008, International Organization for Standardization, Geneva, Switzerland (2008)
16. ISO: ISO/IEC 27001 Information Security Management System (ISMS) standard. ISO 27001: 2013, International Organization for Standardization, Geneva, Switzerland, October 2013
17. ISO: ISO/IEC 27000 Information technology - Security techniques - Information security management systems, Overview and vocabulary. ISO 27000: 2014, International Organization for Standardization, Geneva, Switzerland, May 2014

18. Jin, X., Sandhu, R., Krishnan, R.: RABAC: role-centric attribute-based access control. In: Kotenko, I., Skormin, V. (eds.) MMM-ACNS 2012. LNCS, vol. 7531, pp. 84–96. Springer, Heidelberg (2012). doi:10.1007/978-3-642-33704-8_8
19. Jürjens, J.: Secure information flow for concurrent processes. In: Palamidessi, C. (ed.) CONCUR 2000. LNCS, vol. 1877, p. 395. Springer, Heidelberg (2000)
20. Jürjens, J.: Modelling audit security for smart-card payment schemes with UMLsec. In: 16th International Conference on Information Security (IFIPSEC 2001), pp. 93–108. IFIP, Kluwer (2001)
21. Jürjens, J.: Secure Systems Development with UML. Springer, New York (2005). Chinese translation: Tsinghua University Press, Beijing 2009
22. Jürjens, J.: Verification of low-level crypto-protocol implementations using automated theorem proving. In: 3rd ACM & IEEE International Conference on Formal Methods and Models for Co-Design (MEMOCODE 2005), pp. 89–98. Institute of Electrical and Electronics Engineers (2005)
23. Jürjens, J., Wimmel, G.: Formally testing fail-safety of electronic purse protocols. In: 16th International Conference on Automated Software Engineering (ASE 2001), pp. 408–411. IEEE (2001)
24. Jürjens, J., Wimmel, G.: Security modelling for electronic commerce: the common electronic purse specifications. In: Schmid, B., Stanoevska-Slabeva, K., Tschammer, V. (eds.) Towards the E-Society: E-Commerce, E-Business, and E-Government. IFIP, vol. 74, pp. 489–505. Springer US, New York (2001)
25. National Institute for Standards and Technology: The NIST Definition of Cloud Computing. Technical report, Special Publication 800–145 of the National Institute of Standards and Technology (NIST), September 2011. http://csrc.nist.gov/publications/nistpubs/800-145/SP800-145.pdf
26. Nist, Aroms, E.: NIST Special Publication 800–53 Revision 4 Recommended Security Controls for Federal Information Systems and Organizations. CreateSpace, Paramount, CA . (2012). http://nvlpubs.nist.gov/nistpubs/SpecialPublications/NIST.SP.800-53r4.pdf
27. Ratiu, D., Feilkas, M., Jürjens, J.: Extracting domain ontologies from domain specific APIs. In: 12th European Conference on Software Maintenance and Reengineering (CSMR 2008), pp. 203–212. IEEE (2008)

Two Case Studies on Generating Administrative Process Applications with AdminDSL

Antonio García-Domínguez[1]([✉]), Ismael Jerez-Ibáñez[2],
and Inmaculada Medina-Bulo[2]

[1] Department of Computer Science, University of York, York YO10 5GH, UK
`antonio.garcia-dominguez@york.ac.uk`
[2] Department of Computer Science, University of Cadiz, Av. Universidad de
Cádiz 10, 11519 Puerto Real, Spain
`ismael.jerezibanez@alum.uca.es`, `inmaculada.medina@uca.es`
`https://www-users.cs.york.ac.uk/~agd516/`

Abstract. Some organizations end up reimplementing the same class of
business process over and over: an "administrative process", which consists of managing a form through several states and involving various roles
in the organization. This results in wasted time that could be dedicated
to better understanding the process or dealing with the fine details that
are specific to the process. Existing virtual office solutions require specific
training and infrastructure and may result in vendor lock-in. In this paper,
we propose using a high-level domain-specific language (AdminDSL) to
describe the administrative process and a separate code generator targeting a standard web framework. We have implemented the approach
using Xtext, EGL and the Django web framework, and we illustrate it
through two case studies: a synthetic examination process which illustrates the architecture of the generated code, and a real-world workplace
survey process that identified several future avenues for improvement.

Keywords: Model-driven engineering · Domain-specific languages ·
Business modeling · Code generation

1 Introduction

In many organizations, there is a recurrent kind of business process which we call
an "administrative process". These administrative processes involve managing
a document with a certain structure and tracking it through different states. In
each state, different parts of the document have to be viewable or editable by
people with different roles in the organization. State transitions usually happen
due to human decisions (possibly after a meeting, a review or some kind of
negotiation), deadlines or a combination of both. The process usually concludes
by reaching a "final" state (e.g. "accepted" or "rejected").

These processes are usually kept within a single organization and are not
particularly complex by themselves, but their sheer number within some organizations can produce a high amount of repetitive work. Implementing each of

© Springer International Publishing Switzerland 2016
B. Shishkov (Ed.): BMSD 2015, LNBIP 257, pp. 96–116, 2016.
DOI: 10.1007/978-3-319-40512-4_6

these processes from scratch wastes precious time on writing and debugging the same basic features (form handling, state tracking, internal directory integration and so on) which should have been invested in obtaining a better understanding of the process desired by the users and fine tuning the process-specific business logic. In some cases, the developer tasked with implementing the process is not familiar with some of the best practices of the target technology, needing more time and producing less than ideal solutions.

Another problem is that even after the process is correctly implemented, the framework the implementation is based upon may become obsolete to the point of requiring a complete rewrite. This is compounded by the fact that since the processes may have needed urgent changes and tweaks, they may not be well-documented anymore and may require careful reverse engineering, which is time consuming and prone to mistakes. It would have been much better if most of the code had been produced from a process description: changing the target framework of several obsolete applications would only require writing a different code generator and adding some customizations.

Our organization has evaluated various generic "virtual office" solutions for implementing these administrative processes and having them run in a high-level process engine. While these solutions were acceptable for the simplest cases, adding process-specific UI and business logic and integrating them with in-house systems would have required learning yet another technology that may become obsolete or lose support in the long run. It would be much better if the resulting implementations were based upon a standard web framework chosen by IT, so it could be maintained by regular staff.

This paper is an extended version of a BMSD 2015 conference paper [1]. In the original paper, we presented the first version of AdminDSL and provided a short description of the synthetic examination process and the generated Django [2] website. This version provides a better conceptual introduction to the language, a detailed description of the architecture of the generated code, and a discussion of which parts will usually need to be customized and how. It also provides a new real-world case study in which the authors collaborated with a contractor for the University of Cadiz to develop a workplace satisfaction survey web application. This case study covers not only the initial generation of the application, but also its later evolution until it was deployed to production and what was learned from it.

2 Related Work

There exist several business process management systems (BPMSs) that include some support for form-based steps within workflows, such as Bonita [3] or Intalio [4]. These engines are usually tightly integrated with a design tool which uses a graphical notation (usually BPMN-based) to describe the processes. This graphical notation is normally extended with engine-specific annotations to provide the full semantics of the process, and is persisted using XML-based formats.

While these systems can describe a much larger class of business processes than our DSL, the resulting process definitions are highly dependent on the underlying engine: migrating the same process to a new technology may require a rewrite. Version control is still possible with XML-based formats, but meaningful comparisons and merges require special-purpose tools. In addition, using a BPMS effectively requires a considerable amount of training, consulting and process analysis, which may not be feasible in smaller IT departments. Our approach focuses on a specific kind of business process (manage a complex document through multiple states, with different access rules in each state) and produces a standard web app that can be maintained as any other.

Scaling back from full-fledged BPMS engines, there have been many attempts to simplify the development of form-based applications. One recent initiative in this regard has been the EMF Forms [5] Eclipse project. Using its tools, users can define the domain model and abstract layout once and then render it in various technologies, such as SWT or JavaFX for desktop apps or Tabris for mobile apps. On the one hand, EMF Forms allows developers to specify the concrete layout for the resulting forms, unlike our DSL, which delegates on the generator for the presentation aspects. However, a DSL could cover aspects that EMF Forms does not, such as access control and state transitions.

Another related topic is domain-driven design (DDD): an approach on software development that asserts that the primary focus in most software projects should be the creation of an adequate model that abstracts the problem domain, and the implementation of the relevant business logic around it [6]. In this regard, several frameworks have been implemented to support DDD, enabling rapid iterations by generating a large portion of the application from a "pure" domain model (e.g. a set of Plain Old Java Objects or POJOs), such as Apache Isis [7] or OpenXava [8]. In a way, a DSL conforms to the same view of producing software from a description of the problem domain: the only difference is that the DSL is focused on a specific kind of problem domain, rather than the generic approach of a DDD tool, making it more productive in that particular case.

In the context of e-government, several works have identified some differences in the way e-government processes should be modeled, in comparison to the business processes in the private sector. Klischewski and Lenk argued that in the public sector, many processes involve unstructured decision making (whether by a single official or after a meeting) and negotiations, so officials would need to be able to alter the course of the process [9]. Later in the same work, Klischenski and Lenk proposed a set of "Admin Points" as reusable process patterns that could be used as a shared vocabulary for e-government business processes. In a DSL, many of these admin points which involve negotiation and unstructured decision making could be modeled using decision-based transitions.

3   Language Definition

This section will present AdminDSL, our domain-specific language for defining administrative processes. Before describing the abstract and concrete syntax in a more formal way, we will provide a conceptual introduction to the language:

- An administrative process is understood as a succession of states through which a structured document is viewed and edited by users with certain roles in the organization.
- A structured document contains a sequence of fields, which may be aggregated together into sections and then groups. Sections and groups are useful for presentation and for access control. In addition, groups can be repeated if desired, which may be useful for representing master/slave records such as order line items, student grades and so on.
- Roles are defined separately: users can belong to one or more of them, and the assignments are assumed to be changeable on the fly through the generated web applications. AdminDSL is decoupled of how these roles are actually implemented (e.g. through a database or an LDAP server), but it should allow generic key-value pairs that a generator might understand.
- Finally, a collection of states is defined for each process: the form is implicitly in the "initial" state when it is being created, and then immediately transitions to a different state. Later transitions can be done by user decision or by deadlines. In each transition, roles can be given permission to view or edit certain fields, groups or sections of the document. AdminDSL can limit permissions to the user with a certain role that participated in a previous transition: this allows for process isolation between users with the same role.

3.1   Abstract Syntax

Figure 1 shows a UML class diagram with the abstract syntax of our DSL (the underlying concepts). An APPLICATION is divided into ELEMENTs. There are five kinds of ELEMENTs. SITE is the simplest one: it only declares the name of the application (e.g. "Billing"). OPTIONS elements contain key/name pairs (PROPERTY instances) that may be useful to external generators.

Next are ROLEs. These represent particular roles within the organization (such as "Accountant"). These elements provide a name and a set of PROPERTY instances which may be used by the generator to integrate the role with in-house user directories (such as an LDAP directory).

ENTITY elements represent data entities that must have been created before any documents can be filled in, such as "Country", "State" and so on. An ENTITY contains FIELD instances with the information to be stored about it. Every FIELD has a name and a domain-specific type (such as "currency" or "identity document") and zero or more PROPERTY instances providing additional information to generators.

Finally, the main and most complex kind of element is a PROCESS. These represent entire administrative processes (e.g. "Request for Leave"). They can contain three kinds of PROCESSELEMENTs:

- ENTITY instances, which will be specific to the process in this case. In the "Request for Leave" process, "LeaveReason" instances could be the various reasons for the leave.

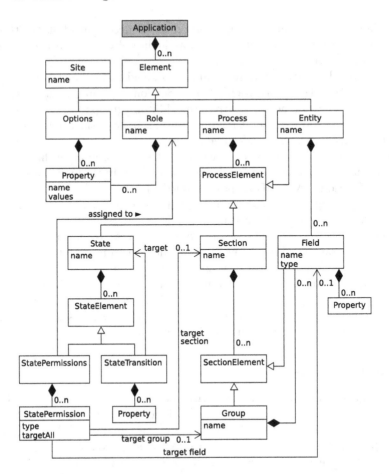

Fig. 1. UML class diagram of the DSL's abstract syntax.

- SECTION instances contain the FIELDS of the managed document, which can be optionally subdivided into GROUPS. A section could be "Billing information", and a group could be "bill item" (containing the "Price", "Quantity" and "Description" fields, for instance). This structure is useful for generating code and specifying access rules.
- STATE instances represent the states that the managed document can be in. It can contain a set of STATEPERMISSIONS for each role of interest, which in turn contain STATEPERMISSION instances that describe the kinds of actions that are available to the role. A role can receive all permissions at once, or it can receive the ability to edit or view a single section, group or field.

  A STATE can also contain STATETRANSITIONS to other states. A transition can activate when all the conditions (specified using PROPERTY instances) are met: these conditions could combine explicit decisions by users ("Accepted" or "Rejected"), dates ("Past deadline") or custom business logic. Alternative paths to the same state can be modeled with several STATETRANSITIONS.

Listing 1. Simplified concrete syntax for our DSL

```
1   site SiteName;
2   options { (Property;)* }
3   (role RoleName { (Property;)* } | role RoleName;)*
4   (entity EntityName {
5     (Type ((Property (, Property)*))? Name;)*
6   })*
7
8   (process ProcessName {
9     (entity EntityName {
10      (Type ((Property (, Property)*))? Name;)*
11    })*
12    (section SectionName {
13      (Type ((Property (, Property)*))? Name;
14      | group GroupName {
15        (Type ((Property (, Property)*))? Name;)+
16      } )*
17    })+
18    (state StateName {
19      (permissions RoleName (from StateName->StateName)? {
20        ((editable|viewable) all;
21        | (editable|viewable) SectionName;
22        | (editable|viewable) SectionName.GroupName;
23        | (editable|viewable) SectionName.FieldName;
24        | (editable|viewable) SectionName.GroupName.FieldName;
25        )*
26      })*
27      (transition (Property (, Property)*) StateName;)*
28    })+
29  })*
```

3.2 Concrete Syntax

Since editing and version control should not require any special-purpose tools, we have picked a textual notation for the DSL which is mostly a one-to-one mapping to the model entities.

Listing 1 shows a simplified version of our original EBNF grammar for the concrete syntax. As usual, (x)+ means "one or more x", (x)* means "zero or more x", (x)? means "zero or one x" and x|y means "x or y". Whitespace is ignored. Literal (and) and keywords are shown in bold, to avoid confusion. A *Property* is of the form Name = Value (, Value)*.

As the grammar can fit into less than 40 lines after some simplifications, we can conclude that it is a rather simple DSL that should be easy to learn by the IT staff. However, it has a considerable number of cross-references in it, so it will require good tooling support to ensure that these references are not stale.

4 Case Study: Exam Process

In this section, we will illustrate AdminDSL by presenting a case study that describes a simple examination process and then generates a web application that implements it. After outlining the process itself, we will present the features, general architecture and design of the generated application, and evaluate the results obtained.

4.1 Description

The process in this case study is a test, involving two roles ("student" and "teacher") and these steps:

1. The student starts the test by introducing their personal information and answering the first part. Some of the questions are free-form, some have a predefined set of answers, and one of the questions pull answers from the database. Students cannot see each other's answers.
   The teacher can already see all the partially filled-in exams, but cannot enter any grades yet.
2. After a certain date, the second part of the test (with two numeric questions) becomes visible and the first part of the test is no longer editable by the student. Students can also fill in what they think about the test. Again, students cannot see each other's answers. Teachers can still see everything, but cannot enter any grades yet.
   The test can be turned in for examination before a certain deadline: after that deadline, it is turned in automatically and is no longer editable.
3. Once the test has been turned in, the teacher can grade it, but the student cannot see the grade yet: they only see their own answers.
4. After the teacher confirms the final grade, the examination is "closed". Every student can see their own answers and everyone's grades. All fields are now read-only.

A simplified version of the DSL-based description of the process is shown in Listing 2. Some of the dates and field names have been shortened to save space.

Line 1 declares that the application to be generated has the name "School". Lines 2–5 include several options for the code generator that targets the Django web framework: in particular, they suggest using a certain base template that follows the organizational image, which is included in a Django app available at a certain URL. Line 6 declares the previously mentioned "student" and "teacher" roles.

The rest of the listing from line 8 onwards is dedicated to the "exam" process. An entity "Answers3" is declared at line 9: its instances are used for the answers for question 3. In lines 10–27, the fields of the document are organized into three sections. The "test" section is divided into two groups and one additional field: using groups simplifies access control specifications later on. The optional fields have "blank" set to "True".

Lines 29–61 describe the 5 different states the process can be in. The "initial" state is a special case: it represents the state before the process starts, and its transitions describe who can start the process and when. The other 4 states match the four stages of the examination which were described before.

Line 36 illustrates the **from** A->B syntax that AdminDSL uses to limit the granted permissions to the user that triggered a certain state transition, providing process isolation between users with the same role. In this particular example, it ensures that students cannot see each other's answers. It is possible to have multiple **permissions** blocks for the same role, with different restrictions: for instance, the "closed" state allows students to see their own answers and each other's grades.

Listing 2. DSL-based examination process

```
1    site School;
2    options {
3      django_base_template ="template/base.html";
4      django_extra_apps = "template = https://.../";
5      }
6    role student; role teacher;
7
8    process exam {
9        entity Answers3 { string answer; }
10       section personal {
11        fullName studentname;
12        identityDocument(label="National ID:") nid;
13        email(label="Email") mail;
14       }
15      section test {
16        group part1 {
17          string(blank="True") q1;
18          choice(values="A1,A2,A3",blank="True") q2;
19          choice(table="Answers3",blank="True") q3;
20        }
21        group part2 {
22          currency(label="Q4 (euros):",blank="True") q4;
23          integer(label="Q5 (integer):",blank="True") q5;
24        }
25        choice(values="Good,OK,Bad",blank="True") opinion;
26      }
27       section evaluation { float grade; }
28
29       state initial {
30        transition(decision_by="student",
31        after_date="2015/03/01-14:00:00",
32        before_date="2015/03/07-14:00:00") part1;
33       }
34      state part1 {
35        permissions teacher { viewable all; }
36         permissions student from initial->part1 {
37          editable personal, test.part1; }
38        transition(after_date="...") part2;
39       }
40      state part2 {
41        permissions teacher { viewable all; }
42        permissions student from initial->part1 {
43          viewable test.part1;
44          editable personal, test.part2, test.opinion;
45        }
46        transition(decision_by="student",
47        before_date="...") evaluation;
48        transition(after_date="...") evaluation;
49       }
50      state evaluation {
51        permissions teacher { viewable all;
52          editable evaluation; }
53        permissions student
54        from initial->part1 { viewable personal, test; }
55        transition(decision_by="teacher") closed;
56      }
57      state closed {
58        permissions teacher { viewable all; }
59        permissions student
60        from initial->part1 { viewable all; }
61          permissions student { viewable evaluation; } }
62    }
```

Available Process List

Action	Name	Can start it	After date	Before date
Start	exam	Student	2015/03/01-14:00:00	2015/03/07-14:00:00

Active Process List

Action	Name	Init user	Current state	Creation date	Last modification date
Edit	exam	student	evaluation	March 5, 2015, 8:07 p.m.	March 5, 2015, 8:09 p.m.
Edit	exam	student	closed	March 5, 2015, 8:10 p.m.	March 5, 2015, 8:15 p.m.

Fig. 2. Generated web app: process list

4.2   Implementation in AdminDSL

The parser and editor for the language in Sect. 3 have been implemented using Xtext [10]. From an EBNF grammar, Xtext generates a metamodel with the abstract syntax of the language and a set of Eclipse plugins which provide a parser and an advanced editor with live syntax checking and highlighting, auto-completion and an outline view.

We have also implemented a separate code generator that takes an APPLICATION described with our DSL and produces a web application in the Django framework. The generator is written in the Epsilon Generation Language [11], which provides modularity and the ability to have "protected regions" that are preserved when overwriting an existing file. Our current version of the EGL source code for the Django generator has 3045 LOC.

4.3   Generated Application

The code generator produced from the example in Sect. 4.1 a ready-to-use Django site backed by a PostgreSQL relational database (shown in Figs. 2 and 3). The generated site is largely divided into two parts:

- A support library that extends Django with the building blocks for implementing forms with fine-grained stateful permissions. This library was written manually in tandem with the code generator and is essentially copied into the project.

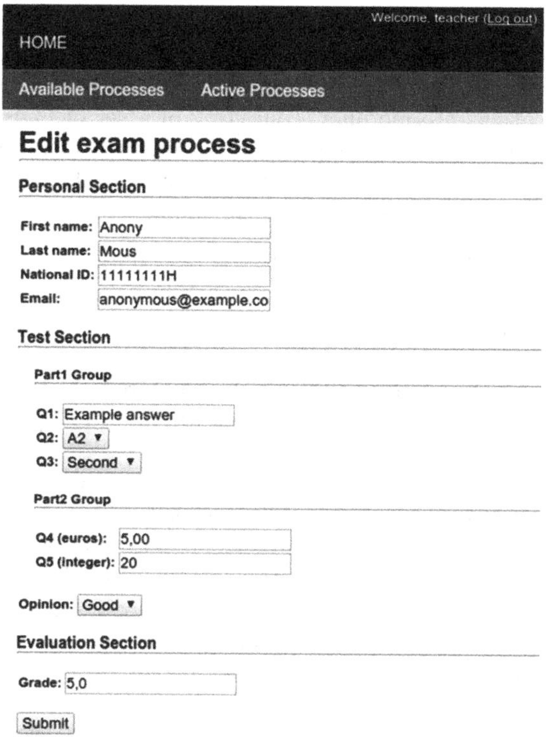

Fig. 3. Generated web app: process form

– A set of modules that are generated automatically, using the above support
library to implement the processes defined in the AdminDSL description. Most
elements in AdminDSL map directly to various combinations of the components in the support library.

This structure makes it possible to produce a high-quality web application
based on a well-tested set of components, which can be rearranged by advanced
users that need a different user interface or additional functionality. The generated code can be more concise and thus be closer to what a developer would
write manually.

This section will introduce the basic concepts behind the Django framework
and present the key details of the support library and the generated modules.
The section will then discuss the features included by default and the various
ways in which the application can be extended.

Background: Django Framework. Django[1] is a web development framework
that follows the Model-View Controller (MVC) pattern [12], providing a clear

---
[1] https://www.djangoproject.com/.

separation between the data managed by the application (the *models*), the ways in which users interact with this data (the *views*) and the logic that redirects incoming requests to the appropriate views (the *controllers*).

Django applications are modular, consisting of a set of *apps*: most applications combine a set of pre-built apps for common functionalities (e.g. forums or blogs) with a set of custom apps for application-specific logic (e.g. business logic). Every module can provide some of the following:

- *Models*: data entities that are persisted to the database. Most models are directly translated into database tables. Django provides its own object-to-relational mapping facilities and an incremental database migration framework.
- *Views*: Python functions that handle an incoming request for certain URLs in the web application. Most functions will then render a response by passing a *context* to a Django *template*.
  Django applications generally use a hierarchical approach for dispatching incoming requests to views: a global dispatcher forwards requests to an app-specific dispatcher, which then forwards the request to the appropriate view.
- *Forms*: in-memory representations of the data managed by a web form. These forms provide the required cleanup and validation logic. Developers can extend the Django form library with new fields and form types.
- *Administration pages*: apps can extend the built-in administration area with new pages for managing their models.
- *Signals and receivers*: some apps may want to react to events produced by other apps. In order to keep these apps decoupled, Django makes it possible to define *signals* that apps can send and *receivers* that can handle those signals.

The Django library also provides most of the basic functionality required by current web applications, such as user authentication and authorization, session management and internationalization, among others.

Support Library. The support library is a Django app (called "base_admindsl") that was manually written together with the Django code generator, making it possible to increase the abstraction level of the generated code and make it more readable and maintainable.

First, the support library contributes a set of Django models for persisting the processes and their instances. The most important ones are shown in the UML class diagram in Fig. 4, and reuse some of the default models provided by the Django framework (shown in the "Django" package). The models are organized roughly into three groups:

- The TRANSITION, STATE, and MAXPROCESSINSTANCE models operate at the process description level. Every process has a collection of TRANSITIONs that link together various STATEs. MAXPROCESSINSTANCE models can limit the number of instances of a process that a certain group of users may create. These models allow administrators to configure parts of the processes without having to regenerate the code.

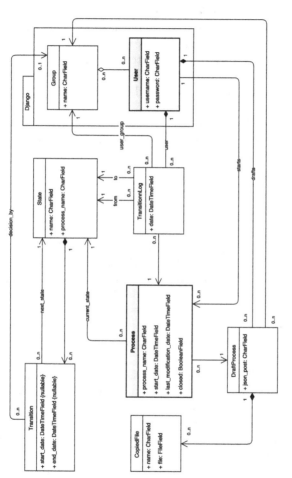

Fig. 4. Excerpt of the base Django models defined by the support library.

– The PROCESS, BASEPERMSECTION, BASEPERMGROUP, TRANSITIONLOG,
  DRAFTPROCESS, and COPIEDFILE models operate at the process instance
  level.
  PROCESS is an abstract superclass for all the process models that represents
  a single instance of a process and stores the current state of the process, the
  start and last modification dates and whether it is closed (i.e. cannot trigger
  any more transitions).
  BASEPERMSECTION and BASEPERMGROUP are abstract superclasses for all
  the generated models that implement the various sections and groups, respectively. These classes provide various utility methods that deal with permissions, such as is_editable, can_view and can_edit.
  TRANSITIONLOG keeps track of every state transition triggered by a process
  instance, storing the date, source and target states, and the user and group
  that triggered the transition. They are used to implement the process isolation
  restrictions that were shown in Listing 2 (see line 36).
  DRAFTPROCESS and COPIEDFILE store draft process forms and uploaded files
  before they are persisted to the real models. Draft process forms are serialized
  as JSON data, so DRAFTPROCESS is kept decoupled from the structure of the
  real models.

The support library also contains various building blocks for the functionality
required by the generated processes:

– Utility classes that extend the Django form handling components with new
  field types and the stateful permissions system required by AdminDSL.
– Generic views that can be reused from the app-specific dispatchers: these
  include user authentication, role switching and process management.
– Signals and default receivers for three kinds of events: process creation, manual process updates and automatic process updates.
– A command-line tool (update_states) that can be run periodically to
  perform automatic state transitions based on the current date.

Generated Processes. Every PROCESS in the AdminDSL description is turned
into a Django app that combines the building blocks provided by the support
library to implement the described process.

Every process-specific app defines its own set of Django models based on
the abstract superclasses provided by the support library. As shown in Fig. 5,
the mapping is relatively straightforward: AdminDSL processes are turned into
subclasses of the PROCESS model, AdminDSL sections are turned into subclasses
of BASEPERMSECTION and AdminDSL groups are turned into subclasses of
BASEPERMGROUP.

The generator also produces default HTML templates for rendering the forms
and extends the Django administration area with pages for managing the various
process instances. The generator does not need to produce any Django views:
instead, it generates an app-specific dispatcher that reuses the views in the support library.

The rest of the AdminDSL elements are mapped as follows:

- AdminDSL roles are mapped to Django roles, created through database migrations that ensure these roles exist in the database.
- Global AdminDSL entities are added as extra models to the support library.
- Process-specific AdminDSL entities are added as extra models to the process-specific Django app.
- AdminDSL states are mapped to instances of the STATE model of the support library.
- AdminDSL transitions are mapped to instances of the TRANSITION model of the support library.
- AdminDSL permissions are mapped to Django permissions, which are assigned to the appropriate Django roles. This makes it possible to change the permissions of the various states without regenerating the code.

4.4   Observed Limitations

The DSL, its tooling and the evaluated generator currently present several limitations. One self-imposed limitation is that they do not aim to produce 100 % of the required code in all cases: the generated code will usually need to be customized in some way, due to additional requirements on the user interface, custom business logic that has to be added, or unexpected integrations with legacy systems. Following the accepted approach in the existing literature [13],

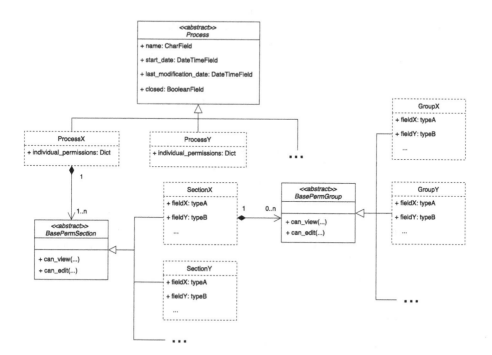

Fig. 5. Django models generated for each process

we have chosen to keep the DSL small and focused on describing administrative processes.

As shown in Sect. 4.3, the resulting web applications are divided into a manually written support library with all the required building blocks and a set of automatically generated components that arrange these blocks according to the AdminDSL description. These generated components are further divided into code (for the parts that do not need to change as often) and data (for the parts that must be editable by regular users). This separation allows users with special requirements to rearrange or further extend the generated applications, while helping produce quickly a first version that can be validated with the end users.

The DSL is focused on describing the current process, and does not have any provisions for migrating running processes to a new version with different states or very different information. Our current approach is to delegate on the target framework of the generator: for instance, since version 1.7 the Django framework has built-in data and schema migrations.

Since we transition to a new state as soon as its conditions are met and ignore all other transitions in the old state, we implicitly only allow one state to be active at a time. While this makes the DSL less general than a full-fledged business process modeling language such as BPMN [14], largely based on Petri nets, it is on par with some of the "virtual office" platforms we evaluated and the legacy applications it is intended to replace.

States do not enforce preconditions, invariants or postconditions yet, beyond simply checking that the mandatory editable fields have been filled in. We intend to add support for the most common conditions to the DSL in the short term: the most advanced cases will be delegated to a protected region, which will have to be filled in by the developer.

5   Case Study: Workplace Satisfaction Survey

This section presents a different case study in which a web application for performing workplace satisfaction polls was developed. Unlike the previous synthetic example, this application has been successfully deployed within the University of Cadiz and is currently under active use.

Similarly to the previous section, this section starts by describing the first version of the process and showing how it was translated to AdminDSL. The section will then discuss how the generated application evolved through several iterations, adding new variants of the original processes and acquiring custom features coded manually. Finally, the overall experience of using AdminDSL will be evaluated and future avenues of improvement will be identified.

5.1   Description

The original intent of the system was collecting the impressions of the staff at the University of Cadiz about their work environment, in order to evaluate the current situation and make plans for improvement. The system would collect information initially from each employee, which would then be revised by their line manager and their area supervisor, and if necessary go through several iterations until there was mutual agreement between all parties. The system would be monitored by external observers, which would make sure that the necessary data quality concerns were being addressed.

The form itself consisted of 16 sections, some of which would be filled in through external systems and some of which would be filled in manually. Forms would go through five states:

1. On the "initial" state, the employee would fill in most of the form and transition it into the "revision" state.
2. On the "revision" state, the line manager would review the form and pass it on to the area supervisor (state "arearevision"). In this state, the employee and the observer could still read the form, but not edit.
3. On the "arearevision" state, the area supervisor would review the form and add some special comments if necessary, and then either close the form (state "closed") or return it to the employee for further improvement (state "emprevision"). The employee, line manager and observer would still have read-only access to the form.
4. On the "emprevision" state, the employee would correct some of the issues identified by the area supervisor and return it to the "revision" state.
5. On the "closed" state, the form would be read-only for all the parties involved, and no further transitions are allowed.

An excerpt of the resulting AdminDSL description is shown in Listing 3. One minor detail is the requirement for a "Month" entity, as some of the sections require indicating the specific months in the year in which certain work sites are used.

5.2   Evolution

The first prototype of the application was developed and validated in record time, thanks to the AdminDSL code generator. However, as anticipated in Sect. 4.4, it required various iterations and manual adjustments before a final version could be deployed to production.

The first set of manual changes integrated the system with third party systems. Some of the sections in Listing 3 are never editable manually, such as the employee identification section. Instead, the BASEPROCESSFORM superclass of all forms was modified to implicitly fill in this section based on the logged in employee. The Django templating system was extended with new tags that pulled in from these third party systems as well.

Another set of manual changes dealt with the user interface: help texts were added, and the layout was changed to use the Bootstrap library for a more attractive appearance. The UI was simplified from a generic "virtual office" arrangement to a closer match with the underlying process, hiding some of the internal complexity in the stateful forms implemented in AdminDSL. A screenshot of the final UI is shown in Fig. 6.

Listing 3. First version of the UCA Workplace Satisfaction Survey process

```
1    site WorkplaceSurveys;
2    ...
3    role admin; role manager;
4    role employee; role observer;
5
6    process survey {
7      entity Month { string name; }
8      section(label="1. Workplace ID") id { ... }
9      section(label="2. Work schedule") schedule { ... }
10     section(label="3. Work description") desc { ... }
11     ...
12     section(label="6. Work conditions") cond { ... }
13     ...
14     section(label="14. Workload metrics") load { ... }
15     section(label="15. Other aspects") other { ... }
16     section(label="16. Manager comments") obs { ... }
17
18     state initial {
19       permissions employee {
20         editable desc, ..., cond, load, other;
21         viewable idworkplace, schedule, ..., obs;
22       }
23       transition(decision_by="employee",
24       max="1") revision;
25     }
26     state revision {
27       permissions manager {
28         editable desc, ..., cond, load, other;
29         viewable idworkplace, schedule, ..., obs;
30       }
31       permissions employee from initial->revision {
32         viewable all;
33       }
34       permissions observer { viewable all; }
35       transition(decision_by="manager") arearevision;
36     }
37     state arearevision {
38       permissions admin {
39         editable desc, ..., cond, load, other, obs;
40         viewable idworkplace, schedule, ...;
41       }
42       ... rest can only view ...
43       transition(decision_by="admin") closed;
44       transition(decision_by="admin") emprevision;
45     }
46     state emprevision {
47       permissions employee from initial->revision {
48         editable desc, ..., cond, load, other;
49         viewable idworkplace, schedule, ..., obs;
50       }
51       ... other roles can view all ...
52       transition(decision_by="employee") revision;
53     }
54     state closed {
55       ... all above can only view ...
56     }
57   }
```

Fig. 6. Screenshot of the final user interface for the workplace satisfaction survey web application

After a pilot run, it was found that the sheer number of responses to the survey required reorganizing the approach into a hierarchy of forms rather than a simple collection. Employees would fill in a form, and the forms would be first grouped by work area and campus, then by campus and then finally for the university. The original process in the AdminDSL was turned into four processes (one per level):

– The "employee form" process: the employee fills in the form, and in the other the form is read-only to all parties.
– The "campus-area form" process: the system aggregates all responses from each work area in each campus, and the line manager reviews the form.
– The "area form": the system aggregates all responses from each campus, and the area supervisor reviews the form.
– The "general form": the system aggregates all responses from the area forms, and the central administrators review the form.

AdminDSL does not directly support this concept of "aggregate" forms, so the developers had to manually implement Django views that would produce them. In addition, since AdminDSL could not capture the relationships between line managers and employees and between area supervisors and line managers, it was necessary to extend the data model to include this information and use it to assign the appropriate aggregate forms to the relevant line managers and area supervisors.

5.3   Evaluation

In this case study, AdminDSL helped produce the first prototype in record time. In addition to the process form itself, the code generator took care of the routine setup work that consists of defining the base models, configuring Django and bringing in dependencies. With the prototype in hand, the project managers were able to quickly ascertain that a different approach based on aggregate forms would scale better with the available personnel for the survey.

As expected, the code generated by AdminDSL had to be customized to cover for the aspects that are not covered by the language: a simplified user interface, integration with third party systems and starting new processes by aggregating results from others. Perhaps some of these aspects could be covered by other small DSLs in the future.

As iterations went on, many protected regions were added to the code generated by AdminDSL, so the customizations could be preserved across regenerations. This approach did not scale as well as intended, as in many cases it was necessary to add code outside the protected regions. Rather than a limitation of AdminDSL, this would be a limitation of the code generator itself, which is purely text-based: perhaps a language-aware generator could detect most manual changes and merge newly generated code with them.

In fact, having done most of the work, the final refinement iterations stopped using the AdminDSL code generator and instead manually recombined the building blocks in the support library from Sect. 4.3. This backs our assertion that using a support library is a best practice for generating code, as the inevitable manual iterations at the end of a project will still take advantage of it.

One issue that we identified during the manual iterations is that the generated per-section and per-group Django models (shown in Fig. 5) introduced an unnecessary level of complexity when writing manual code or SQL queries. We are currently working into simplifying our approach, using a single model per process and leaving sections/groups to the user interface.

The case study also highlighted several limitations in the current version of the AdminDSL language, which could be revised in later revisions:

- The **permissions** block did not allow for specifying multiple roles at once, which results in repetition in some states in which several roles had the same permissions.
- The "initial" state could not be reused in Listing 3, as it is a special case: instead, a new copy named "emprevision" had to be defined.
- The aggregate form processes mentioned in Sect. 5.2 were mostly the same: it may be useful to allow for process inheritance or reuse, to avoid these repetitions.
- The application had to be manually extended to support employee-manager relations, in order to limit the employee forms that each manager could see. It would be useful to be able to limit a **permissions** block not only by the transition log, but also by relations between users.

6   Conclusions

A simpler class of business processes (administrative processes) are very common in many organizations today: these processes basically consist of managing a form through many states, involving various roles in the organization. Implementing the basic logic and infrastructure for them again and again wastes precious time that could be used on understanding better the process and implementing the fine details correctly.

This paper has presented an approach to improve the efficiency of implementing these solutions, while avoiding lock-in into a particular technology: using a high-level domain-specific language (DSL) for describing the process and writing a separate code generator for each target technology. The approach has been illustrated by describing an examination process, and has been implemented with Xtext [10] on the DSL side and EGL [11] on the code generation side. The code generator produces a ready-to-use site that follows the best practices of the Django web framework [2], accelerating the implementation of the process. The generated code is based on a manually-written support library: when later iterations hit the limits of our code generator, developers are still able to extend and reuse its building blocks.

After the synthetic case study, a real-world case study for a workplace satisfaction survey developed within the University of Cádiz was discussed. The first version of the original survey was quickly developed with AdminDSL, and the developers were able to ascertain in the early stages of development that an alternative approach based on aggregating multiple levels of forms was needed. After rapid iteration of prototypes of AdminDSL, developers then manually extended the application to cover for the aspects that AdminDSL did not cover (custom user interface, external system integration, form aggregation and so on). While the experience with AdminDSL has been positive, it has highlighted the need for a smarter code generator that is friendlier to manual modifications, and has shown several ways in which AdminDSL could be improved or assisted by other small DSLs.

We are currently running two more case studies within the University of Cádiz and studying their results. After taking into account the feedback from our first real-world case study, we intend to use these two case studies to obtain more detailed metrics of the usability and productivity of AdminDSL. Once the Django support in AdminDSL is mature, we will open the tool to the general public and start working on generators for other web frameworks that are common in our organization (e.g. Symfony 2).

Acknowledgments. This work was funded by the research project "Mejora de la calidad de los datos y sistema de inteligencia empresarial para la toma de decisiones" (2013-031/PV/UCA-G/PR) of the University of Cádiz.

References

1. García-Domínguez, A., Jerez-Ibáñez, I., Medina Bulo, I.: Domain-specific language for generating administrative process applications. In: Proceedings of the 5th International Symposium of Business Modeling and Software Design, pp. 178–183. SciTePress, Milan, July 2015

2. Django Software Foundation: Home page of the Django web framework. https:// djangoproject.com. Accessed 6 March 2015
3. Bonitasoft: Homepage of the Bonita BPM project. http://www.bonitasoft.com/. Accessed 3 March 2015
4. Intalio, Inc.: Homepage of the Intalio|BPMS project. http://www.intalio.com/ products/bpms/overview/. Accessed 3 March 2015
5. Eclipse Foundation: Homepage of the EMF Forms project. https://www.eclipse. org/ecp/emfforms/. Accessed 3 March 2015
6. Evans, E.J.: Domain-Driven Design: Tackling Complexity in the Heart of Software, 1st edn. Addison Wesley, Boston (2003)
7. Apache Software Foundation: Apache Isis. http://isis.apache.org/. Accessed 3 March 2015
8. OpenXava.org: OpenXava homepage. http://www.openxava.org/web/guest/ home. Accessed 3 March 2015
9. Klischewski, R., Lenk, K.: Understanding and modelling flexibility in administrative processes. In: Traunmüller, R., Lenk, K. (eds.) EGOV 2002. LNCS, vol. 2456, pp. 129–136. Springer, Heidelberg (2002)
10. Eclipse Foundation: Xtext project homepage. http://www.eclipse.org/Xtext/. Accessed 2 March 2015
11. Eclipse Foundation: Epsilon project homepage (2015). https://eclipse.org/epsilon/. Accessed 5 March 2015
12. Gamma, E., Helm, R., Johnson, R., Vlissides, J.: Design Patterns: Elements of Reusable Object-Oriented Software, 1st edn. Addison Wesley, Reading (1994)
13. Fowler, M.: Domain Specific Languages, 1st edn. Addison-Wesley Professional, Boston (2010)
14. Object Management Group: Business Process Model and Notation 2.0.2. http:// www.omg.org/spec/BPMN/2.0.2/. Accessed 2 March (2015)

A Financial Approach for Managing Interest in Technical Debt

Areti Ampatzoglou[1], Apostolos Ampatzoglou[1(✉)], Paris Avgeriou[1], and Alexander Chatzigeorgiou[2]

[1] Department of Mathematics and Computer Science, University of Groningen, Groningen, Netherlands
{areti.ampatzoglou, a.ampatzoglou}@rug.nl,
paris@cs.rug.nl
[2] Department of Applied Informatics, University of Macedonia, Thessaloniki, Greece
achat@uom.gr

Abstract. Technical debt (TD) is a metaphor that is used by both technical and management stakeholders to acknowledge and discuss issues related to compromised design-time qualities. Until now, despite the inherent relevance of technical debt to economics, the TD community has not sufficiently exploited economic methods/models. In this paper we present a framework for managing interest in technical debt, founded on top of *Liquidity Preference,* a well-known economics theory. To tailor this theory to fit the TD context, we exploit the synthesized knowledge as presented in two recent studies. Specifically, in our framework, we discuss aspects related to technical debt interest, such as: types of TD interest, TD interest characteristics, and a proposed TD interest theory. Finally, to boost the amount of empirical studies in TD research, we propose several tentative research designs that could be used for exploring the notion of interest in technical debt practice.

Keywords: Technical debt · Architecture · Software quality · Interest

1 Introduction

The term *Technical Debt* (TD) was coined in 1992 by Ward Cunningham [8] to describe the technical compromises being made while coding, in order to speed up product delivery and meet release deadlines. Research on technical debt is currently an active field, since around 90 % of articles on the subject have been published after 2010 [15]. Remarkably, this research effort is performed both within academia and industry: according to Li et al. [15], from the current corpus of research efforts in technical debt, 43 % is performed in academia, 40 % in industry and 17 % in both. Apart from the fact that TD is a problem of paramount importance for software

---

This paper is an extended and revised version of the paper entitled "Establishing a framework for managing interest in technical debt", published in BMSD 2015 [4].

B. Shishkov (Ed.): BMSD 2015, LNBIP 257, pp. 117–133, 2016.
DOI: 10.1007/978-3-319-40512-4_7

development, another possible explanation for its prominence in both academia and industry, is its interdisciplinary nature (software engineering and economics), which facilitates the communication among technical and non-technical stakeholders [3]. To achieve this, the TD community *borrows* terms from economics and maps them to software engineering ones.

Based on two recent literature reviews on the subject [3, 15], the two most frequently used financial terms in TD research are: *interest* and *principal*. Principal is a well-defined and accepted concept, which is characterized as the effort required to address the difference between the current and the optimal level of design-time quality, in an immature software artefact or the complete software system [3]. Therefore, it is quantifiable as long as one agrees on the concerned properties (i.e., specific qualities). On the other hand, interest (associated with many definitions, which in some cases are controversial) cannot be measured in a straightforward way, since it involves the valuation of future maintenance activities. Measuring interest becomes even more complicated since its occurrence is not certain, in the sense that maintenance activities might not take place, and therefore interest will not need to be paid off. To partially alleviate these problems, in this study we conduct a systematic literature review which results in a Framework for managing Interest in Technical Debt (FITTED). The goals of FITTED are:

(G1)   *to identify types of TD interest, and the parameters that affect its valuation.* Identifying the types of interest, which can occur along evolution, is the first step towards more formal Technical Debt Management (TDM). Until now, the definitions of interest are rather high-level, and interest measurement is often not applied in practice.

(G2)   *to explore how various characteristics of interest in economics apply in TD interest.* An example of such a characteristic is whether interest is simple or compound. However, these characteristics have not been fully exploited in research state-of-the-art, yet. Therefore, in this study we first discuss the different opinions stated in the literature, and take them into account when presenting our proposal.

(G3)   *to propose a TD interest theory.* Until now, no study has used the economic interest theories for modelling technical debt interest. We will rely on the Liquidity Preference Theory, for modelling the evolution of TD.

The application of FITTED is expected to support software engineers to determine the change of technical debt amount in the future, by describing the parameters that affect its future value (i.e., anticipated maintenance effort, interest, etc.). This can in turn allow the use of elaborate financial methods in different TDM activities, i.e., repayment, monitoring, and prioritization. Additionally, we expect that FITTED can support further research in the field of TD, in the sense that it can facilitate a common understanding on TD interest and point to interesting research directions.

The rest of the paper is organized as follows: In Sect. 2, we discuss related work, i.e., the secondary studies from which we gathered our data (see Sect. 2.1), and background information on interest theory from economics (see Sect. 2.2). Next, in

Sect. 3, we present the research method used in this study. In Sect. 4, we introduce the proposed framework for managing interest in TD. In Sect. 5, we discuss possible paths for further research in the field of TD by employing the proposed framework, whereas in Sect. 6 an illustrative example of its application. Finally, in Sects. 7 and 8, threats to validity and conclusions are presented.

2 Related Work

In this section we present research efforts that are related to this study, and on which the development of the proposed framework is built upon. In particular, we discuss:

- *The corpus of existing research on Technical Debt*, by examining existing systematic literature reviews [14] (see Sect. 2.1). These will provide the primary studies that are reused in the reported systematic literature review.
- *The existing economic interest theories* (see Sect. 2.2). We intend to apply an existing economic interest theory, i.e., *Liquidity Preference Theory*, to reuse existing knowledge from economics, on how interest should be handled, and learn from accumulated experiences.

2.1 Literature Reviews in Technical Debt

Several systematic literature reviews on technical debt have been published during the last three years; a fact suggesting that the issue of technical debt management has become of great interest to both practitioners and academics. Firstly, Tom et al. [26] have published a study in which they explore the nature of technical debt and its implications for software development. In order to achieve this goal they have conducted a multi-vocal literature review and a set of semi-structured interviews among industry practitioners. This research aims at providing indications on how the concept of TD is exploited by both researchers and practitioners. However, the use of non-peer-reviewed reports or articles raises significant reliability and validity issues [21].

In 2015, two secondary studies have been published. Li et al. [15] have performed a mapping study on technical debt and its management (TDM). In this study, the authors present research efforts concerning the concept of technical debt, any related notions and TD management. As a result of the research, TD has been classified into 10 different types, whereas 8 TDM activities have been identified. In addition, Ampatzoglou et al. [3] have conducted a systematic literature review in order to analyze the state of the art on technical debt, by focusing on its financial aspect. Particularly, the analysis is carried out in terms of the definition of financial aspects of TD, and their relation to the underlying software engineering concepts. Finally, even more recently (2016), Alves et al. [2] published the outcomes of a mapping study that aimed to characterize the types of technical debt, identify indicators that can be used to find technical debt, identify management strategies, understand the maturity level of each proposal, and identify what visualization techniques have been proposed to support TD identification and management activities.

Each one of these secondary studies attempts to chart the whole area of TD, while none of them focuses particularly on the topic of interest; this is the aim of our study. In addition to that, since the body of work on TD has already been well scrutinized by the four aforementioned secondary studies, we can build on top of them by reusing the identified primary studies and focusing on interest (see stated goals in Sect. 1).

2.2   Interest in Economics

Regarding the way interest rate is defined in the market; various models have been suggested, by different schools of economics [18]. The mainstream theories are the *Loanable Funds Theory*, developed by the neoclassical school, and the *Liquidity Preference Theory*, proposed by the Keynesian theory [18]. Interest rate is the price paid for borrowing money or vice versa (the payment received to loan money). Therefore it can be considered as the price of money. Interest rate, as any other price, can be defined in the market at the equilibrium between supply and demand. According to the Loanable Funds Theory, interest rate specification takes place in the market of loanable funds. On the one hand, individuals or enterprises, who want to invest, form the demand for loanable funds. They ask for loans in order to proceed with an investment. As interest rate gets higher, borrowing becomes more expensive. As a result, demand for loanable funds decreases as interest rate increases. On the other hand, the supply of loanable funds comes from people or enterprises that use the loanable funds market to save their money. Instead of consuming part of their income, they choose to put it into the loanable funds market in order to save it for later. In this case, higher interest rate means higher return on savings. Therefore, supply of loanable funds rises as interest rate increases.

In the diagram of Fig. 1, the equilibrium in loanable funds market is presented. We note that, in economic theory, all kinds of supply – demand diagrams represent the dependent variable on the horizontal axis and the independent variable on the vertical axis. Therefore, in this case, the vertical axis depicts interest rate (r), while the horizontal axis represents the quantities of supply and demand for loanable funds. The quantity of loanable funds supplied at any level of interest rate is presented by line S. Line S depicts the positive correlation between interest rate and loanable funds supply. Likewise, the quantity of loanable funds demanded at any level of interest rate is presented by line I. The negative correlation between interest rate and loanable funds demand is indicated by the negative slope of line I. When interest rate is higher than r^*, then it is more profitable to save, or it is more profitable to lend than to borrow, and supply of loanable funds is higher than demand. On the other hand, when interest rate r is lower than the level of r^*, then it is more profitable to invest, or it is more profitable to borrow than to lend, and demand for loanable funds is higher than supply. When $r = r^*$, then both the investors and the savers have no motivation to change their position in the market and equilibrium is achieved. Consequently, interest rate is determined at $r = r^*$. Equilibrium in the market is achieved at interest rate r^*, when every other factor, that could influence savings or investment, is considered stable

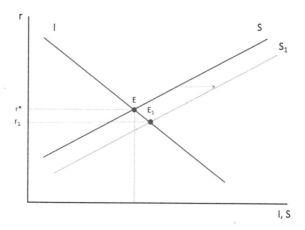

Fig. 1. Loanable funds theory

(ceteris paribus[1]). However, interest rate level may move upwards or downwards in case of changes to savings or investments, due to exogenous factors (e.g., income). For example, an increase in income would cause an increase in the quantity of savings. That would result in a shift to the right of the savings curve (S), which is the supply of loanable funds. In Fig. 1, the new line S_1 depicts such a change. As shown in the diagram, the new equilibrium is now achieved at point E_1 and interest rate is defined at r_1, lower than r^*.

The Liquidity Preference Theory determines interest rate level through the mechanism of supply and demand for money (cash), which is performed in the money market. In this case, supply of money (M) is a constant at any point of time and is determined by the central bank, according to the needs of the economy. In other words, supply of money is not dependent on interest rate and it is exogenously defined. On the other side, demand for money (L) represents the quantity of cash that people prefer to hold for purposes of transactions, precaution or speculation. In this case, as interest rate increases, it becomes more profitable for people to invest money than to hold it. Consequently, an increase in interest rate leads to a decrease in the quantity of money demanded in the market and a decrease in interest rate causes an increase in demand for money. Similarly to the Loanable Funds theory, interest rate is determined by the equilibrium point of the market.

The diagram of Fig. 2 shows the equilibrium in the market of money. Interest rate is represented on the vertical axis, whereas money supply and demand are shown on the horizontal axis. The supply curve is vertical to the horizontal axis, and represents the stable money supply, provided by the central bank, independently of the interest rate level, as mentioned above (this assumption consists the main difference with the loanable funds theory). Demand for money is negatively related to interest rate (because in this case interest rate is the cost of holding money against investing in a bond)

---

[1] A Latin phrase often used in economics to suggest that all other factors are constant, in order to examine the relationship between two variables.

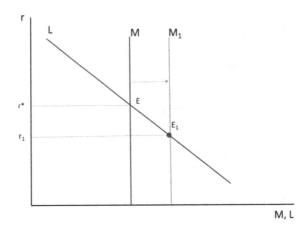

Fig. 2. Liquidity preference theory

and line L shows the quantity of money demanded at any given interest rate, ceteris paribus. The intersection of the two curves, M and L, represents market equilibrium and determines the level of the interest rate at r^*. When interest rate is higher than r^*, then it becomes more profitable for people to invest than to hold their money, so demand for money (cash) is lower than the quantity of money that circulates in the market (excess supply). On the other hand, when interest rate r is lower than the level of r^*, then the opportunity cost of money is lower, and people demand for more money than the central bank currently supplies (excess demand). When $r = r^*$, then people want to hold exactly the amount of money they currently have and equilibrium is achieved. In case of a change in demand for money because of a change in another determining factor, e.g. income, or in case of a change in the quantity of money supplied by the central bank, the equilibrium rate will change. For example, if the central bank decides to increase money supply, then M would increase to M_1 and the curve in the diagram of Fig. 2 would shift to the right. Consequently, equilibrium would be defined by point E_1 and the new interest rate in the market would be r_1, lower than r^*.

3   Research Method

This work is a systematic literature review that synthesizes knowledge from existing primary studies. The systematic literature review has been designed and executed according to the guidelines presented by Kitchenham et al. [14]. Due to lack of space we do not report the design of the full SLR. The goal of this study is to develop the Framework for managing Interest in Technical Debt (FITTED). Based on the framework's goals (see Sect. 1), we set three research questions[2]:

---

[2] The mapping between research questions and goals is one-to-one. Therefore, RQ_1 has been set to achieve G1.

[RQ₁] *What are the types of TD interest and the parameters of its valuation?*
[RQ₂] *How characteristics of interest in economics are applied in TD interest?*
[RQ₃] *Can we define a TD interest theory?*

In order to select the studies to be explored in this research effort, we consider the primary studies investigated by Ampatzoglou et al. [3] and Li et al. [15] (see Sect. 2.1). Both these secondary studies are recent and have explicitly investigated the concept of interest, so they can provide a valid and up-to-date set of primary studies. We considered the union of the two sets of primary studies and select those that are related to interest. On the completion of this process, we ended up with *36 studies that focus on TD interest*. In Table 1, we present the reference numbers of the selected studies (as provided by the original secondary studies). In the last column, the total number of primary studies retrieved from every literature review is provided. In the parenthesis, we note the number of studies reported by only one of the two literature reviews, also indicated by the boldface reference numbers. Note that the two secondary studies have obtained different sets of primary studies since they applied different inclusion criteria (e.g., Ampatzoglou et al. [3] excluded all studies that were not using any material from finance).

Table 1. Studies included in this review

Source of reuse	Reference in the original secondary study	Study Count
Ampatzoglou et al. [3]	P1, P2, P7, P8, P9, P10, P12, P13, P15, P16, P17, P22, P23, P24, P26, P30, P35, P37, P38, P41, P42, P51, P52, P53, P57, **P58**, P67, P68, P69	29 (1)
Li et al. [15]	S1, S2, S9, S10, S11, S12, **S15**, S16, S17, S20, S22, S23, S24, S34, S35, S39, **S40**, **S42**, S50, **S53**, S55, S56, S61, S62, S65, S71, S72, S73, **S75**, **S77**, S78, **S85**, S91, S93, S94	35 (7)

The study selection process of the two secondary studies surveying primary studies on TD can be summarized as follows:

Ampatzoglou et al.

• Queried 7 digital libraries (IEEE, ACM, Scopus, Springer, Science Direct, Web of Science, and Google Scholar), with the term *technical debt*. The search returned 1,173 primary studies
• Applied Inclusion/Exclusion Criteria (e.g., the study should focus on the financial aspect of TD). The process returned 69 primary studies.

Li et al.

• Queried 6 digital libraries (IEEEXplore, ACM, Science Direct, Web of Science, Springer Link, Scopus, Inspec, with the term *debt*, in the area of computer science or software engineering. The search returned 1,665 studies
• Applied Inclusion/Exclusion Criteria (e.g., paper should focus on some specific types of TD). The process returned 94 primary studies.

To answer the RQs and construct FITTED (see Sect. 4), we extracted data from the primary studies and combined this information with theory from Economics (see Sect. 2.2). In particular, in order to answer RQ_1, we have isolated all definitions of interest, and the parameters used for its valuation. To answer RQ_2, we have extracted and analyzed all statements regarding how interest evolves over time. To answer RQ_3, we have looked into the accumulation and repayment of interest, as well as the Liquidity Preference Theory. Eventually we performed a synthesis of the data in the primary studies and the aforementioned economics theory. Therefore, to some extent, FITTED represents our own ideas that aim at covering gaps in literature.

4 Framework for Managing Interest in TD

In the next sections we present FITTED, i.e., the proposed framework for managing interest in technical debt, structured based on the set RQs.

4.1 Types of Interest and Parameters of Its Valuation

According to Ampatzoglou et al. [3] and Li et al. [15], interest is the most prominent financial term that is used in TDM research. Note that in economics, interest theories are used for calculating interest rate (not interest per se), since interest is calculated based on interest rate. However, in TDM, interest is not calculated based on interest rate, but it is assessed in various other ways, as explained later in this section. Specifically, from TD research, it is not clear if interest rate can be defined at all. Based on the selected primary studies, technical debt interest is perceived as a risk for software development, in the sense that it has a specific effect (i.e., *interest amount*) and a probability to occur (i.e., *interest probability*). Concerning these two terms:

- 28 % of primary studies describe **interest amount** as the extra effort during maintenance, whereas 50 % as the extra maintenance cost. However, since in software economics, cost is usually defined as a function of effort, we can safely assume that 78 % of studies refer to interest amount as the extra effort/cost that is required during maintenance activities, due to the presence of technical debt. The rest of the studies, either provide more high-level definitions—e.g., [9, 16] —or define technical debt interest similarly to economics, i.e., the increase rate of technical debt amount [10], or define interest as a change in a design-time quality attribute—see for example [23, 28].
- 25 % of the studies acknowledge the existence of **interest probability**. According to Seaman and Guo [22], interest probability refers to the possibility that interest will occur in one item, i.e., that extra effort will be demanded during future maintenance. It should be noted that Technical Debt Items might not be need to be maintained and thus no interest will be paid. From the studies that deal with interest probability, [11, 25] adopt a financial risk management approach where interest probability is calculated as the standard deviation of past interest rate; [13] suggests that interest probability is time sensitive; the rest, as [12] or [22], adopt a risk

management approach, i.e., they consider interest probability as the probability of the TD incurring event to occur.

In addition to the amount and probability of incurred interest, it is useful to distinguish between two different situations when interest can manifest itself:

- *Interest while performing maintenance activities—IM*: Performing maintenance tasks is more time/effort consuming in software with accumulated TD, compared to the same software if it had no TD (see for example [1, 20] or [23]). The difference between the two amounts of effort is the amount of the *IM* interest. This type of interest will occur, and will be simultaneously paid, when maintenance tasks are performed (i.e., while undertaking the effort to perform the maintenance task).
- *Interest while repaying TD—IR*: The effort for repaying technical debt at any time point *t* (i.e., enhancing the quality of a Technical Debt Item - TDI to partially or totally remove TD) is higher than the effort needed for repaying technical debt for this item, at any time point prior to *t*, supposing that the TDI has been extended along software evolution—see for example [17, 19]. Therefore, *IR* is calculated as the difference between the two aforementioned efforts. This type of interest will occur when (and if) the amount of TD is to be paid off. For example, consider a long method bad smell that initially consisted of 500 lines of code. During evolution, the same method grows to 750 lines. Thus, the time needed for refactoring it (TDI repayment) increases over time.

Both of the aforementioned types of interest are in agreement with the most established definitions of interest amount (i.e., extra cost/effort); however they add more details on when these extra costs/efforts can occur. Thus, for each technical debt item, interest (I_{TDI}) should be calculated, based on the following high-level formula:

$$I_{TDI} = IR_{TDI} + IM_{TDI}$$

$$= PR_{TDI} * ER_{TDI} + PM_{TDI} * EM_{TDI},$$

in which P denotes the probability of a repayment (R) or maintenance (M) event to occur, and E the effort needed to perform the action. For example, ER_{TDI} corresponds to the effort required for repayment in the technical debt item: TDI. To transform the aforementioned formula from the TDI level to the system-level, we propose the use of the sum aggregation function, since the total TD of a system is the sum of TD of all items with incurred TD. Therefore, interest at system level (I) can be calculated, as:

$$I = \sum_{j=1}^{j=count(TDI)} PR_j * ER_j + PM_j * EM_j$$

We note that to use the aforementioned formulas, one needs to assign estimates for the *PR*, *PM*, *ER*, and *EM* factors; these can either come from experience or from empirical data. For examples and interesting research directions on this issue, see Sect. 5.

4.2   Mapping of Interest Characteristics in Economics on TD Interest

Based on economics, interest is classified over two dimensions: its method of calculation and its variation over time. For these purposes, interest or interest rate can be:

- *Simple* or *Compound*: Interest is simple when it is calculated only as a function of the principal; whereas it is compound when it is calculated over the principal, plus the incurred interest; and
- *Fixed* or *Floating*: Interest rate is fixed, if it does not change along time; whereas it is floating when it can increase or decrease based on circumstances.

The primary studies we looked into, discuss these characteristics of interest, but only superficially, without empirical evidence on the real-world evolution of interest. As already explained in Sect. 4.1, the concept of interest rate does not apply for technical debt. Therefore, the distinction between floating and fixed interest rates is not applicable. Specifically, 19 % of primary studies deal with the evolution of interest along time and either characterize it as compound, or continuously increasing. As an exception to this, Chin et al. [7], propose that the cost of the organization to hold on TD is stable across time and neither increases nor decreases. Finally, only 14 % of the studies propose a specific way of measuring interest. The estimation is commonly performed by using historical data, documentation, and maintenance models.

From the primary studies, we observe that technical debt interest is perceived as *compound*, in the sense that it is increasing, since the additional effort to repay technical debt and perform maintenance on a technical debt item increases as software grows and design-time quality is compromised (see for example [1, 5]). It is suggested that the level of compromised design-time quality (CQ) (e.g. higher complexity or coupling) can be used to calculate the increase of interest. However, it is rather problematic to decompose the level of compromised design-time quality of the system to the level of the original system at time $t1$, $CQ(t_1)$, i.e., the one that existed in the system when the principal incurred, and the additional level of the system at (t_2), i.e., the one that incurred due to system evolution (system larger in size, more functionality, etc.): $\Delta Q = CQ(t_2) - CQ(t_1)$. Therefore, the calculation of the effort needed to perform any maintenance action in t_2, can only be assessed based on current level of compromised design-time quality of the system $CQ(t_2)$. However, in case that some repayment activity is performed (at t_2), we expect that the level of compromised design-time quality of system after partial repayment $CQ(t_2)$ to decrease (i.e., $CQ(t_2) < CQ(t_1)$), leading to a decreased amount of both types of interest, in future maintenance—i.e., ER and EM. These claims are valid for TDIs, in which no additional technical debt has been incurred between timestamps t_2 and t_1.

4.3   Interest Theory

Based on the above, and by borrowing the rationale of the equilibrium achievement from the existing economic interest theories, we developed an interest theory for managing TD interest. Specifically, we adopt the concept of the *Liquidity Preference Theory*. The reason for selecting the *Liquidity Preference Theory* and not the *Loanable Funds Theory* is that in TD the amount of money that is available to the company for

TDM is stable, i.e., the principal (the amount that has been saved, while incurring TD supposing that principal is not invested to provide extra benefits). The assumption that the available money for TDM is the principal is based on the fact that principal is the maximum amount that can be saved without spending any additional effort.

In the proposed interest theory, we map *money supply* to *principal*, in the sense that principal is the amount of money that is available to the software development company, after incurring TD; and we map the *money demand* to the *accumulated amount of interest*, in the sense that this is the extra amount of money that is demanded by the company when performing future maintenance activities, caused by the TD. In Fig. 3, where we present the FITTED Interest Theory, the *x-axis* represents *time*, whereas the *y-axis* represents *amount of money*. Therefore, the equilibrium point (E_0) denotes the time stamp (t_0), in which the company has spent the complete amount of money from the internal loan (i.e., initial principal – P_0) in extra maintenance activities because of the incurred TD. We note that the specification of the equilibrium point is achieved through an analysis based only on effort, i.e., the effort saved when taking on TD and the extra effort required for any future maintenance activity because of its accumulation. Any other related costs or benefits related to technical debt occurrence (e.g. gains from launching the product earlier) have been excluded from the model for simplicity reasons. Thus, if the expected lifespan of the specific TDI is shorter than t_0 then undertaking technical debt is a beneficial choice, whereas if not, technical debt becomes harmful for the company. The aforementioned discussions, in the case that no repayment actions are performed, are summarized in the blue lines of Fig. 3.

Additionally, in Fig. 3, we consider $\Sigma(IM)$ as *continuously increasing*, since it is a sum of positive numbers and because TD interest is compound (see Sect. 4.2). In case that some repayment occurs at some timestamp (t_r), the line of the accumulated

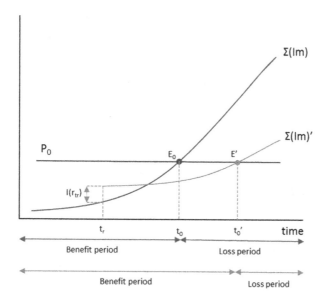

Fig. 3. FITTED interest theory

interest $\Sigma(IM)$ is moved upwards, due to the interest paid for repayment – i.e., $IR(t_r)$ but its slope is decreasing, since the interest is expected to lower for future maintenance activities (IM). This in turn leads to a shift of the equilibrium point (E') to the right, increasing the benefit period (t_0'). The money supply line (P_0) is not moved, because the originally available budget of the company is not affected, assuming zero investment or inflation. The proposed interest theory can help practitioners in their decision making by:

- Identifying the timestamp in which incurring TD, becomes harmful for the company. Thus, they can decide if they should undertake the debt.
- Supporting the continuous monitoring of the interest that has been paid so far.
- Evaluating the repayment activity, based on the time-shift of the equilibrium point that it offers.

5 Research Implications

Research on TD is rather theoretical and lacks empirical evidence. In particular, according to Li et al. 49 % of the complete corpus of TD research presents no empirical evidence, or only toy examples, whereas this number rises to 56 %, when focusing on interest [15]. Thus, in this section we provide future work directions, which could provide empirical evidence on TD interest and support the realization of FITTED.

Types of Interest & Evolution:

- Which one of the two types of interest $(IR$ or $IM)$ produces higher interest amounts when it occurs? Answering this question would suggest which type of interest would be more profitable to manage.
- How can IR and IM amount be modelled, as a function of the principal, or the underlying structure of the TDI? Answering this question would open new research directions in TD management, since more elaborate management approaches could be employed.
- What is the relationship of the decay of quality in the underlying system and the increase in EM or ER? Answering this question could guide practitioners on how to model the increase of interest during software evolution.

So far, these questions have been partially explored by Guo et al. [12], Nugroho et al. [20], and Siebra et al. [24], by exploring historical changes and documentation. The research state-of-the-art lacks real-world evidence on effort allocation.

FITTED Interest Theory:

- What is the expected time (t_0) when the equilibrium will be reached?
- What is the average time-shift from performing specific repayment activities?
- What factors influence this time-shift?
- What is the relationship between IR and the average decrease in the IM of future maintenance activities?

Answering these questions, would enable researchers to instantiate the proposed theory, based on context-specific data, and offer FITTED as a useful tool for practitioners (see Sect. 6).

6   Application of FITTED Interest Theory

As an illustrative example of how the FITTED interest theory can be applied, Chatzigeorgiou et al. [6] proposed an ***empirical setting for calculating the expected time (t_0) when the equilibrium will be reached*** (see first question on FITTED Interest Theory in Sect. 5)[3]. Based on this study, the time point at which the equilibrium is reached has been termed as the *breaking point of technical debt*. To formulate principal and interest, Chatzigeorgiou et al. [6] used the rationale depicted in Fig. 4. In particular, it is assumed that the quality of every system can be calculated with the use of a fitness function. Also, using search-based optimization a design that optimizes the value of this function can be obtained. The effort needed to transform the original system to the optimal one is the ***principal***. Furthermore, it is reasonable to assume that the effort needed to perform any feature addition (EM) on the actual system will be higher than the effort to add the same feature to the optimum system. This difference in effort is ***interest*** (more details can be found in [6]).

To instantiate this approach with a specific implementation, Chatzigeorgiou et al. [6] performed the following actions/assumptions:

- ***Fitness function (FF):*** Ratio between coupling and cohesion, i.e., two well-known software quality characteristics.

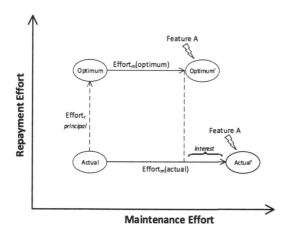

Fig. 4. Increased maintenance effort for technical debt item

---

[3] We note that for this illustration we have not considered the equilibrium point shift that is described in FITTED, but we only calculate the equilibrium point without any refactoring. (In this illustration we assume that while adding features quality does not further decay.)

- *Principal*: Number of simple refactorings (move methods, extract class, etc.) nee-ded to transform the actual design to the optimal one. The cost of a simple refac-toring according to the literature is 5.73$ [27]
- *Interest*: The ratio of the levels of design quality (fitness function) is correlated to the ratio of the two EM (the actual and the optimum). Thus, and by considering that on average the addition of one line of code costs 1.83$, interest can be calculated as $1.83 * LOC_{added} * (1 - FF_{ratio})$.

The application of this approach in an open source system, namely Junit, has shown that an interest of 243$ is accumulated per release and its principal in version 4.10 (starting version) is 1,891$. Therefore, the breaking point will be reached in approx-imately 8 versions after the start version, i.e., about 5.5 years from the time of analysis (see Fig. 5). We note that for simplicity, Chatzigeorgiou et al., have assumed that interest is a linear function of the FF, therefore, the growth of interest, i.e. $\Sigma(IM)$, is linear as well, in contrast to Fig. 3.

Consequently, if no TD repayment activities are performed in this time period the difficulty of maintaining this system (interest) will be as high as the effort saved from not having developed the optimal system (principal). However, we need to note that 5.5 years is a long period, and thus, the project is considered to have a sustainable amount of TD.

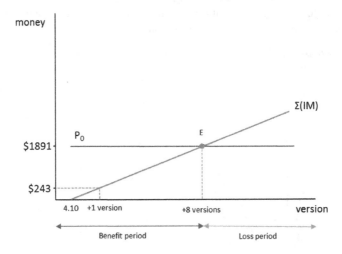

Fig. 5. Application of FITTED interest theory in Junit

7   Threats to Validity

In this study, we report threats to the validity of this research. Since some parts of the research method application are inherited from the secondary studies of Ampatzoglou et al. [3] and Li et al. [15], their threats to validity are also inherited. Therefore, the following threats have been identified:

- *Possibility of missing primary studies.* We believe that although this threat still exists, we have substantially mitigated it, by considering the union of primary studies reported on the two secondary studies. Also, the fact that their overlap was quite high indicates that their coverage was adequate.
- *Publication bias.* As both secondary studies report, in many cases research areas in their infancy are biased by the fact that most of the studies are published by a small community. However, we believe that this fact is currently changing in TD, since more and more researchers are getting actively involved in the last years.

Concerning data extraction, since we independently performed this step, the corresponding threats are related only to this study. To mitigate bias while extracting data, two researchers performed data collection independently, compared the results and discussed possible differences. The final dataset was built through the consent of all authors. Finally, as a threat we acknowledge that the construction of the presented formulas, is to some extent based on the understanding of the authors on TD interest.

8 Conclusions

Nowadays, Technical Debt (TD) is receiving increasing interest by both academia and practitioners, leading to an explosion of studies in this field. The cornerstones of TD are two notions borrowed from economics: i.e., *principal* and *interest*. Although principal is a well-established term, interest has so far been discussed in a rather coarse-grained way, with several contradictions among researchers. In this paper, we propose *FITTED*, i.e., a framework for managing interest in TD, which takes into account existing TD literature and economic interest theories. The framework comprises of: (a) the parameters that are used in TD interest valuation, (b) a classification of TD interest types, (c) a characterization of TD interest evolution, and (d) a TD interest theory, based on the Liquidity Preference Theory. The proposed framework is expected to aid in the decision making of practitioners, and points to interesting research directions. The main emphasis of the future research directions is on empirical studies, which until now are underrepresented in the TD research corpus.

References

1. Allman, E.: Managing technical debt. Communication **55**(5), 50–55 (2012). ACM
2. Alves, N., Mendes, T., de Mendonça, M., Spínola, R., Shull, F., Seaman, C.: Identification and management of technical debt: A systematic mapping study. Inf. Softw. Technol. **70**(2), 100–121 (2016)
3. Ampatzoglou, A., Ampatzoglou, A., Chatzigeorgiou, A., Avgeriou, P.: The financial aspect of managing technical debt: a systematic literature review. Inf. Softw. Technol. **64**, 52–73 (2015). Elsevier
4. Ampatzoglou, A., Ampatzoglou, A., Avgeriou, P., Chatzigeorgiou, A.: Establishing a framework for managing interest in technical debt. In: 5th International Symposium on Business Modeling and Software Design, BMSD 2015, Milan, Italy (2015)

5. Buschmann, F.: To pay or not to pay technical debt. Software **28**(6), 29–31 (2011). IEEE Computer Society
6. Chatzigeorgiou, A., Ampatzoglou, A., Ampatzoglou, A., Amanatidis, T.: Estimating the Breaking Point for Technical Debt. In: 7rd International Workshop on Managing Technical Debt, MTD 2015. IEEE Computer Society (2015)
7. Chin, S., Huddleston, E., Bodwell, W., Gat, I.: The Economics of Technical Debt. Cutter IT J., September 2010
8. Cunningham, W.: The WyCash Portfolio Management System. In: 7th International Conference on Object-Oriented Programming, Systems, Languages, and Applications, OOPSLA 1992 (1992)
9. Eisenberg, R.J.: A threshold based approach to technical debt. ACM SIGSOFT Softw. Eng. Notes **37**(2), 1–6 (2012). ACM
10. Ernst, N.: On the role of requirements in understanding and managing technical debt. In: 3rd International Workshop on Managing Technical Debt, MTD 2012. IEEE (2012)
11. Guo, Y., Seaman, C.: A portfolio approach to technical debt management. In: 2nd International Workshop on Managing Technical Debt. ACM (2011)
12. Guo, Y., Seaman, C., Gomes, R., Cavalcanti, A., Tonin, G., da Silva, F., Santos, A.L., Siebra, C.: Tracking technical debt - an exploratory case study. In: 27th International Conference on Software Maintenance, ICSM 2011. IEEE Computer Society (2011)
13. Izurieta, C., Griffith, I., Reimanis, D., Luhr, R.: On the uncertainty of technical debt measurements. In: Proceedings of the 4th International Conference on Information Science and Applications, ICISA 2013, pp. 1–4. IEEE, Suwon, South Korea (2013)
14. Kitchenham, B., Brereton, O.P., Budgen, D., Turner, M., Bailey, J., Linkman, S.: Systematic literature reviews in software engineering – a systematic literature review. Inf. Softw. Technol. **51**(1), 7–15 (2009). Elsevier
15. Li, Z., Avgeriou, P., Liang, P.: A systematic mapping study on technical debt and its management. J. Syst. Softw. **101**, 193–220 (2015). Elsevier
16. Letouzey, J. L.: The sqale method for evaluating technical debt. In: 3rd International Workshop on Managing Technical Debt, MTD 2012. IEEE Computer Society (2012)
17. McGregor, J.D., Monteith, J., Zhang, J.: Technical debt aggregation in ecosystems. In: 3rd International Workshop on Managing Technical Debt, MTD 2012. IEEE Computer Society (2012)
18. Mishkin, F., Eakins, S.: Financial Markets and Institutions, 7th edn. Prentice Hall, Upper Saddle River (2012)
19. Nord, R., Ozkaya, I., Kruchten, P., Gonzalez-Rojas, M.: In Search of a metric for managing architectural technical debt. In: 2012 Joint Working IEEE/IFIP Conference on Software Architecture (WICSA) and European Conference on Software Architecture (ECSA). IEEE Computer Society (2012)
20. Nugroho, A., Visser, J., Kuipers, T.: An empirical model of technical debt and interest. In: 2nd International Workshop on Managing Technical Debt, MTD 2011. ACM (2011)
21. Ogawa, R.T., Malen, B.: Towards rigor in reviews of multivocal literatures: applying the exploratory case study method. Rev. Educ. Res. **61**(3), 265–286 (1991). SAGE Publications
22. Seaman, C., Guo, Y.: Measuring and monitoring technical debt. Adv. Comput. **82**, 25–46 (2011). Elsevier
23. Seaman, C., Guo, Y., Zazworka, N., Shull, F., Izurieta, C., Cai, Y., Vetró, A.: Using technical debt data in decision making: Potential decision approaches. In: 3rd International Workshop on Managing Technical Debt, MTD 2012. IEEE Computer Society (2012)
24. Siebra, C.S., Tonin, G.S., Silva, F.Q., Oliveira, R.G., Junior, A.L., Miranda, R.C., Santos, A. L.: Managing technical debt in practice: an industrial report. In: 6th International Symposium on Empirical Software Engineering and Measurement (ESEM). ACM (2012)

25. Snipes, W., Robinson, B., Guo, Y., Seaman, C.: Defining the decision factors for managing defects: a technical debt perspective. In: 3rd International Workshop on Managing Technical Debt, MTD 2012. IEEE Computer Society (2012)
26. Tom, E., Aurum, A., Vidgen, R.: An exploration of technical debt. J. Syst. Softw. **86**(6), 1498–1516 (2013). Elsevier
27. Wake, W.C.: Refactoring Workbook, 1st edn. Addison-Wesley Professional, Boston (2003)
28. Zazworka, N., Seaman, C., Shull, F.: Prioritizing design debt investment opportunities. In: 2nd International Workshop on Managing Technical Debt, MTD 2011. ACM (2011)

Classifying Business Model Canvas Usage from Novice to Master: A Dynamic Perspective

Boris Fritscher[1(✉)] and Yves Pigneur[2]

[1] Information Systems and Management Institute, HES-SO,
University of Applied Sciences Western Switzerland,
HEG Arc, 2000 Neuchâtel, Switzerland
boris.fritscher@he-arc.ch
[2] Faculty of Business and Economics, University of Lausanne,
1015 Lausanne, Switzerland

Abstract. When designing and assessing a business model, a more visual and practical ontology and framework is necessary. We draw lessons from usage by practitioners around the world of the Business Model Canvas (BMC) method to define three maturity level. We propose new concepts to help design the dynamic aspect of a business model. On the first level, the BMC supports novice users as they elicit their models; it also helps novices to build coherent models. On the second level, the BMC allows expert users to evaluate the interaction of business model elements by outlining the key threads in the business models story. On the third level, master users are empowered to create multiple versions of their business models, allowing them to evaluate alternatives and retain the history of the business models evolution. These new concepts for the BMC which can be supported by Computer-Aided Design tools provide a clearer picture of the business model as a strategic planning tool and are the basis for further research.

Keywords: Business model canvas · Computer-aided business model design · Guidelines

1 Introduction

Competition for companies and start-ups has evolved in the past decade. Today, success cannot be achieved on product innovation alone. At a strategy level, having the means to improve the design of business models has become a real issue for entrepreneurs and executives alike. Business models methods are a good way to share a common language about part of a strategy across a multidisciplinary team. These methods enable quick communication, and help improve the design of a new business model, as well as assess existing ones.

There are many different business model ontologies which focus, for example, on economics, process, or value exchange between companies. One such business model tool which is getting popular is the Business Model Canvas (BMC) [1].

© Springer International Publishing Switzerland 2016
B. Shishkov (Ed.): BMSD 2015, LNBIP 257, pp. 134–151, 2016.
DOI: 10.1007/978-3-319-40512-4_8

Its visual representation and simple common language are two essential characteristics which have helped spread its adoption and make its book a bestseller. The current version of the BMC is an evolution from the original academic work the Business Model Ontology (BMO) [2]. The need to evolve the model took place to better fit the needs of practitioners over academics. The visual representation was improved under the influence of design thinking practice.

Through observation gained from, giving workshops, teaching to students and a survey, it appears that the building blocks of the BMC are covering the main needs, however usage itself of the model seems very basic and is limited to static analysis of one business model at a given time. This can be linked back to its original ontology which is used to describe a static model.

In reality, companies have to change and adapt to internal and external changes which impact their business. Therefore, a business model method should also consider the dynamic nature of transformation and evolution of the model.

This brings us to the following research question:

How to represent and help to design the dynamic aspect of a business model with the Business Model Canvas?

In order to answer the question, we first contribute to a definition of the maturity level of BMC users. Based on the three identified levels: novice, experts and master, we split the main question into three sub questions. For each, we contribute to a concept on how to handle a particular dynamic aspect. Having a classification of levels and demonstrating how they fit together will help inventors of new BMC extensions to target the right users. We also highlight the implication of these concepts for computer-aided design support functions.

On the first level, the BMC supports novice users as they elicit their models; it also helps novices to build coherent models. On the second level, the BMC allows expert users to evaluate the interaction of business model elements by outlining the key threads in the business models story. On the third level, master users are empowered to create multiple versions of their business models, allowing them to evaluate alternatives and retain the history of the business models evolution.

We adopted the following design science structure for our paper: After this introduction, we present the related work on business model languages, dynamic perspectives and present the result of a survey of BMC users. Followed by a short presentation of the methodology and how we address the research question in multiple parts. The main artifact section presents two new concepts: business model mechanics and business model evolution, to help address designing the dynamic aspect of a business model. In the evaluation section we present the validity of the concept. We end the paper with a discussion and a conclusion on the implications for future research in business model design.

2   Related Work

In this section we present the choice of the BMC over other business model languages, present how a dynamic perspective is addressed in similar domains as business modeling. In addition, the importance of a dynamic perspective for BMC is highlighted through the presentation of results of a survey of practitioners.

2.1   Business Model Languages

Whilst many other business model languages exist, this paper does not include a detailed comparison of them. We have, however, sought to highlight the differences between Business Model Ontology (BMO) and its closest alternatives. Starting around the same time as BMO, e3-value [3] includes many similar concepts, many of which can be mapped between them [4]. In particular, e3-value goes into more detail about the interactions between the components. In addition, it specifies the value which is exchanged in both directions and the way in which it flows. Using e3-value, it is possible to go beyond creating a single business model; indeed, it is also possible to model the interactions between business models within a sector. This detailed modeling of interactions comes with the necessity to specify ports through which the connections flow. Consequently, this makes visual representation more complex. The relationship between elements can further be described with types and values that allow for the basic financial calculation of the model.

Whilst BMO is concerned with providing a small but complete set of strategic components to describe a business model, another modeling language, known as SEAM [5] also exists. SEAM focuses on enterprise architecture and addresses the issue by providing a hierarchical decomposition. It uses a visual representation to handle the encapsulation of its hierarchies, which allows an exploration of the underlying resources and processes that contribute to the high level element. In the past few years, SEAM [6] and BMO [7] have both evolved ways to better describe and explore the connection between the value proposition and customer segments. An essential part of both models is to be able to visually display the elements and show their connections at the same level as the concepts. The visual handling of encapsulation does, however, generate complex diagrams, which can be hard to read for the non-initiated.

Weill and Vitale [8] illustrated a method for the schematic description of e-business models. The focus is on the simple interactions between the firm and its customer and suppliers, which are drawn on a blank canvas. An indication of the direction of interactions is given, along with the type of flow. Thus, it adds value to an interaction in a way that is similar to e3-value; however, it is more general since it does not define ports or go into more detail about the flow itself.

Business model ontology has evolved since its initial design. Retrospectively, we can distinguish there distinct stages: (1) the creation of Business Model Ontology (BMO), (2) followed by its first confrontation with reality, (3) which then paved the way for its design-influenced redevelopment as the BMC incorporating its visual canvas and simplified components. Other communities, such as Customer Development [9], have started using the BMC as a supporting model for their theories.

2.2   Dynamic Perspectives

Having a dynamic perspective on the BMC can be interpreted in several different fashion: (1) considering the interactions between its components, (2) different representation of one model depending on the focus or the stakeholder, (3) transformation of the model into another version of itself (versioning).

Interaction Between Components is seen in strategic business model ontology (SBMO) [10]. It introduces a strategy layer which reasons about alternative strategies with the i* model. Focus is on its ability to express the overall decision making process. It illustrates that making interactions explicit helps in strategic reasoning about business models.

Different Perspectives for a process model are explored by [11]. They show how different perspectives of the same model can be provided to different stakeholder through CAD tooling.

Versioning of work was first introduced in development environments and has proved successful in handling a variety of change tracking that goes far beyond the initial source files [12]. In fields such as database modeling, schema evolution is well known in relational and object-oriented systems [13]. These solutions are too technical and not easily adapted to high-level and managerial-level business illustrations. In enterprise architecture, versioning is also something well known, especially the concept of making an as-is and a to-be model. An ontology to describe transformation from one state into another exists, but lacks any visual representation [14]. At its core, versioning serves to guarantee the integrity of the changes, giving the business model an immutable history. However, whilst this works for documenting the history of an evolution, it does not support creative prototyping, where a flexible and dynamic back-and-forth way of idea exploration is required. More complex versioning such as tree or graph based variations can help [15]. A lot of work has been done in business process modeling, but their models are more formal than the BMC which is closer to brainstorming. Some kind of variant management [16] to handle what-if exploration should be possible and would provide more than linear versioning of a models history.

2.3 Practitioners' Survey

Business Model community members participated in a survey. The participants confirmed that visual aspects and the use of a common language to facilitate group discussion were key reasons for opting to use the BMC (as shown in Table 1). One interviewee summarized it clearly by stating that: It makes an integrated discussion, focused on the interrelationships of essential building blocks possible (Survey 2013 - Why did you choose to use the Canvas?)

The BMC gained the strongest foothold in the entrepreneurial community, who have in an interest in building new business models. However, the BMC is not limited to only design such models. A common language can also be used to analyze a current situation and then help with strategic reorientation towards a better performing business model. Table 2 shows that whilst a new business

Table 1. Survey question

Why did you choose to use the Canvas?		N= 1,229
Visual aspects	65.3 %	803
To facilitate group discussion	61.0 %	750
Intuitive	54.3 %	667

Table 2. Survey question

What has been your primary reason for using the Canvas?		N= 1,120
Development of an entirely new business	35.8 %	401
New product/service development within existing business model	21.3 %	238
Strategic reorientation	19.6 %	219
Renovate old business model	14.8 %	166

Table 3. Survey question

What type of organization do you primarily work for?		N= 1,616
Corporation	29.1 %	470
Start-up (younger than 5 years)	21.3 %	345
Self-employed	15.4 %	249
Boutique consultancy	14.6 %	236
University	8.6 %	139
NGO/non-profit	5.3 %	85

model is the primary activity, the desire to work on an existing business model is non-negligible.

As can be seen in Table 3, the participants came as much from corporations as from the entrepreneurial world; meaning that neither has biased the previous result.

From this survey we can see that the simplicity of the one page visual layout is a key component from its adoption. But the results also show that a third of the use is focused on improving / transforming an existing business model. A usage which is not best served by the static BMC, a more dynamic approach to move between as-is and to-be state is needed. Additionally, the current design method and recommendation focus on breaking innovation, while maybe a more traditional methods focus on renovation with planned transformation is needed.

3   Methodology

In this study, we used Design Science Research (DSR), as described by Gregor &Hevner [17]. They defined a process in which artifacts are built and evaluated in an iterative process in order to solve the relevant problems. The need to take a visual approach to creating the BMC was driven by design-thinking theories and we identified need for practitioners to have better tools that can be easily integrated into daily practice. Existing knowledge of business model ontology has been described in the previous section. It was shown that Information Systems (IS) has the necessary body of knowledge to handle *strategizing as designing* [18].

3.1   Users Maturity Level of Business Model Canvas Modeling

The BM canvas method was evaluated using data and evidence from its use in the real world, books, canvas, workshops and lectures helped to inform the following three maturity levels inspired by the Common European Framework of Reference for Languages (CEFR), which also has three groups.

Novice use the BMC as a simple common language and visualization help.

Expert use the BMC as a holistic vision to understand and target a business models sustainability. They understand the models methods, such as high level links and colors, which helps to connect ideas and follow the interactions.

Master use the BMC in the global Strategy, which is a process that evolves and adapts to its environment. They understand that the design of a model has to accompany such a process by supporting concepts of iteration, transformation (mutation) and choosing alternatives (selection).

Having defined these three level of proficiency we use it to decompose the research question into three sub-questions:

Novice level usage is the most commonly observed and fully applies to the static use of the BMC. Before moving to a dynamic representation of a business model, it should be guaranteed that at a static level it is already a coherent model. Which leads us to the following sub-question:

How can the static design usage of the business model canvas be improved (in relation to its coherence)?

Expert and Master level design of BMC are not observed frequently and lack representation due to their requiring a more dynamic aspect of the BMC.

For the expert with a focus on internal interactions this leads us to the following sub-question:

How to represent the dynamic aspect of interactions happening inside the business model?

Handling multiple states of a business model, due to internal or external changes, at the master level leads to the following sub-question:

How to represent the transformation from one state to another of a business model?

In the next section, we address these questions individually each with their own artifact.

4   Artifact

In the next three subsection we consider each business model canvas design task of each mastery level by looking first at a metaphor of a similar design task in another design domain. Transposing the metaphor of house planning in architecture, plane building in engineering and evolution in biology to business model designing, we propose a concept to help answer each sub question. Each level builds on the previous and comes with their respective concept: BM Canvas Coherence, BM Mechanics and BM evolution, to address the dynamic nature of business models. We then illustrate how each concept applies to a small common example: the case of Apples iPod business model. Each Artifact also describes in a short summary the essence of the mastery level to further offer a clear way to differentiate the three levels.

The following three concepts are presented below:

BM Canvas Coherence helps the novice to improve static business model modeling by way of using guidelines to check coherence of the business model.

BM Mechanics helps the expert by proposing to use colors and arrows to outline the interactions happening inside the business model.

BM Evolution helps the master by offering a way to visualize business model transformation from one state into another. Applying these transformation multiple times results in a tree showing the evolution of the business model.

A mapping between level and concept can be seen in Table 4.

4.1   BM Canvas Coherence

At the novice level, the focus is on the concepts of the ontology, meaning the nine building blocks that define a business model. The main task consists of designing a business model by filling in elements for each block. Designing a business model can be best described using the metaphor of an architect engaged in designing a house. The architect needs to know about the various components of a house, such as the walls, doors, windows, roof and stairs, and also how they relate to each other. A wall can have windows and doors. A room has four walls with at least one door. Beyond such constraints, however, the architect is free to produce a variety of designs for a house. During the design process, the architect puts forwards his ideas using sketches and prototype models. These prototypes are not finished products, but are specifically aimed at testing the interaction of a selection of concepts in the specified context of the prototype. Transferring this design technique to a business model design means creating different business model variations of component interactions. For example, when prototyping a specific customer segment, the value proposition set could have its revenue stream type switched from paying to free, or from sales to subscription. This could then lead to further prototype changes to dependent components. This iterative validation of ideas leads to a business model that has all its components matching to become a usable business model. Checking the coherence between the elements is a key requirement for a valid business model. It is not enough to only produce a checklist of items without verifying their compatibility. Again, with reference to our architecture metaphor, stairs should be used to connect floors, and a door should lead to a room rather than nowhere. We call this usability. Similarly, in a business model, a value proposition needs to offer added value to a customer segment requiring it. A value proposition without a customer segment indicates a non-coherent business model. The iterative validation of design ideas can go as far as getting out of the building and test the assumptions directly with the potential customer as is done in Customer Development [9]. The gained insights may help to validate the hypothesis of the prototype or else offer new ideas to make a pivot of the model to target different customers.

In order to facilitate the checking of coherence, there are a series of guidelines which we have proposed to help validate the business models elements and interaction [19]. They are split into three categories from element, to building block and interactions:

Guidelines applying to individual elements for example that the meaning of the element is understandable by all stakeholders.

Guidelines applying to individual blocks for example that the detail level of the elements are adequate (there are not too many detailed elements, nor too few which are too generic).

Guidelines applying to connections between elements in different blocks for example that there are no orphan elements: all elements are connected to another element (in a different block to themselves).

4.2   Novice Level in Summary

At the novice level, the concepts of the model identify the right elements and how they are related to one another. An iterative process that explores detailed features of the elements helps to adjust the elements that make up the model in order to solve real problems. This leads to a coherent model that addresses the right job.

4.3   Apple iPod BM Canvas

In this example, we focus on Apples iPod business model. A model can be described by its elements, with keywords for each of the nine building blocks. Alternatively, illustrations can be used, as shown in Fig. 1. The value proposition is a seamless experience that includes listening, managing and buying music. It is targeted at consumers who want to listen to music wherever they go and have access to a computer. The distribution channels to reach these consumers is a store or online-shop where the device can be bought along with iTunes software to manage the music library. Sales of the device generate revenue with higher margins than sales of the songs, where most of it goes to the majors. The customer relationship is oriented towards the lifestyle experience of Apple products. In order to offer these services, the key activity is the design of the device. Key resources are the device itself, music contracts, the developers and the Apple brand which strengthens the customer relationship. Marketing and developers are the key cost structures. Music licensing and device manufacturing is carried out through the partners.

This business model slice is coherent since as described each element is connected to another. There are no orphan elements, nor any combination of elements not connected to the rest of the business model.

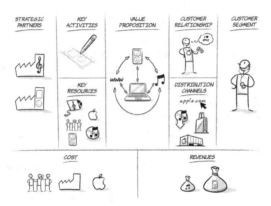

Fig. 1. Apple iPod BM Canvas XPLANE 2008

4.4   BM Mechanics

At the expert level, knowledge about the BMC and the requirement to design a coherent model is well incorporated into practice. The focus is on analyzing the interaction of the models elements beyond the relationships between them. It is not just about how one element relates with its connected elements, but about how they contribute to the overall thread of the business model story. A chain of interactions must be built from one element to another throughout their relationship. To continue with our comparison with other design domains, we move from architecture to engineering, where it is not enough to just know about the concept. An engineer needs to know about the underlying physics that supports the concepts. For example, it is not enough to know about the concepts that make a plane; we also need to know about their interactions. Without knowing how the aerodynamic properties of a wing generate lift, it would be impossible to design a plane that flies. Trial and error with prototypes that are not based on physical calculation would result in a large number of failures. Whats more, the end result could not be explained fully. Similarly, in the design of business models, the activity has to move beyond prototyping and try to simulate the model to see if it is workable. A good business model needs to both do the right job and be sustainable. Business model mechanics, outlines how elements influence each other beyond their relationship. The story can illustrate the flow of the exchange value between customers and the product and how it is produced. It is about understanding the underlying interactions which make the business model possible. In this context, explaining a revenue stream can for example depend on a partner (a relationship which is not defined in the basic ontology). These connections can be drawn using arrows at the top of the canvas to show the story. Elements can also be added to the canvas one after another while telling the story; this helps to strengthen the illustration. Another way to highlight the connectedness of elements is to use colors.

4.5   Expert Level in Summary

At the expert level, the business model concepts of the canvas are well understood, and analysis has moved beyond the elements towards the interactions
based on their relationships. The business model is coherent and does the right
job. Above all, the interactions needed to make it work are understood. Thus,
the model is the right one and has the potential to be sustainable if implemented
correctly.

4.6   Apple iTunes BM Mechanics

In the case of the Apple iTunes, two stories can be identified (see Fig. 2): the
music part (shown using dotted lines), and the device (iPod) and brand part
(shown using dashed lines).

In order to make the platform attractive, Apple had to offer a broad selection
of titles, including all the popular songs. This was achieved by making deals with
all the big majors. Skill and leverage were required to be able to make deals which
will make the platform competitive on pricing and title selection. Initially, to get
the majors on board Apple added Digital Rights Management (DRM) to protect
the digital music files; this had the side benefit of locking the user in to Apples
devices and software platform.

On the device side, functionality and esthetics had to be combined in the
design activity to create a product which is in line with the customers brand
expectations.

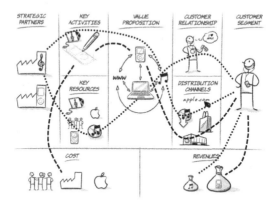

Fig. 2. Apple iPad BM Mechanics adapted from XPLANE 2008

4.7   BM Evolution

At the masters level, any considerations go beyond the current business model.
Masters are not afraid of the unknown and are ready for anything. There is an

understanding that the strategy has to have a longer-term vision that extends beyond the current business model, and that to survive, it has to be able to evolve. The focus is on actions that can be taken to evolve from one business model to another. In order to be aware of incoming changes, observation of the business models environment is key. Our architecture and engineering metaphor has its limits; indeed, we would need to use analogies from the realm of science fiction to illustrate transforming behaviors. Therefore, a better analogy is the concept of biological evolution. Individual business models can become obsolete and die off; however, the species evolves and survives through mutation and selection. This means that in order to survive decay, new business models (mutations from existing ones) have to be tested continuously. When proven successful, they are selected. Sometimes, the previous business model might even be cannibalized by it.

A business model can do the right job and be sustainable and still fail if it is not adapted to its environment. Unlike our biology analogy, the variations of a business model can be planned so that it can be ready to adapt when the environment changes. This involves planning different business models for a range of scenarios [20] and then being ready to switch to them depending on the environment. The adaptability of a business model to its context is key.

Various external occurrences may affect the business model at any time; thus, different alternatives need to be kept should one of them become a reality. Keeping track of the mutation in relation to external stimuli necessitates the management of different versions of the business model. The creation of multiple versions of a business model to address different external environments is a first step. Another step is to know how to adapt from one version of a model to another. In this case, the transformation between them needs to be highlighted. For that purpose, we propose to use the concept of transparent layers to stack business models parts on top of each other. On paper this can be done with tracing paper, each new layer can show new elements and reuse of element which are visible in a semi-translucent fashion from lower layers.

Together, the two steps allow us to evaluate a model in the light of external factors, thus enabling us to select the business model that fits best.

The combination of multiple transformation from a given state help form a graph or a tree with branches of possible evolution paths to follow for the future business model. As well as to visualize the past transformations which lead to the current state of the business model.

4.8   Master Level in Summary

At the masters level, business model concepts and interactions (story) are well understood, both in terms of a single model and the analysis of multiple models. Decisions are made with the environment in mind in order to deploy the right model in the right context. Using this strategy, business models can be evolved to adapt to any change.

4.9   BM Evolution: From Apple iTunes to Apple App Store Business Model

The transformation from a music service to a software platform has many innovation drivers. A major one which can be highlighted in Apples case was their capability to create a touch-based screen for a phone device by combining new external technology (touch hardware) with internal knowledge of the design of human friendly interfaces (custom software).

To create the App Store business model (seen in Fig. 3), Apple evolved their iTunes business model by reusing existing components, expanding others and adding new ones. Apple capitalized on its knowledge of design, value chain management and store to build and distribute a new touch based phone (iPhone). New components included the extension of the distribution channel to also include the new partner, the mobile phone operators. Taking advantage of their knowledge of building software development kits for computers, Apple created a development kit for the phone which is targeted at a new customer segment of developers to create mobile apps. To manage the quality of these apps and handle financial transactions, a validation process and revenue sharing model had to be put in place. Putting these pieces into place helped to create an eco-system that connects phone users in need of specialized apps with a large developer community willing to provide them for a small price. This transformation was much more than a product innovation; rather, the whole business model moved to a double sided business model [21], connecting the developers with the phone users.

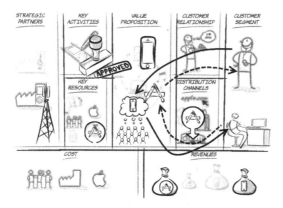

Fig. 3. Apple iTunes to App Store adapted from XPLANE 2008

5   Evaluation

The first evaluation of the proposed concept is their instantiation into cases. Being able to use the concept to represent real world business models demonstrates the validity of the artifact. The second part is to show their utility having user employing the proposed techniques to represent their own business models. Since the proposed concept are still very early ideas, a further step would be to refine them. This would allow for them, for example, to be implemented into a computer-aided design tools for business models. Providing advantages of automating some of the concepts more tedious interactions such as validating constraints, editing arrows paths and changing visibility of elements.

For each of the BM concepts explained in the previous section we present the goal solved by an artefact we built to demonstrate its instantiation. We give a summary of our related work findings and propose some further possible evaluations.

5.1 BM Canvas Coherence

Goal: evaluate how rules can help beginner build more coherent business models.

Useful validation questions and best practices emerged during the years of teaching workshops on the business model canvas. Some of which have been formalized into guidelines and applied to build an expository case business model [19]. This could then be evaluated to see how automated validation of the coherence of a business model can assist the creation of better business models. In the process of testing user experience and idea generation differences between paper and digital business model design, we also did initial testing on coherence guidelines on paper with a group of students. This showed that they lacked the perseverance to rigorously apply them manually and highlights the need to perform experiments with computer aided systems.

5.2 BM Mechanics

Goal: evaluate how visual help such as color tagging can help provide a clearer picture.

Drawing arrows on top of business models is also something that emerges naturally in design session. Therefore it is already somewhat in use although not in a guided fashion. However, it is not always used as described in the bm mechanics technique. Previous work has shown that formalized links do not get adopted by the users, instead color tagging of elements can be used [22]. We tested how tagging elements with different color can help get a better visual picture without increasing the visual legibility. This suggests that for formalizing the BM mechanics feature, attention should be focused on not making the arrow interaction too constraining or complicated.

5.3 BM Evolution

Goal: Evaluate the usefulness of the layer concept to represent business model transformations.

The business model evolution concept with its two parts: transformation (mutation) and path of possible (selection) is a somewhat complicated concept.

Especially to create the visual representation on paper. Wanting to explore alternatives can lead to a lot of copy work and stacking multiple versions of transformation on top of each other can get visually cluttered. An initial instantiation into a Computer Aided Design (CAD) tool has been attempted and shows promising results [23]. The creation of the prototype tool lead also to the building of a case which describes a real world business model evolution over seven transformations and two business models evolving in parallel[1]. This illustrate the potential of using a layered visual approach to represent the dynamic nature of business model evolution.

The connected layered view concept defined in BM evolution is very versatile and can cover more than one type of the dynamic perspective. In the current evaluation, we mainly proved the feasibility of following the transformation (history) of a business model and its forking into parallel models. But the technique can also apply to scenario planning such as a what-if exploration of multiple future models. Having the advantage of being connected to the original model from which they were forked, thus they are kept up to date with the current models changes. The perceived value of such automatically updated brainstorming tool has still to be tested in a real world application. Layers can also be combined with concepts of other levels as we describe in the next section.

6   Discussion

Although we presented the three concept separately, each successive level of maturity builds on top of the previous ones. A business model has to be coherent in itself before exploring its dynamic aspect. The prototype built to support BM evolution visualization also supports drawing of arrows for BM mechanics. This shows that the feature of drawing arrows combines itself nicely with the layers that support the transformations of the evolution. For example, instead of decomposing versions of a business model, layers can be used to highlight the temporal decomposition of BM mechanics. Its story, if it has multiple parts, such as the Dell computers business model which first sells the product and then in a second phase makes it. This can be visualized with layers as an *evolution* (chapter) of the story.

Implementing prototypes to support the concept required to identify how the different design technique can be support by CAD functions. We summarize them in the next section.

Documenting the transformation which BMO went through to get adopted by practitioners gave us some insight into elements which made it possible. We present our observation in the section entitled: Lessons learned for business model methods designers.

---

[1] Valve Corporation: Business Model Evolution Case http://www.fritscher.ch/phd/valve/.

6.1   Design Techniques and Supporting CAD Functions

In Table 4 we provide a summary of the key design techniques and supporting CAD functions for each concept of the three maturity levels.

At the novice level, BM Canvas Coherence can be improved by following guidelines. It is possible to formalize these guidelines into verifiable rules. This in turn allows to perform validation or trigger contextual hinting assistance with a CAD tool. In order for the tool to get a better model, it is needed to indicate some of the elements relationship. This can be accomplished by tagging them into different colors, which is simpler for the user than explicitly connecting them with links.

At the expert level, BM mechanics helps to provide a clearer picture on the internal interaction of the business model. In order to support such storytelling, functions like color and arrows can be used on top of the BMC. In addition, a CAD tool can help by toggling the visibility of elements as the story progresses allowing for a dynamic representation of another ways static canvas. This temporal execution of the models story can then be tailored to the individual stakeholders, the dynamic management of the visibility allowing to support multiple stories on the same canvas.

At the master level, BM Evolution helps to address the transformation required by renovation and exploration of possible future states envisioned by scenario planning. Through layers, versioning and by allowing to compute custom views of superposing layers CAD tools offer dynamic visualization showing any chosen past, present or future state of a business model. Also by chaining the transformations, it can be known which change affects any descendant elements future state. A new computation of these updated views can be performed by the tool without any work from the designer.

Table 4. Summary of concept, design technique and CAD functions

Maturity	Concept	Design Technique	CAD functions
Novice	BM Canvas Coherence	Guidelines, rules	Colors, validation, hinting
Expert	BM Mechanics	Storytelling	Colors, arrows, elements visibility
Master	BM Evolution	Renovation, what-if, scenario planning	Layers, versioning, computed views

6.2   Lessons Learned for Business Model Methods Designers

Based on the lessons gained from our experience we can share the following observations on the possible influences on the success of a business modeling methods. These will help to broaden the adoption of an academic enterprise ontology by practitioners:

Designing a method that can scale in complexity for various proficiency levels, from novice to masters, helps its adoption.

Performing design science evaluation cycles and evolving the method after each evaluation is key to identifying the right balance between simplification and the re-addition of elements at different proficiency levels.

Finding the right community is important: people need to be willing to quickly test and iterate the models concepts. (In our case, entrepreneurs were the ideal test participants; it is in their nature to try out business model concepts, which allowed for quick iterations).

Providing a tool (free canvas and book) empowers teaching at a university level as well as in workshops, thus helping to spread the method.

7   Conclusion

Starting from observation on the evolution and adoption of the BMC we identified the need to address the issue of **how to represent and help to design the dynamic aspect of a business model with the Business Model Canvas**. Based on observations we *identified three maturity levels* of business model canvas design and addressed the issue by splitting the question into three sub-questions.

We not only provided three clearly defined level of usage of the BMC through concept, design technique and CAD functions, but also showed how each levels builds on and combines with the previous ones. Furthermore, we illustrated how the current concepts, can fit together into the bigger picture of Business Model under a dynamic perspective. Together addressing the sub-questions:

How can the static design usage of the business model canvas be improved (in relation to its coherence)?

At the novice level, the simple nature of the canvas helped in its adoption. This simplicity lends to the use of building blocks as a checklist. It is however necessary to keep in mind the relationship between the elements in order to maintain the underlying ontological nature of the business model theory. *Guidelines can help to verify these relationships and thereby help to create more coherent models.*

How to represent the dynamic aspect of interactions happening inside the business model?

At the expert level, it is necessary to understand the big picture. Showing a completed model to a person for the first time would overload them with information. Thus, design-thinking mechanics, such as storytelling, have to be used to present the BM mechanics of a model one step at a time. This allows users to understand all the elements of a business model, as well as the way they interact with each other. *These interactions can be further strengthened by drawing arrows to outline the main story thread in what we call BM Mechanics.*

How to represent the transformation from one state to another of a business model?

At the master level, it was found that making different versions of a business model could help in analyzing its reaction to its environment. The management of these versions quickly became a constraining factor, particularly if only part of the business model changed. *Using layers to illustrate only the changes is a design technique that helps to overcome some of these constraints. Having the means to describe transformation from one state into another, can then be combined to form a chain of transformation leading to a tree of possible path of evolution for the business model in what we call the BM Evolution.*

To conclude, we provide several opportunities that could be further investigated for each of the discussed levels.

7.1 Opportunities

The business model ontology can be directly extended in several ways. However, it is most advantageous to capitalize on the diffusion and knowledge of the current version. We argue that it is helpful to develop extension as a plugin. For example, a customer segment can be analyzed through the lens of such tools as personas and customer insight or through the framework of jobs to be done [24]. The current focus on plugins is mainly on the value proposition and the customers, or the connection between the two. There are many more elements, however, that could benefit from in-depth analysis at a component or relationship level. Those that come to mind include categorizing the channel based on the time and type of interaction of the client-to-customer relationship for this particular event; this would make better use of the customer relationship component. Key activities can be decomposed into types and supporting applications. This allows us to better align the enterprise architecture, its business processes and infrastructure to the business model [25].

Beyond small transformation of business model, research into a theory of evolution for business models is of great interest, particularly in identifying why some business models survive change better than others.

References

1. Osterwalder, A., Pigneur, Y.: Business Model Generation: A Handbook for Visionaries, Game Changers, and Challengers. Wiley, Hoboken (2010)
2. Osterwalder, A.: The Business Model Ontology-a proposition in a design science approach. Academic Dissertation, Universite de Lausanne, Ecole des Hautes Etudes Commerciales (2004)
3. Gordijn, J., Akkermans, H.: Designing and evaluating e-business models. IEEE Intell. Syst. **4**, 11–17 (2001)
4. Gordijn, J., Osterwalder, A., Pigneur, Y.: Comparing two business model ontologies for designing e-business models and value constellations. In: Proceedings of the 18th Bled eConference, Bled, Slovenia, pp. 6–8 (2005)
5. Wegmann, A.: On the Systemic Enterprise Architecture Methodology SEAM. In: Proceedings of the 5th International Conference on Enterprise Information Systems, pp. 483–490 (2003)
6. Golnam, A., Ritala, P., Viswanathan, V., Wegmann, A.: Modeling value creation and capture in service systems. In: Snene, M. (ed.) IESS 2012. LNBIP, vol. 103, pp. 155–169. Springer, Heidelberg (2012)

7. Osterwalder, A., Pigneur, Y.: An eBusiness model ontology for modeling eBusiness. In: 15th Bled Electronic Commerce Conference, Bled, Slovenia, 17–19 June 2002
8. Weill, P., Vitale, M.R.: Place to Space: Migrating to eBusiness Models. Harvard Business Press, Boston (2001)
9. Blank, S.G., Dorf, B.: The startup owner's manual: the step-by-step guide for building a great company. K&S Ranch, Inc., Pescadero (2012)
10. Samavi, R., Yu, E., Topaloglou, T.: Strategic reasoning about business models: a conceptual modeling approach. Inf. Syst. E-Bus. Manag. **7**(2), 171–198 (2008)
11. Delfmann, P., Knackstedt, R.: Towards tool support for information model variant management-a design science approach. In: Proceedings of the Fifteenth European Conference on Information Systems, University of St. Gallen, pp. 2098–2109 (2007)
12. Tichy, W.F.: RCSa system for version control. Softw. Pract. Experience **15**(7), 637–654 (1985)
13. Nguyen, G.T., Rieu, D.: Schema evolution in object-oriented database systems. Data Knowl. Eng. **4**(1), 43–67 (1989)
14. Purao, S., Martin, R., Robertson, E.: Transforming enterprise architecture models: an artificial ontology view. In: Mouratidis, H., Rolland, C. (eds.) CAiSE 2011. LNCS, vol. 6741, pp. 383–390. Springer, Heidelberg (2011)
15. Clever, N., Holler, J., Pster, J., Shitkova, M.: Growing trees - a versioning approach for business process models based on graph theory. In: ECIS 2013 Proceedings, p. 157 (2013)
16. Kumar, A., Yao, W.: Design and management of flexible process variants using templates and rules. Comput. Ind. **63**(2), 112–130 (2012)
17. Gregor, S., Hevner, A.: Positioning and presenting design science research for maximum impact. MIS Q. **37**(2), 337–355 (2013)
18. Osterwalder, A., Pigneur, Y.: Designing business models and similar strategic objects: the contribution of IS designing. J. Assoc. Inf. Syst. **14**(5), 237–244 (2013)
19. Fritscher, B., Pigneur, Y.: Business model design: an evaluation of paper-based and computer-aided canvases. In: Fourth International Symposium on (BMSD) Business Modeling and Software Design. Scitepress (2014)
20. Schoemaker, P.J.H.: Scenario planning: a tool for strategic thinking. Sloan Manag. Rev. **36**(2), 25 (1995)
21. Eisenmann, T., Parker, G., Van Alstyne, M.: Strategies for two-sided markets. Harvard Bus. Rev. **84**(10), 92 (2006)
22. Fritscher, B., Pigneur, Y.: Computer aided business model design: analysis of key features adopted by users. In: Proceedings of the 47 Annual Hawaii International Conference on System Sciences. Computer Society Press (Ed.) (2014)
23. Fritscher, B., Pigneur, Y.: Visualizing Business Model Evolution with the Business Model Canvas: Concept and Tool. In: Proceedings of the 16th IEEE Conference on Business Informatics (CBI2014). IEEE Computer Society Press (2014)
24. Johnson, M.W.: Seizing the White Space. Harvard Business Press, Boston (2010)
25. Fritscher, B., Pigneur, Y.: A visual approach to business IT alignment between business model and enterprise architecture. IJISMD **6**(1), 1–23 (2015)

Exploring Business - IT Nexus: Make the Most of IT-Enabled Capabilities

Ivan I. Ivanov[✉]

Empire State College of the State University of New York,
Hauppauge, NY 11788, USA
ivan.ivanov@esc.edu

Abstract. Increasingly the business success and economic opportunities stea-dily depend on IT-enabled capabilities and IT-driven business transformations. The strategic alignment of IT capabilities to organizational business strategy, as content and processes, ensures further IT governance to seize opportunities for improvements and to maximize revenue. Utilizing a well deliberated framework -Operating model, Enterprise architecture, and IT engagement model- the paper explores the impact of emerging technologies on the alignment process. Cur-rently, companies across the globe are going through a very disruptive tech-nology development: Consumerization of IT. Consumerization of IT, along with workforce mobility, reliable, accessible and affordable remote computing, are forcefully reshaping the corporate IT lanscape, affecting the relationship between enterprise IT, knowledge workers, corporate users, and consumers. The paper confers the impact of these trends on the IT domain and specifically emphasizes on the dynamic forces interlinking IT capabilities with the business agility, growth and asset utilization.

Keywords: Socio-technical system · Systemic effect · Enterprise architecture · IT architecture · IT governance · Emerging technologies · Cloud computing · Mobile computing · Consumerization of IT

1 Trends in Business-IT Nexus

Increasingly we have witnessed how business success and economic opportunities steadily depend on IT-enabled capabilities and IT-driven business transformations. In today's global digital economy, the technology and business domains are colliding forcefully than ever and new business models and growing prospects emerge. The IT and especially emerging information technologies profoundly change how companies create value both within specific industries, and through industry boundaries.

Large number of surveys indicates that IT has mature and increased greatly its capability despite the fact business stakeholders' satisfaction with IT continues to decline in the last several years. This discrepancy could be attributed to rising expectations of IT capabilities – as IT improves the business demands more. This is most notably in categories related to revenue generating objectives such as new product creation and entering novel markets – see Fig. 1 [1].

© Springer International Publishing Switzerland 2016
B. Shishkov (Ed.): BMSD 2015, LNBIP 257, pp. 152–170, 2016.
DOI: 10.1007/978-3-319-40512-4_9

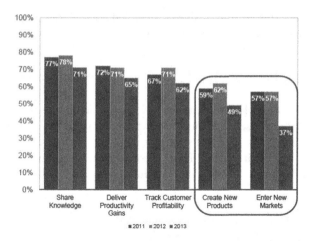

Fig. 1. IT effectiveness and enabling business objectives (Color figure online)

In the recent CIO Trend Report 2016, the Info-Tech Research Group identified four high level strategic pillars to provide the foundation to approach informative decision making in 2016. Among the most substantial challenges for IT executives are leading the digital transformation, building a culture of innovation leadership, fostering a data-driven IT strategy, and utilizing security analytics. The authors of the Info-Tech 2016 report highlighted the fact that the most IT leaders suffer from focusing solely on maximizing IT efficiencies and keeping IT running, while over 60 % of the C-suite stakeholders believe IT does not understand their business goals and only 23 % of them confirmed the developed IT strategy is effectively aligned with their corporate strategy and desired capabilities [2]. With the growing reliance on technology to drive business innovations, logically IT leaders should be involved discussing and planning the business initiatives. As McKinsey analysis "Why CIOs should be business-strategy partners" revealed IT performance and capabilities increase significantly when CIOs are involved in shaping the business strategy. In addition, there is a very high correlation between IT's ability to innovate and the level of overall satisfaction with IT [1]. Continues innovation is a force driving not only IT ecosystem forward, but delivering new methods to collaborate and do business over-all. More and more organizations consider IT success as delivering benefits by generating revenue and creating value for the business stakeholders, who constantly demand better metrics around business value and satisfaction reporting. It is time for the IT leaders to use data-driven methods, to prioritize and manage these metrics when take direction from business objectives and strategy and align with them.

This paper is structured as follows. Section 2 discusses a possible Framework for Aligning IT to Business strategy and more specifically the business strategy core components and the notion of socio-technical system. It also highlights the role of IT and how it bridges with the organization's operating model. Section 3 determines the key domains of aligned enterprise architecture followed in terms of directing IT towards business objectives. Section 4 summarizes and analyzes key findings and explains how the interrelations between identified factors and Business-IT Nexus. Section 5 summarizes and concludes the paper.

2   Framework for Aligning IT to Business Strategy

In order to understand why corporations develop IT architecture, it is important to know their business mindset when doing so, which ultimately begins with a discussion on *strategy*. Some authors state that strategy cannot be planned, since doing so would suggest a controlled environment. These theorists state that strategy happens in an uncontrolled environment, thus it is more useful to consider it to be *an art* or *tool* over *a plan*.

2.1   Core Components of Business Strategy

In the 1970s, the strong competition in several key industries (appliances, automakers, and banking sector) up surged a new concern about the business operating environment. The traditional long range planning lost its position to strategic planning, which allowed businesses to consider changes to its surroundings.

Strategic planning forced businesses to look beyond its own walls into the greater fluidity of the ever growing global marketplace. A holistic analysis of the factors correlated to: the external environment – customers and competitors - and the internal environment –the organization- is needed for establishing and maintaining finest management practices. According to the online business dictionary "…the objective of strategic management is to achieve better alignment of corporate policies and strategic priorities." "A brilliant strategy or breakthrough technology can put any company on the competitive map, but only solid execution can keep it there" [3]. Through structural changes or efforts focused on performance improvement produce normally short-term gains. Instead, concentrating on the three major sections formulating this process: *Strategic Thinking*, *Strategic Planning*, and *Strategic Momentum* is far more powerful and successful [4]:

Strategic Thinking: This is a stage the organization should grasp both the detailed view of itself: what it does well, and what seems to be lacking; and the systematic picture of the external environment.

Strategic Planning: First at this phase a situational analysis should be performed based on the previous stage SWOT -Strengths, Weaknesses, Opportunities, Threats- findings. Next steps will include formulating a strategy, and determining ways of its implemention.

Strategic Momentum: The final stage should evolve the strategic plan implementation. The organization needs to not only keep in mind who has been working towards strategy implementation, but must also take into consideration the ongoing changes in the external environment.

The essence of **Strategy** according to Harvard Business School professor and one of the world's most advanced thinkers on strategy - Michael Porter is *"about being different."* Which means a company to choose for their core business different and unique set of activities or to perform already known activities in a different way. With a set of activities, different from those of the other competitors in an industry, a company winning strategy means creation of "unique and valuable position" on the market. Creating strategy also means making tradeoffs and combing the unique activities to fit well together and reinforce one other.

Industry Analysis. Referring again to Michael Porter, the structure of an industry is embodied in five forces that collectively determine industry profitability and should be considered in strategic formulation: Rivalry among Existing Competitors, Bargaining Power of Buyers, Threat of Substitute Products or Services; Bargaining Power of Suppliers; Threat of New Entrants. The shared power of the five forces varies for different industries as does the profitability [5]. The model exposes comprehensive outer view of the organization with its traditional direct competitors and the correlation with four other forces within its market environment.

The Rivalry among Existing Competitors force represents the magnitude to which fierce battling for position and aggressive competition occur in the industry. The term *hyper-competition* refers to industries characterized by fierce rivalry among existing firms and very rapid pace of innovations leading to fast obsolescence of any competitive advantage and a consequent need for a fast cycle of innovations. The consumer electronic industry -mobile smart devices in particular- is the most current example as *hyper-competition*, as is the ICT industry in general. The Bargaining Power of Buyers force signifies the extent to which customers of those organizations in the industry have the ability to put downward pressure on prices, highly concentrated buyers (such as Wal-Mart) and low switching costs typically conspire to increase the bargaining power of buyers. The Threat of Substitute Products or Services force denotes the extent to which the products or services marketed by the company are subject to potential substitution by different products or services that fulfill the same customer needs and expectations. The Bargaining Power of Suppliers force represents the magnitude to which the firms or individuals who sell production input to the organizations in the industry have the ability to maintain high prices. The Threat of New Entrants force represents the extent to which the industry is open to entry by new competitors, or whether significant barriers to entry make it creates comfortable shelter so the existing firms need not to worry about competition from outside.

The industry analysis framework suggests that industry differences can be analyzed a priori by managers using the Porter's analytical framework, and based upon the results of this analysis, executives can decide whether to enter an industry or forgo investment.

Industry Analysis and the Role of IT. Scholars and experts who have embraced industry analysis to search and identify IT-dependent strategic initiatives and opportunities advise to consider information systems effects on one or more of the industry forces, thereby tipping it to the company's advantage or preventing foreseeable losses.

Investment in and the use of specialized emerging technologies and applications could raise or increase barriers to entry in the industry. In so doing the existing firms would reduce the threat of new entrants. This particular option is most likely applicable in IT intense and highly regulated industries such as Healthcare, Banking, and Finance.

The far and wide adoption of Internet technologies, and more specifically products and services searches, e-commerce and online transactions utilization, contribute steady to dynamically shifting power away from suppliers, so toward buyers. As much as the Internet based systems and applications help firms strengthen their bargaining position toward either suppliers or buyers, they also could reduce their bargaining power just before either one. Innovative implementations of emerging technology and services by creative companies, whether incumbents or new entrants, could speed up immediate changes in industry competition. Noticeable examples of this dynamic were presented by the advent of online retailing in the late 90-ties and early 2000, and later with the individualized entertaining industry.

Essentially advances in the IT are transforming any industry structure and alter each of the five competitive forces, creating the need and opportunity for change, hence, industry attractiveness as well.

While Porter's five competitive forces model is truly important when strategic planning and managerial decisions are taken, the impact of the key internal forces clearly associated with the information technology are particularly critical to the operational effectiveness and shapes the organizational business strategy and benefits.

2.2   The Socio-Technical System Model

Technology has become the heart and soul of every business and it has a powerful effect on competitive advantage in costs optimization, enhancing product and services differentiation, or spawning new business options. Every product on the market has physical and information content and the tendency today is towards increasing the information component of products. Naturally, IT is deeply involved in all aspects of the information component, and yet IT is increasingly involved in the physical component likewise – manufacturing processes become automated, faster, more efficient and precise with IT. The IT transforms the products and affects the overall value activities of an industry. Starting from traditionally information intensive accounting, and continuing to performing optimization and control functions, and furthermore - judgmental, executive decision functions, the significance of IT is becoming ever more strategic for companies' competitive advantage. How to align the IT to the business strategy and to gain value turning the great strategy into a great performance is a "mature way of doing business" in the information age.

To explore the complexity of the problems inside organizations, and to avoid unrealistic expectations when aligning the IT to the business strategy, a formal methodology of examining and evaluating IT capabilities in the organizational context should be applied. In IT world, "*capability* is the ability to marshal resources to affect a predetermined outcome" [6]. The core IT capabilities are discussed later in the paper and they are critical to meet the enduring challenges of uniting business strategy and IT vision, designing an IT architecture, and delivering IT services.

The contemporary Information Systems approaches incorporate multidisciplinary theories and perspectives with no dominance of a single discipline or model. Gabriele

Picolli in his Information Systems for Managers text features IT as a critical component of a formal, sociotechnical information system designed to collect, process, store, and distribute information [7]. Kenneth and Jane Laudon in Managing the Digital Firm, define Information Systems as Sociotechnical Systems incorporating two approaches: *Technical* and *Behavioural*, with several major disciplines that contribute expertise and solutions in the study of Information systems [8].

The notion of above definitions is based on the Sociotechnical theory work developed by Tavistock Institute in London about the end of the fifties. The IT Sociotechnical approach not only visualizes the concept, but reveals the impact of new technologies and processes –the technical subsystem- on the entire organization system, and the dependencies and interactions between all other facets and components of the sociotechnical system. According to Picolli any organization Information System can be represented as a Sociotechnical system which comprises four primary components that must be balanced and work together to deliver the information processing and functionalities required by the organization to fulfill its information needs. The IS Sociotechnical model validates the most important components, and at the same time illustrates primary driving forces, within organizations: structure, people, process, and technology. The first two – *people* and *structure* – shape the *social subsystem*, and represent the human element of the IS. The latter two – *process* and *technology* (more specifically IT) – contour the *technical subsystem* of the IS and they relate to a wide range of IT resources and services intertwined with a series of steps to complete required business activities.

The sociotechnical system approach is instrumental in helping policy and decision makers to strategize and manage organizational change particularly when introducing and implementing new IT. The easiest to envision, justify and manage change is *automation*. It occurs when an IT innovation modifies existing processes without affecting the social subsystem sphere. Thus, this change requires little executive sponsorship and involvement, while the financial benefits can be estimated with some precision. The further change impacts primarily on the people component of the sociotechnical model. It takes place when the information intensity of the processes being performed is substantially changed due to introduction of new IT. This level of change – *informate* - affects mainly employees and most likely the customers, and would require executive sponsorship and greater management involvement to provide appropriate training and overcoming the human tendency to resist changes while at the same time seeking to take advantage of available market opportunities.

The advanced change incorporates the previously described changes, while also causes organizational structure disruptions. The magnitude of this – *transform* – change shakes all dimensions of inner components interactions: it transforms the way how organization selects, utilizes and manages IT; it results in a change in the reporting and authority structure of the organization; it manifests a novel way of tasks' accomplishment or/and a new set of tasks or processes. The later change requires significant managerial and executive involvement with a steady championship by the top management team for both signaling purposes and to provide the necessary political impetus to complete the transition.

The Sociotechnical system approach not only validates the four critical components of the Information System interdependency, but proves that none of them works in isolation. They all interact, are mutually dependent, and consequently are subject to *"systemic effects"* - defined as any change in one component affecting all other components of the system. "Every business decision triggers an IT event," this quote from 2003 by Bob Napier, former HP's CIO is still valid: when addressing business issues like productivity, service quality, cost control, risk management, and ROI the decision-makers have to consider the appropriate corresponding modifications in the IT domain.

The process of changes and reciprocal adjustment of both technical and social subsystems should continue to interplay and growing closer until a mutually satisfying results are reached. However, the model in reality could not be with equal subsystems' changes. It should grow from micro to macro level to reflect crucial influences of the external environment, including regulatory requirements, social expectations and business trends, competitive pressures, and to some extend - interoperability of the IT systems within partnering institutions.

2.3   The Notions of Operating Models and Digitized Platform

The process of enterprise architecture design requires a holistic view of the organization. Following such approach makes possible to explore how business processes, information flow, systems, technology and predominantly business strategies interact and contribute value to the organization. Hence, understanding the organization synergy in detail provides the means to define two important choices related to the organization's business operations:

- How *standardized* its business should be across operational units?
- How *integrated* its business processes should be across those units?

Based on the business processes selection, any organization operates in one of the four possible operating models. The models are well-illustrated by Weill and Ross from MIT Center for Information Systems Research in their IT Savvy textbook [9]. Which one is considered as "the right one," depends on the organization executives' strategic decision:

- Within the *diversification model* - low standardization and low integration - organizations operate in a decentralized mode with independent transactions, unique units with few data standards across local autonomies, most technological (IT) decisions are made within the units;
- The *coordination model* - low standardization, high integration - is used by organizations that deliver customized services and solutions by unique business units, while accumulating and providing access to integrated data across the divisions. The decisions are made in consensus for designing the IT infrastructure and integrated services, while IT applications decisions are processed within individual units;
- Organizations implementing the *replication model* - high standardization, low integration - typically provide high operational autonomy to their business units while requiring highly structured and standardized business processes. All decisions related to IT infrastructure, applications and services are centrally mandated;

- Organizations operating in *the unification model* - high standardization, high integration - are centralized managed with highly integrated and standardized business processes. The Enterprise IT is highly centralized and all decisions are made centrally.

In the information age, when the business decisions and success depend on precise and quickly delivered information, IT unquestionably needs to serve as a platform for the business operations. For that reason, the Weill and Ross describe the cocept of Digitized Platform (DP) as an "integrated set of electronic business processes and the technologies, applications and data supporting the processes." Therefore the DP becomes a prerequisite to compete in the digital economy and it should be used for achieving growth and profitability.

The Digitized Platform and the Operating Model are multi facets interrelated. First, a company needs to have a vision what they want to do (business strategy), and then to think over how IT can help to create a platform to accomplish their vision for progress and profit. Weill and Ross exemplify the IT role in this process as "… IT can do *two things* very well – *integration* and *standardization*." The integration – delivers data access across the business, while the standardization – reduces variation in business processes and increases quality, efficiency, and predictability in the operations [10]. By identifying what the company wants to integrate and standardize, actually defines its Operating Model. In fact, the Operating Model establishes the objectives and the requirements for the company's specific Digitized Platform.

Let makes this real by illustrating with two examples how two different well-defined operating models bring together specific requirements to their company's Digitized Platform and to achieve remarcable success. In order to support its business strategies to innovate and remain on leading position in the industry, Procter & Gamble (P&G) not only spends 3.4 percent of revenue on innovation, more than twice the industry average, but has created the most efficient and effective IT architecture by employing a "Diversification" operating model. To accomplish that feat, P&G created Global Business Services (GBS) as internal shared services organization, to provide a base of over seventy common, repetitive, non-unique services for the company's 250 world-wide units. GBS delivers shared services ranging from core IT systems to advanced collaborative tools that allow researchers, marketers, and managers to gather, store, and share knowledge and information, such as: Web 2.0 based social networking and collaborative tools; integrated services that include unified communications, instant messaging, live video meetings, web conferencing, and content management. The listed above collaborative systems illustrate how well-planned advanced technologies stimulate sharing knowledge, ideas, innovations and support teamwork across company's world-wide spread autonomous businesses. All these systems help P&G to accelerate the decision making and increase the speed of new producs to the market, while reducing the operational costs and increase resource utilization. Clearly P&G business success is derived from its efforts in product innovation and collaboration, developed and supported by company's constantly evolving digitized platform.

A further example of a different operating model is the ING DIRECT Bank *replication* operating model. The Bank operates internationally, and it doesn't offer any tangible product, but primarily on-line or phone bank products and services. Although the business processes/services in the bank's branches world-wide are the same, there is no need of interaction between the separate offices as they serve primarily local clients. So there is low need of business processes integration. However, the offered services in all counties are identical and by standardizing the core business activities, ING DIRECT establishes a Digitized Platform that includes standard systems and processes which are very easy to replicate. As a result, ING DIRECT implements its systems for weeks only, avoiding any risks and downtime caused by untested or unknown applications, and thus significantly reduces IT implementation costs, increases its business efficiency and gainful outcomes.

3 Key Domains of Aligned Enterprise Architecture

Generally speaking "... Enterprise Architecture (EA) is a holistic design for an organization, aligning the current state of IT capabilities, processes, and resources to enable business strategy" [11]. In the Federal Enterprise Architecture document, the CIO Council refers to the EA as the "glue" that ties business and IT strategy together and that allows them to drive each other. The best practice to conceive and manage EA function is by identifying the key domains, specific for every company.

At times, these key architectural domains are shaped with a broader vision in mind and consist of different sub-fields. Randy Heffner from Forrester Research in his report depicted four interrelated facets of EA that provide short- and long-term effectiveness of delivering business technology solutions: business architecture, information architecture, application architecture, and infrastructure architecture [12]. In the Common Approach to Federal EA, six sub-architectural domains delineate the types of analysis and modeling that is necessary for an EA to meet stakeholders' requirements: strategic, business services, data and information, enabling applications, host infrastructure, and security [13]. Peter High in his World Class IT Strategy book illustrates seven facets in cascading logic from strategy to technology: strategic intentions, business context, business value, business process, data architecture, application architecture, systems (IT) architecture [11]. In all three previously described models, and likewise in others not specified here, the two key EA domains are actually: the Business architecture and the IT architecture. And for each of them we may add particular sub-domains reflecting organization's or industry's specifics. Such approach will simplify and will provide better alignment of different architectures' life-cycles in some of these domains, while will reflect more precisely diverse business requirements.

Later on, the business of IT will be discussed emphasizing how IT architecture could be designed, built, utilized more efficiently and with greater value for the company. With escalating IT operational costs and the inability to get adequate value from the IT investments, firms are striving to convert their IT from a strategic liability to strategic asset. According recent surveys from Gardner, Forrester, and CISR most of the IT budgets are spent for keeping the existing applications and infrastructure running. Many firms typically spend over 80 % of their IT budget for supporting existing systems, and the budget for renovation or new systems, if exists, is below 20 %. The widely adopted piecemeal approach results in set of isolated systems wired together to meet the next immediate need. And while there are some valuable IT-based products and services in every company IS environment, the organizations find that it takes longer and longer to test and integrate the new patches with the existing systems, increases vulnerability to systems outages, and makes more difficult to respond to changing business conditions. Reversing such IT fortunes requires different thinking from the type that "helped" the organization to create its messy legacy.

The current digital economy has introduced urgency around the need to plan and manage IT strategicaly. To succeed in this approach and with evolving business transformations, the management must pursue four activities to ensure that the company generates stratigic business value from IT. These four activities – Commit, Build, Run, and Exploit - constitute the "IT value creation cycle" [14].

In recent years, the IT divisions have professionalized their *Build* and *Run* IT activities by developing service catalogs, calculating and monitoring unit costs, standardizing project methodologies, defining and implementing technology standards, and working with business partners to manage current demands. While improved IT *Build* and *Run* activities generate measurable business benefits, they are just the first step in producing sustained business success. Companies that have achieved a reasonable level of maturity in their *Build* and *Run* activities can greatly enhance the strategic value of IT by developing more effective *Commit* and *Exploit* activities and as a result to excel at all four category by implementing seamless handoffs from one activity to the next.

Commit involves allocating business and IT resources to enact the company's strategic priorities. This requires the firm to articulate its stratigic priorities in terms of its operational requirements and to direct its resources accordingly. This activitiy actually demostrates how well the Business – IT alignment works in every company. At the enterprise level, *Commit* can be political challenging as the senior executives have to fix what is broken in their management and the use of IT. In a nutshell, IT and business leaders have to introduce new ways of thinking about and funding IT that would later lead to building a digitized platform. As previously has been difined the IT architecture domain could be consider interchangeable as Digitalized Platform (DP). *Exploit* involes driving additional benefits from existing business architecture and technology capabilities. Effective *Exploit* category leverages digitized platforms to continuously improve corporate performance, profitable growth and business opportunities.

The IT unit of the future will not own all *Commit*, *Build*, *Run*, and *Exploit* activities, hence IT and business leaders will need to coordinate and balance well all four activities to ensure that the company generates strategic value from IT. Every company can decide which accountabilities belong inside the IT unit, and which can best be enacted outside IT unit. Maturing the four IT value creation activities would demand development and coordination of new capabilities, not only in IT but throughout the enterprise. However the firms are not equally successful in harvesting dividends from the advanced IT capabilities, or driving benefits from their digitized platforms.

3.1   Directing IT Funding to Business Objectives and Strategic Needs

The IT funding and investment decisions are important and challenging part of the previously discussed Commit activities. Since the systems have been implemented, they become part of the company's legacy: their ongoing support requires time and money, their influence and constrains dictate how business processes are performed. IT funding decisions are long-term strategic decisions that implement the company's operating model.

Weill and Ross intense research on successful or failed firms shows that three key factors are critical for the IT funding and investments in any IT-savvy company:

- *Defining clear priorities and criteria for IT investments* - the operating model of the company defines the business priorities and how products and services will be delivered. The top executives and IT leaders respectively must clarify the IT investments priorities. All companies are different, but what the IT savvy have in common is that they "create a central point for business change efforts" - and this central point helps them to prioritize the IT investments on high-value projects.
- *Establishing transparent process of project prioritization and resource provisioning* - in well-advancing with IT companies, the senior management is responsible for strategic business initiatives and respectivelly for project prioritization. The prioritization criteria must be clear and must specify how the IT project team will be held responsible for the project outcomes and deliverables. The transparency in project approval will guarantee that not individual or political decisions would influence project's approval, but pure economic and business efficiency.
- *Monitoring the projects through the phase of implementation and afterwards* - only few companies track their IT projects from the idea –all through putting into practice, including post-implementation. By applying post-implementation projects' review (PIR), companies can obtain valuable information about accomplished outcomes, and how further to improve their IT funding cycle.

There is a splendid example of how British Telecom revamped its IT funding model based on the newly developed business strategy around three lines of business: retail, wholesale, and global services. At that time (2004), BT was running above 4000 systems, and over 6000 IT employees were working on more then 4300 projects world-wide. The new appointed company management examined the existing IT environment and concluded it is not designed for integration or low cost. To endorse IT to be a critical tool for enabling BT's business transformation, the top management established "One IT for One BT" to consolidate the systems environment and to optimaze the project portfolio management. Actually BT rebuilt the company's project portfolio by targeting three core business processes: lead-to-cash ("selling stuff"), trouble-to-resolve ("fixing stuff"), and concept-to-market ("innovating stuff"). These three processes defined the key elements of BT's *unification operating model* and provided the management focus and clear methodology for IT spending and resource allocation. Furthermore, the projects were monitored following approved metrics periodically in ninety-day cycle, and beyond the implementation phase if they generate the expected business ROI. The company succeeded to reduce its total IT costs by 14 percent and to cut the unit cost of IT services while tripling output and doubling delivery speed. The new IT funding processes, aligned well to the company business strategy and operating model, helped BT to be transformed from a very traditional and conservative telecom company to a competitive and innovative firm.

The intents of IT advancing companies are to change the funding ratio *new projects vs existing systems* from 20 % to 80 % to 40 %:60 % and to force the company to a new more competitive level.

3.2   Building IT Architecture

Once the company takes charge of directing IT funding to the strategic business needs, it is ready for the second component of the *Commit* activities: to build a digitized platform for enhanced business performance.

The IT architecture or the Digitized Platform of a company is the computer hardware and infrastructure, software applications and data which all together provide and support the core business processes of the firm. In today's highly technological world, the DP is a company instrument to achieve an efficient operating model which will guarantee the company long term prosperity and success. According Weill and Ross from MIT CISR based on their extended research around the globe the companies' IT experience of building their DP as a "journey" that can be divided into four stages:

- Stage 1 - *Localizing* – this stage illustarates a dynamic, energetic and innovative approach of any new company or IT unit, when the firm's priority is rapidly grow of new systems or customized solutions as they respond to customer demands and seek establishing their unique proposition. The stage helps in local and functional optimization, however it raises complexity and expensive localized IT solutions that respond to instant business needs, and soon alter the stage name as *Business silos* where business processes lack consistency and costs/performance gaps become commonplace.
- Stage 2 - *Standardizing* – firms retreat from the rapid-fire responces and focus on IT efficiencies through shared infrastructure and resources and technology standardizations. The stage succeeds to discipline processes in IT service delivery and investment prioritization, and to achieve IT functional efficiency as to low OpEx and high reliability, however soon after its adoption it limits opportunities and become incapable to meet new strategic needs.
- Stage 3 - *Optimizing* – firms implement disciplined enterprise processes and share data as required by their operating model. In this stage firms define enterprise priorities, invest in core packaged or customized integrated platforms and systems, and most likely accomplish high operational efficiency. In general IT spending is increasing, but not the IT unit costs, the project priorities are established based on enterprise requirements, rather than isolated ROI estimates, however focusing on standardization and integration provides little if any opportunity for innovations.
- Stage 4 - *Reusing* – firms exploring the opportunities to utilize their business processes as reusable components that they customize for new, but related, business prospects. In this stage firms achieve *Business modularity* based on synchronized strategic and operational decisions with clear rules, reliable data, and business intelligence tools, these all result in gaining the most of IT capabilities towards assets utilization, new business opportunities and growth.

The successful DP creates a set of reusable IT modules, and the business agility allows the IT advanced companies promptly to address the following four business opportunities:

- empowering the employees with information they need, and optimizing the processes for maximum performance;
- speeding up product/services innovations;
- reorganizing the business processes to meet better the customers and business needs;
- improving merging and acquisition processes for business growth.

If the company strategy to growth is by acquisitioning businesses, the process of integrating the IT infrastructures and information systems of the new and the old structures is often extremely challenging task. That is why many companies choose "rip and replace" strategy to completely change the old IT infrastructure in the acquired firm with their existing DP which already has proven success.

One great example of a company that has reached the fourth stage of its journey to build advanced DP and successfully reusing it in many differnet ways is Amazon. Initially Amazon business strarted in dot com era as online C2C bookstore. Their strategically evolving IT architecture, well aligned to agile business strategy, created a successful and growing business. Soon after the beginning, Amazon has expanded the range of selling goods far beyond books, and proffered its advanced wide-spread digital platform to large number of businesses and independent retailers. At present, over 3 million retailers are using the Amazon DP and are part of its enormous marketplace with over 300 million global customers. Amazon did not stop with the first previously described transformation from direct sales business model to sales-and-service model. The company has capatalized on its advanced IT capabilities and succeeded to build one of the largest in the world cloud computing platform, creating and launching the Amazon Web Services in late 2006. In short, with this new business model, based on innovative utilization of existing DP and enhancing it with new applications and higher computing performance, Amazon targets and serves new customers and different business processes, providing computing resources on demand, and applying diverse profit formula. AWS is an explicit example of IT advanced firm where the investments in IT are used for building digital platform that can be used and reused multiple times by the company itself, its direct customers or resellers to reap the benefits and to enhance the growth.

Evolving through the four stages of building DP is a challenging experience for organizations and their IT units. As it has been said at the beginning - the radical changes impact the organizational mindsets in rethinking and reengineering the traditional IT resources. Indicators for such transformations can be seen analyzing the latest Gartner CIO Agenda Report from 2015. It is based on survey gathered data from over 2500 CIOs from 84 countries across the globe. The results represent how IT domain is moving beyond IT craftsmanship (focusing on technology) and IT industrialization (focusing on process efficiency and effectiveness) into a third era of enterprise IT, where digitalization is transforming business models and provides continual opportunities for growth, innovation and differentiation – see Fig. 2 [15].

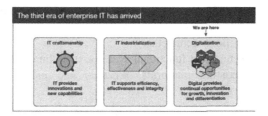

Fig. 2. New IT domain - "Digital first"

As one CIO is cited "we stopped thinking of the IT as a bad, and started thinking of it as what keeps the business running." And this is a pivot point for the modern organizations how to plan and manage IT stratigically. By closing the loop with the *Exploit* activities in the "value creation cycle" the companies would maximaze the gain from reused ingredients, will steady advance in performance and profitable growth, and at the same time will be chasing new business opportunities – see Fig. 3 [14].

Fig. 3. The it value creation cycle

Common practice for the organizations is to have a dedicated enterprise-architecture (EA) entity to oversees the entire system architecture, including business processes, IT infrastructure, and technology-enabled services to be delivered effectively. There are different approaches how to constitutes best practice in EA management. One is to perform continually measuring IT performance and adjusting business processes and systems as needed. Others tout the importance of aligning the overall IT architecture with those of the individual business units. More structured approach can be determine following the four stages: Localizing, Standardizing, Optimizing and Reusing. In such approach, the organization of EA should reflect the organization of the business, who is accountable for EA decissions and how to measure the effects of EA on the business, how to keep strategy-related tasks separate from operational ones, how to collaborate closely with the business and IT organizations.

4 Insights on Shaping IT-Capabilities to Business Strategy

For the benefit of any company it is most important to define and establish the IT architecture underneath the organization's business strategy. A well-formulated IT architecture typically consists of *content* and *processes* and describes the following key components of the enterprise IT architecture:

- Technology planning and management: strategy, governance and operations aligned to business processes
- Information and data flow architecture
- Applications architecture and functional systems, including correlated interfaces
- IT infrastructure: existing platforms, services, and industry regulations and standards.

The "IT/Business Alignment Cycle" is a frequently used methodology which introduces a set of well-planned process improvement programs that systematically address a broad range of activities to permeate the entire IT organization and its culture. The four phases of the alignment cycle are [16]:

- The *Plan* phase translates business objectives into measurable IT services and helps close the gap between what business needs and expects and what IT delivers;
- The *Model* phase designs infrastructure to optimize business value and involves mapping IT assets, process, and resources, then prioritizing and planning to support business critical services;
- The *Manage* phase drives results through consolidated service support and enables the IT to deliver promised levels of service based on pre-defined business priorities;
- The *Measure* phase verifies IT commitments and improves its cross-organization visibility into operations.

Following the above IT/Business alignment cycle fosters organization-wide shared IT expectations and defines a common framework for a broad range of activities forcing alignment of IT and business objectives. This simple framework should be revisited periodically when there is a significant course correction in corporate directions or in the key components of the IT architecture.

In the evolving IT/Business alignment process several significant points should be considered.

The first finding reflects **the lead on driving value from IT** and the following critical steps should be executed:

- Set the directions for the IT-Business alignment process – define the company operating model, identify the key components of the IT architecture, articulate the strategic vision that the OM and IT is intended to realize;
- Lead the IT-business transformations – straight the activities to build the DP, complete the organizational changes needed to execute the vision;
- Preserve technology, data, and process standards – supervise the technology implementations conforming to the operating model, the platform enabling it, and adopted standards;
- Exploit the value – gain the advantage of the business agility provided by the adopted IT platform, reuse and innovate constantly to achieve sustaining technology S-curve.

The second finding reinforces **Structure rationalization** to transform IT from a costs center to strategic assets with business intelligence capabilities. The Gartner analysis on Future Directions of the IT industry from 2011, exemplifies where the transformations are the most appropriate – from lessening the *After the Sale* IT spending to substantial increase the investments in *Before the Sale* and in *The Sale* sectors – see Fig. 4 – The IT Money Spending Model [17]. The process requires significant alternations in the enterprise requirements to support transformational initiatives such as: content-aware computing, social and semantic computing, information-enabled pattern-based strategy.

Fig. 4. The IT money spending model

Only few years later, the current Gartner analysis shows a new Nexus of Forces – BI/analytics (social and information), cloud and mobile- as leading CIOs investment priorities forcing transformations in the traditional IT money spending model targeting Before the Sales and the Sales sectors – see Fig. 5 – the CIO Priorities [18].

Rank	Investment priority	2014	2015
1	BI/analytics	41%	50%
2	Infrastructure and data center	31%	37%
3	Cloud	27%	32%
4	ERP	26%	34%
5	Mobile	24%	36%
6	Digitalization/digital marketing	17%	11%
7	Security	13%	11%
8	Networking, voice and data comms	12%	12%
9	Customer relationship/experience	11%	8%
10	Industry-specific applications	9%	10%
11	Legacy modernization	7%	7%
12	Enterprise applications	6%	2%

Fig. 5. The CIOs priorities 2014/2015

Based on the CIOs strategies reported in the table, IT and business leaders transform profoundly the role of IT from a strategic liability to strategic asset strengthening the customer experience and pursuing new channels of growth.

The third finding suggests modifying the Latin philosophy "Ex Chaos Facultas" ("From Chaos comes Opportunity") to "From **Consumerization** comes Opportunity" to reflect the current technology trends. Recent tendencies in IT utilization show that new technologies emerge first in the consumer market and then, after mass acceptance, are employed largely by business organizations. The expected consequence of this pattern

Fig. 6. Consumer tools in enterprises

is that across the globe companies are experiencing the most disruptive new technology trend of this decade: Consumerization.

Enterprises are capitalizing on the consumerization of IT and proliferation of mobile devises by developing applications aimed at improving employee productivity and customer satisfaction – see Fig. 6 [19].

Consumerization of IT, along with workforce mobility, and flexible, reliable, accessible and affordable remote computing, change forcefully the corporate IT lanscape affecting the relationship between enterprise IT, corporate users, and consumers. For organizational IT management, consumerization exemplifies the convergence of a demanding set of challenges such as information and infrastructure security, technology policy, data protection, and end-user technology. A new tendency -BYOD (Bring Your Own Device) and COPE (Company-owned, personally enabled)- driven mostly by current Consumerization of IT in the enterpise, is forcing companies to redesign or create their policy and rules on how smart portable devices can be used for both corporate and private purposes, and how the related expenditures should be covered.

For corporate management, consumerization of IT signifies a new strategy which supports business models and process innovations, talent strategy and customers' satisfaction, as well as corporate brand and identity. Consumerization of IT blurs the line between personal and work life, especially for mobile workers. Mobile workers make up about 39 % of the employees in North America, 25 % in Europe, and 42 % in Asia, according to Forrester's analysis [20]. Their cohort benefits the business immensely by increasing productivity, and advancing collaboration and business agility, thereby improving customer satisfaction and climbing the rate of talent retention. Consumerized employees spread the boundaries of the workday and workplace, and it is fair to name them "anytime, anywhere workers."

The fourth finding is that in a digital economy every organization is challenged by **IT constant innovations**, and it should take a look again on the pivotal question: "*What comes first: IT architecture or Business strategy?*" The IT rapid advancement is spawning completely new industries in several different ways:

- IT makes new businesses technologically feasible – advances in nano-technologies made today's mobile industry possible. If we think about Apple's i-products – they came as of technological advancements and miniaturization, however Apple did something unique and far more smarter making not only a great technological product, but wrapped it in a superb business model. The Apple's true innovation was to enter and gain a substantial slice of the personalized entertainment industry – utilizing the technology innovations and make it easy, customers' friendly and demanding the control of all i-products and services.

- IT can spawn new businesses by creating demand on new products such as customized financial services (mortgage, brokerage, and investment) there were not optional nor needed before the spread of IT caused a demand for them. Web 2.0 technologies help social networking and Big Data to flourish as multibillion dollar business, the new coming Web 3.0 with the next digital inspiration: semantic technologies, MDM, Internet of Things, M2 M, would make even beyond the current experience.

- IT creates new businesses within old ones. Many companies take advantage of excess capability of its advanced IT value chain. They create and provide new or modified products and services to others based on surplus capacity.

5   Conclusions

There are many other considerations and challenging implications in the Business-IT Nexus: asymmetric competition, speed of innovations, speed to the market, speed of organizational and operating models' evolution. All these specifics require yet more efforts and analyses on how to integrate technology into the strategic business objectives and to excel on IT-enabled capabilities. The suggested trends, simplified EA framework, and findings for consideration have to provide a consistent, predictable, and agile experience when mapping and executing IT-Business alignment.

Further work is planned in two directions: how consumerization of IT affects the dynamic business objectives and current operating models and what approach can be addopted for approariate evaluation and assessment, and how Web 3.0 technologies would impact the business of IT at a corporate level.

References

1. Khan, N., Sikes, J.: IT Under Pressure: McKinsey Global Survey Results, McKinsey & Company (2014). http://www.mckinsey.com/business-functions/business-technology/our-insights/it-under-pressure-mckinsey-global-survey-results
2. Info-Tech Research Group: Info-Tech's 2016 CIO Trend Report (2015). http://www.infotech.com/research/2016-cio-trend-report-executive-brief
3. Neilson, G., Martin, K., Powers, E.: The Secrets to Successul Strategy Implementation, HBR's 10 Must Reads On Strategy. Harvard Business School Publishing, Boston (2010)
4. Swayne, L., Duncan, W., Ginter, P.: Strategic Management of Health Care Organizations. Blackwell Publishing, Malden (2006)
5. Porter, M.: On Competition. Harvard Business School Publishing, Boston (2008)

6. McKeen, J., Smith, H., Singh, S.: A Framework for Enhancing IT Capabilities. Commun. Assoc. Inf. Syst. **15**, 661–673 (2005)

7. Picolli, G.: Information Systems for Managers: Text and Cases. John Wiley and Sons, Hoboken (2012)

8. Laudon, K., Laudon, J.: Management Information Systems: Managing the Digital Firm. Pearson Education, Upper Saddle River (2014)

9. Weill, P., Ross, J.: IT Savvy: What Top Executives Must Know to Go from Pain to Gain. Harvard Business School Publishing, Boston, (2009)

10. Ross, J., Beath, C.: Maturity Still Matters: Why a Digitized Platform is Essential to Business Success, CISR, Sloan School of Management, MIT, Research Briefing, Volume XI, Number II, Boston, USA (2011)

11. High, P.: Implementing World Class IT Strategy. Jossey-Bass A Wiley Brand, San Francisco (2014)

12. Heffner, R.: The Pillars of Enterprise Architecture Terminology, Report for EA Professionals, Forrester Research, Cambridge, USA (2010)

13. EO of the President of the US: The Common Approach to Federal Enterprise Architecture (2012). https://www.whitehouse.gov/sites/default/files/omb/assets/egov_docs/common_appr oach_to_federal_ea.pdf

14. Ross, J., Beath, C., Quaadgras, A.: The IT Unit of the Future: Creating Strategic Value from IT, CISR, Sloan School of Management, MIT, Research Briefing, Volume XI, Number X, Boston, USA (2011)

15. Gartner Executive Programs: Executive Summary: The 2015 CIO Agenda, Gartner Inc., Stamford, USA (2014). http://www.gartner.com/imagesrv/cio/pdf/cio_agenda_execsum2015. pdf

16. Nugent, M.: The Four Phases of IT/Business Alignment, CIO Update (2004). http://www. cioupdate.com/insights/article.php/3446591/The-Four-Phases-of-ITBusiness-Alignment.htm

17. McGee, K.: The 2011 Gartner Scenario: Current States and Future Directions of the IT Industry, Gartner, ID Number G00209949, Stamford, USA (2011)

18. Gartner Executive Programs: Flipping to Digital Leadership, Gartner, Stamford, USA (2015). http://www.gartner.com/imagesrv/cio/pdf/cio_agenda_insights2015.pdf

19. Columbus, L.: How Enterprises are Capitalizing on the Consumerization of IT, Forbes sites (2014). http://www.forbes.com/sites/louiscolumbus/2014/03/24/how-enterprises-are-capitali zing-on-the-consumerization-of-it/

20. Forrester Consulting: Exploring Business and IT Friction: Myths and Realities, Cambridge, USA (2013)

The Process of Process Management: Enabling High Performance in a Digital World

Mathias Kirchmer[1,2(✉)]

[1] BPM-D, 475 Timberline Trail, West Chester, PA 19382, USA
[2] University of Pennsylvania, Organizational Dynamics, Philadelphia, USA
mathias.kirchmer@bpm-d.com

Abstract. Business strategies and operations are driven by scores of ever-shifting factors: from legal regulations to technological innovations and an all present digitalization. Companies need a powerful management approach to achieve high performance in today's digital world. In effect, they must know how and when to enhance their business processes, which processes are optimal candidates for intervention, and how to move rapidly from strategy to execution.

That's where the Business Process Management-Discipline (BPM-Discipline) helps. It delivers significant business value by converting strategy into people and IT based execution at pace with certainty. The BPM-Discipline is implemented through the "process of process management". An efficient and effective implementation of this management process is achieved using a holistic framework and reference model as well as related tools and templates.

Keywords: Agility · ARIS · BPM · BPM-Discipline · Business process management · Compliance · Digitalization · Execution · Innovation · Management discipline · Reference model · Standardization · Strategy · Value-driven BPM

1 The Challenge: High Performance in a Digital World

In today's business environment organizations' strategies and operations are driven by scores of ever-shifting factors: from demographic changes, capital availability, legal regulations and customers who require something new every day to technological innovations and an all present digitalization. Static business models are no longer able to keep pace with such dynamic change. Companies need a management approach that makes them successful in this volatile environment. Organizations need to achieve high performance by mastering this "new normal" and deal proactively with the opportunities and threats of our "digital world" [1]. Companies need to become "Exponential Organizations" who achieve a significant higher output than peers through the use of new organizational techniques and related technologies [2]. In effect, organizations need to know how and when to modify or enhance their business processes, which processes are optimal candidates for intervention, and how to move rapidly from idea to action.

However, organizations are not sufficiently prepared to meet those challenges to reach high performance in our digital world. According to a study of The Gartner

© Springer International Publishing Switzerland 2016
B. Shishkov (Ed.): BMSD 2015, LNBIP 257, pp. 171–189, 2016.
DOI: 10.1007/978-3-319-40512-4_10

Group, only 13 % of businesses meet yearly their strategic goals [20]. Hence, 87 % of organizations define strategies and goals but don't really execute on them. This trend is accelerated through the current wave of digitalization. According to the same study only 1 % of organizations have business processes in place that are agile enough to realize the full business potential of new digital technologies. So, if they keep on building their strategies based on those digital opportunities, the likelihood of failure increases. A research study conducted by BPM-D, Widener University and the Universidad de Chile shows that organizations are even struggling identifying the right opportunities to really benefit from digitalization, that their business and information technology capabilities are not aligned, and that the necessary decisions are taken too slowly [21].

Those challenges can be explained by examining the definition of digitalization. Digitalization refers to the realization of new business models through the integration of physical products, people and processes through the internet or better the "internet of Everything" [22]. This definition is visualized in Fig. 1. Companies normally have a good management discipline around products and people: product management, human resources, customer and supplier relationship management and more. But they are missing the right management discipline around their processes.

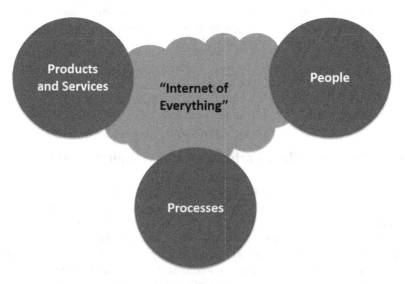

Fig. 1. Definition of digitalization

That's where the Business Process Management-Discipline (BPM-Discipline) helps. It enables organizations to deal with change successfully, drive their growth agenda and create immediate as well as lasting competitive advantage. Companies increasingly invest in areas of "intangibles" such as "business process" [3]. The BPM-Discipline delivers significant business value by converting strategy into people and technology based execution at pace with certainty to achieve high performance and benefit from the opportunities of digitalization [4, 5]. BPM becomes the "value-switch" for digitalization [23].

Existing approaches to BPM focus in general on one or very few aspects of process management, e.g. implementing a process automation engine or setting up an enterprise architecture. There is a need for a comprehensive overarching approach to identify and establish all process management components required to form a simple but successful BPM-Discipline in the context of a specific organization to drive the strategy execution and leverage the opportunities of digitalization. The BPM-Discipline enables high performance in a digital world. This is the topic of the research presented in this chapter.

The BPM-Discipline is implemented through the "process of process management", just as other management disciplines are implemented through appropriate business processes: human resources (HR) through HR processes, finance through finance processes, IT through information technology management processes, to mention a few examples. The process of process management (PoPM) operationalizes the concept of the BPM-Discipline. It applies the principles of BPM to itself by interpreting BPM as a business process by itself.

In the following, the book chapter defines the BPM-Discipline and its value. It explains how this management discipline is further operationalized through the Process of Process Management (PoPM). Then it gives an overview over a reference model for the PoPM, developed to enable a systematic application of the PoPM approach to establish and apply a value-driven BPM-Discipline. Finally the chapter will share first experiences with the practical application of the PoPM, the reference model and related methods and tools.

2   Value and Definition of the BPM-Discipline

Research involving over 90 organizations around the world of different sizes and in different industries has shown that companies who use BPM on an ongoing basis get significant value in return [6, 7]. Basically all surveyed organizations state that the transparency BPM brings is a key effect. This transparency is on one hand a value by itself: It enables fast and well informed decisions which is in the volatile business environment we are living in crucial for the success of a company. On the other hand, BPM and the transparency that it provides also help to achieve other key values and enable the management of the trade-offs between those values. BPM enables four key "value-pairs":

- Quality and Efficiency
- Agility and Standardization (Compliance)
- External Networks and Internal Alignment
- Innovation and Conservation.

Let's look at a few examples. A company wants to improve its call center process. Only few sub-processes are really relevant for clients and their willingness to pay a service fee for them. Hence you improve those sub-processes under quality aspects. Other sub-processes are more administrative. Clients don't really care about them.

Hence, you improve those processes under efficiency (mainly cost or time) aspects, using appropriate BPM approaches. BPM delivers the transparency to achieve both values and end up with a business process that provides the highest quality where it matters and the best efficiency where this counts most. The transparency BPM delivers also helps identify where a company really needs to be agile and where it just must comply with standards and guidelines. Many processes that "touch" clients or are focused on creating new ideas may need a lot of creativity and agility. In other areas, for example in finance, you may not want this creativity: People have to follow compliance regulations and meet legal requirements. BPM provides in both situations the right degree of freedom to the people involved. BPM and the transparency it creates also help to align people internally because they understand how they fit into an end-to-end processes and the value it provides. In the same time BPM supports a better integration with external partners, suppliers and customers because the transparency it creates shows how to best organize the collaboration. Or BPM helps to identify where it is really worth thinking of process innovation and where you can conserve existing good practices. Since an organization only competes with 15–20 % [11] of its processes it is key to identify where innovation pays off. This is again possible though the transparency BPM delivers. The values BPM delivers are shown in Fig. 2 [8].

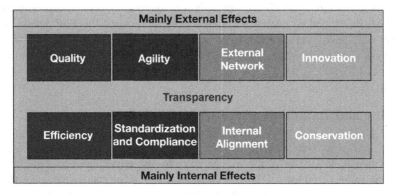

Fig. 2. Values delivered by BPM

In general, all those values are important for an organization. However, depending on the overall business strategy, companies focus on a subset of those values. These values and the underlying strategic objectives need to be realized across organizational boundaries within a company and beyond, while focusing on creating best results for clients.

In order to achieve those values consistently it is required to establish BPM with its infrastructure as an ongoing approach to run an organization [9, 10]. BPM becomes a management discipline.

We define BPM as the management discipline that transfers strategy into execution – at pace with certainty [11]. Hence, we refer to BPM as the BPM-Discipline (BPM-D®). This definition shows that BPM uses the "business process" concept as tool for a cross-organizational strategy execution, including the collaboration with market partners like customers, agents, or suppliers. The execution of the strategy can be people or technology based – or a combination of both. Hence, it includes the use of the opportunities of digital technologies and their connections with physical objects through the internet. This definition is consistent with newest findings regarding BPM definitions in BPM research studies [12]. But our definition stresses the value that processes management produces and its key role as strategy execution discipline.

The BPM-Discipline addresses the entire business process lifecycle, from design, implementation through the execution and control of a process. Hence, it handles the build-time as well as the run-time phase of the lifecycle of a business process. The definition of BPM as a management discipline is shown in Fig. 3. We refer to it as the BPM-D Framework.

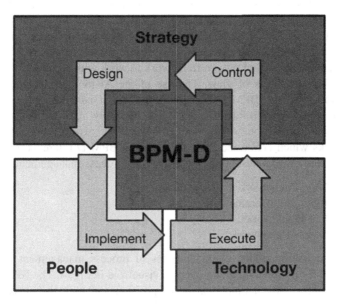

Fig. 3. The BPM-D® framework: definition of BPM as management discipline to execute strategy

3   The Processes of Process Management to Implement the BPM-Discipline

While over years many practitioners, especially executives, questioned the value of BPM, this situation has changed significantly in the past 5-7 years. Most organizations and their leadership at least start understanding the value proposition and the broader dimension of BPM. The challenge has become how to establish this new management discipline in an organization in a pragmatic but systematic way with – fast and with minimal up-front investment. In most cases the BPM-Discipline is expected to deliver fast benefits while developing and offering lasting capabilities.

In order to resolve this issue, we can look at other management disciplines and how they are implemented. An example is the discipline of Human resources (HR), as mentioned before. How do you implement the HR discipline? You introduce it into an organization through the appropriate HR processes, like the hiring process, performance evaluation or promotion process. Each HR sub-process starts delivering value when it is implemented and the organization keeps on suing it over time. Through the appropriate process implementation approach you create the right mix between immediate value-creation and establishing lasting capabilities.

Since BPM is a management discipline, too, you can implement a BPM-Discipline through the "process of process management", the BPM process. You address the BPM-Discipline just like any other management discipline. If you interpret the BPM-Discipline as process itself, you can apply all the process management approaches, methods and tools to it – enabling an efficient and effective process implementation approach. You basically implement BPM using BPM.

In order to identify and address all key aspects of the process of process management we use the ARIS Architecture [13] developed by August-Wilhelm Scheer. This is a widely accepted and proven framework to work with processes by examining them from different points of view. The use of the ARIS ararchitecture enables the operationalization of the BPM-D framework so that it can be applied to different organizations that want to identify, establish or apply relevant capabilities of a BPM-Discipline. Based on ARIS, the BPM-D Framework is decomposed into sub-frameworks which create the basis for a formal BPM-D reference model. Result are four core frameworks describing the process of process management:

- BPM-D Value Framework
- BPM-D Organization Framework
- BPM-D Data Framework
- BPM-D Process Framework

The decomposition of the overall process of process management as shown in Fig. 3 into sub-frameworks based on ARIS is visualized in Fig. 4. The BPM-D Process Framework covers both, a functional decomposition and with the clustering of the functions aspects of the control view of ARIS.

The BPM-D Value Framework is shown in Fig. 2 and has been discussed before. It describes the key deliverables (values) the process of process management (PoPM) produces. The use of this framework enables a consequently value-driven approach to BPM. This is especially important when you establish BPM as a management discipline so that you don't end up just with another "overhead initiative" but an organization that drives systematically value by executing strategy. BPM must focus on the values reflecting the business strategy that has to be executed. These value are identified in a company specific version of the BPM-D Value-Framework.

The earlier mentioned research study about the value of BPM [6] shows that organizations who apply BPM successfully have multiple different process specific roles in place. We identified over 40 of such roles. The segmentation of those roles led to the BPM-D Organization Framework.

There exist two big groups of process-related roles: core roles and extended roles. People with BPM core roles are part of the core BPM organizational unit, for example a

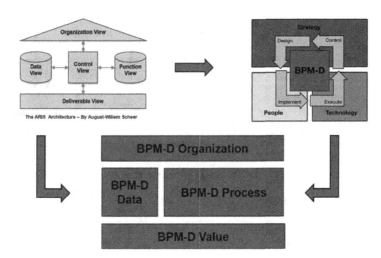

Fig. 4. Operationalizing the process of process management using the ARIS architecture by A.-W. Scheer

center of excellence [9, 11]. People with roles in the extended BPM organization are part of other organizational units. BPM roles can be centralized to achieve best synergies or decentralized to be close to operational improvement initiatives. Roles can be permanent or project based, relevant only for a specific process-led initiative. In most of the cases the roles are internal roles, hence help by employees. However, there is in more and more organizations a tendency to procure more administrative roles, like helpdesk activities or the maintenance and conversion of process models, externally, as a managed service. The BPM-D Organization Framework is shown in Fig. 5.

Very important is an emergent top executive role in the BPM-D core organization: the Chief Process Officer [14, 15]. This business leader owns the overall process of process management, hence leads the overall BPM-Discipline. The empirical research confirmed the trend of such an emerging top management position. Successful BPM organizations report in many cases directly to the board of a company. As a consequence, the lead of such a BPM organization needs to be a top executive who makes a difference for the entire organization. Other BPM core roles are business planning roles, business analysis roles, business-oriented and IT-oriented delivery roles, commercial roles, process-related content development and maintenance roles, IT maintenance and service roles as well as people enablement roles.

The most important role in the extended BPM organization is the process owner, responsible for the end-to-end management of a business process. This role has to make sure things get done with the expected impact on the strategic value-drivers, using the BPM core organization as internal service group. Other groups of core and enabling roles are sponsor and enabler roles. Sponsor roles are important for the process governance, especially the related decision making. Enabler roles are operational support roles, such as project team members in improvement initiatives. They are the "arms and legs" of the process owner.

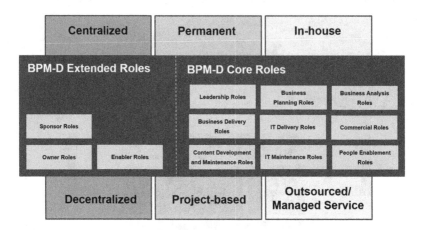

Fig. 5. BPM-D organization framework

In most of the organizations you don't have representatives for all the groups of roles right away or only part time roles. It depends on your overall BPM agenda which roles you need when. The required roles change over time, driven by the specific value the BPM discipline has to provide to execute on an organizations strategy. It is important to have both, core and extended roles in place to be on one hand able to execute, on the other had avoid to re-invent the wheel for every new process-led initiative.

Next "ARIS view" to be discussed is the data view. The information used in or produced by the process of process management is summarized in the BPM-D Data Framework. That view helps to plan information requirements for the process of process management. This includes business strategy related information to enable the link between strategy and execution. Example are strategic goals or value-drivers. But also operational information, like project related information, enterprise architecture, organization or tool and technology related information. The BPM-D Data Framework is shown in Fig. 6 in form of a simplified entity-relationship model.

Most important for the operationalization of the process of process management is the BPM-D Process Framework, covering the function and control view of the ARIS Architecture. It represents basically the first three hierarchy levels of a functional decomposition and a segmentation of the key activities of the PoPM.

The structure of the Process Framework is based on the principle thinking suggested in August-Wilhelm Scheer's Y-Model to segment the processes of an industrial enterprise [16]. In order to make the PoPM happen an organization requires project-related sub-processes (activities), focusing on identifying the best improvement opportunities and improving specific business processes. On the other hand it also needs to have "assets-related processes" in place to identify and execute improvement projects efficiently and effectively. Both, project and asset related sub-processes require planning and execution. This results in four groups of BPM-related sub-processes as shown in Fig. 7.

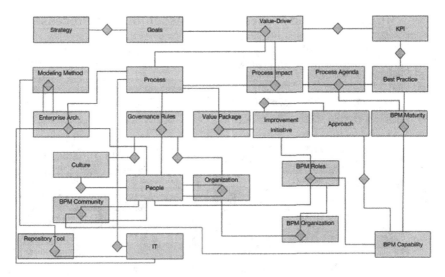

Fig. 6. BPM-D data framework

	Project-focused Processes	Asset-focused Processes
Planning Processes	BPM Project Planning	BPM Assets - Planning
Execution Processes	BPM Project Execution	BPM Assets - Execution

Fig. 7. Segmentation of BPM-related activities

The specific sub-processes of the PoPM were identified based on the analysis of over 200 process management BPM-Discipline initiatives. The result is shown in the BPM-D Process Framework in Fig. 8.

The Process Strategy identifies high impact low maturity processes in regards to the strategy of and organization. Hence it defines how to target real business value by focusing on those processes important for the execution of the business strategy. In order to develop the appropriate capabilities the BPM capability requirements and gaps are identified through a maturity assessment. Those gaps need to be filled to be able to improve the target processes. Finally a BPM agenda is developed. It shows which processes are improved when to achieve specific strategic business objectives and

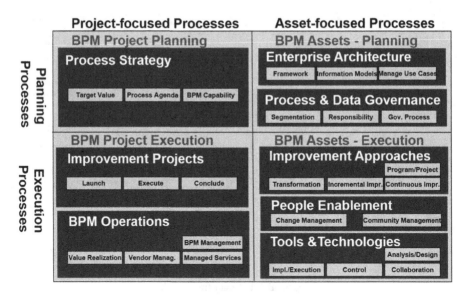

Fig. 8. BPM-D process framework

which BPM capability gaps are closed during each improvement initiative. Hence, every initiative delivers immediate business value while creating lasting process management capabilities.

Improvement projects follow a straight forward project approach: launch, execution, and conclusion of the project. BPM-Operations enable the execution of activities outside specific projects, for example the value realization once a project is already concluded. These "post project" activities are often neglected in traditional process management approaches that are project-centric. As a result improvement targets are not or only partially met.

The Enterprise Architecture related sub-processes handle all activities necessary to create and manage information models, necessary to scope process initiatives and improve specific processes or keep them on track through ongoing adjustments. Those models play an important role in delivering the transparency over an organization. Key is that those information modelling activities are outcome-driven. It must be clearly define how we get which useful results out of those information models. Many organizations create a lot of content but get little actual benefits out of them.

Process and Data Governance sub-processes organize the way process management is executed, hence, grant the power to take decisions, drive action and deal with the consequences of those actions. Important here is the integration of process and data governance [17]. Insufficient master data quality leads in many cases also to ineffective processes. Inconsistent or inaccurate customer master data may, for example, lead to data search and clean-up activities or even to a failed client interaction, hence to significant process performance issues. An integrated process and data governance approach aligns both aspects.

The availability of improvement approaches and of people knowledgeable in those approaches enables the execution of improvement projects which use those capabilities. Those approaches can include continuous improvement tools like Lean or Six Sigma, but also transformational approaches, standardization approaches, creativity approach for process innovation, for example design thinking, or a solid project management methodology.

People enablement is all about information, communication and training. Hence it prepares people to think and work in a process context and deal with process change successfully. In many improvement and transformation initiatives those people-related capabilities are underestimated and not sufficiently addressed. This can lead to significant issues.

Tools and Technology related sub-processes handle the technical infrastructure required for a successful BPM-Discipline, including for example automation engines, rules engines, repository and modelling tools, process mining, strategy execution tools, social media, the internet of things and other internet-based approaches, e-learning applications and other digital technologies. Tools and Technologies include core BPM tools but also additional technology required to increase the performance of a process to the required level. A successful BPM-Discipline needs to integrate People Enablement with Tools and Technologies to come to an optimal process improvement and with that to the desired strategy execution. This enables the appropriate digitalization approaches and related new business models.

While all the sub-processes of the PoPM shown in Fig. 8 can be important in a specific company context, organizations only rarely need all of them in full maturity. The business strategy and the specific objectives of a company's BPM-Discipline determine the importance of a specific sub-process and the required maturity level. Once the relevant sub-processes of the PoPM are selected and their required maturity level is defined, the necessary BPM roles and BPM-related information are identified

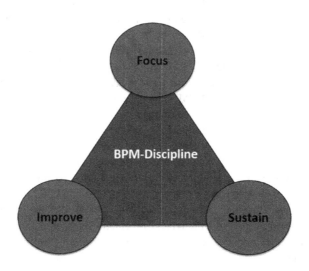

Fig. 9. Key tasks of a BPM-discipline

using the appropriate BPM-D frameworks. All frameworks need to be configured consistently to a specific organization, its strategy and business context. The right application of the BPM-Framework and its sub-components enables companies to focus on what really matters, improve those areas efficiently and effectively as well as to sustain those improvements. These key tasks of a BPM-Discipline are visualized in Fig. 9.

The BPM-D Framework with all its components is patent-pending. It is a strategy execution environment helping organizations to achieve high performance in a digital world.

4   Reference Model for the Process of Process Management

In order to operationalize the BPM-D Framework and its components further, the framework is transferred into a more formalized reference model. Reference models are generalized knowledge, structured and documented in a manner that enables adaptability to specific situations [18, 19]. While the discussed frameworks provide the overall guidance, the reference model provides the detailed information about how the BPM-Discipline works. They are adjusted to a specific company context to establish and apply a BPM-Discipline that provides best value for the organization.

The reference model also allows to identify and develop specific tools and templates that support the BPM-Discipline.

During the development of the BPM-D Reference Model the BPM-D Process Framework is further detailed and integrated with the other BPM-D sub-frameworks. The control flow logic is added to the functional decomposition. Key functions are linked to tools, templates or other job-aids supporting their execution.

The process framework is described on 3 levels of detail. The top level is represented as value chain diagram (VCD), level 2 and 3 as event-driven process chain (EPC). The EPC notation was selected since it is focusing on the description of the business content and has less formal requirements than other methods like the business process modelling notation (BPMN). It is in general easily understood by business practitioners. Also people used to work with other modelling methods can usually quickly adjust and understand the EPC notation. In order to support a potential automation of some of the sub-processes of the process of process management, level 3 processes are also available in BPMN (simple model conversion). These BPMN models can be used as starting point for the specification of application software supporting the PoPM. While this redundancy needs to be managed we feel that at the current point of time it helps to achieve both, easy use of the PoPM reference model content by process practitioners as well as by software developers.

Figure 10 shows level 1 of the process reference model. Examples for levels 2 and 3 are represented in Figs. 11 and 12. On level 3 process models, for example in the model shown in Fig. 12, it is exactly described which BPM roles are required, what the people in those roles have to do, which data (information) they use and in which logical sequence they work. Hence, the process is sufficiently described to be implemented in an organization [18].

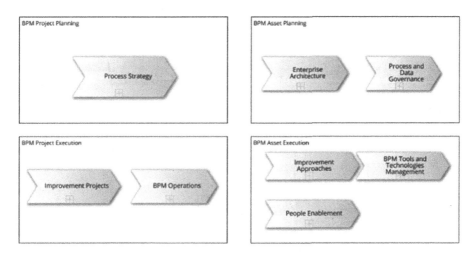

Fig. 10. Level 1 of BPM-D process reference model

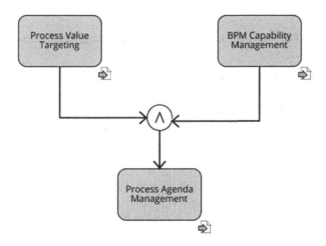

Fig. 11. Level 2 of BPM-D process reference model – process strategy

The reference model is developed in a web-based process repository tool. This enables the easy access from all relevant locations and reduces tool maintenance to a minimum. It can be easily transferred into all market leading modelling and repository applications. The reference model currently consists of 67 individual information models.

The implementation and execution of the level 3 processes is further supported through the link of the models to execution tools, templates and other job aids. The sub-process "BPM Capability" of "Process Strategy" is, for example, linked to a BPM maturity assessment tool, based on the BPM-D Framework. The "Responsibility" sub-process of the "Process and Data Governance" is linked to job aids supporting the

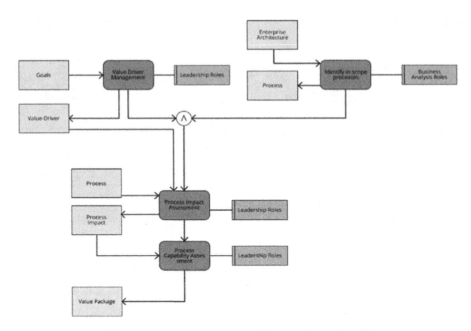

Fig. 12. Level 3 of BPM-D process reference model – targeting value of the process strategy

establishment of a BPM Center of Excellent with its different roles and the introduction of process and data governance to a specific end-to-end process. The reference model links to over 20 tools, templates and other job-aids. It proves the applicability and validity of the BPM-D frameworks and enables the desired application in business practice.

5 First Experiences

The BPM-D Framework and Reference Model or components of it have been applied in 26 organizations of different industries and sizes over the last two and a half years to implement or apply the process of process management. This has been done through a combination of consulting, coaching and educational activities, combined with appropriate research activities to continuously improve the process of process management reference model.

Let's look at a couple of examples: The CEO of a medium-size consumer goods company has focused for several years successfully on a small niche market. The company offers their products at a high price enabling high revenues and profits – in spite of a relatively high cost level. Now competitors entered that niche market and offer similar products at a much lower price. The CEO decided to adjust strategy: reduce prices in the current market and enter new market segments with new products. However, to reduce prices the company needs to reduce cost. None of the functional executives sees significant cost reduction potential in their own areas. They blame other departments for the cost issues. Also the innovation related processes are not performing at the level required. The introduction of two new products in a short is considered challenging. An existing process repository with its process models did not really help: the models are outdated and inconsistent regarding semantic content as well as modelling format. The only person who is somehow familiar with the models and the repository has left the organization. There is no cross-functional management in place with responsibilities beyond department boundaries. It is very difficult or even impossible to identify focus areas for cost reduction or a consistent enterprise-wide approach for the development and launch of new products.

The situation is addressed through a combination of defining and establishing an appropriate BPM-Discipline through the according process of process management, combined with the immediate application of the new improvement capabilities to "no regret" processes. Additional improvement targets are defined when all high impact low maturity processes are identified by the new BPM-Discipline. Key areas of the PoPM addressed in this initial BPM-Discipline launch are the development of a process strategy, introduction of a simple process and enterprise architecture approach, definition of a basic process governance, outline of a straight forward model-based improvement approach and some people enablement through targeted training.

The immediate improvement initiatives have let to measurable results in less than six months. After 12 months clear improvement trends in the identified key areas have been visible. The PoPM has become a part of the "business-as-usual". It forms a value-network around the functional organization.

Another typical example is a large financial organization. They have made significant investments over the last four years into what they call "BPM". However, none of the top executives has seen any business impacts or positive results after all that time and money spent. A stakeholder assessment and BPM maturity analysis showed that almost all BPM related initiatives focus on tools and technologies – for all business units in parallel. There is, for example, a process repository in place with over 2000 models – how to get value out of them is unclear. A flexible process automation is in the works – but business changes faster than the technology can be adjusted. And it is impossible to focus on just one area because business priorities are not or not well enough defined.

The introduction of a value-driven BPM-Discipline, led by a top manager as "Chief Process Officer" and its use for a simplification of processes with known issues as preparation for a more focused and business-driven automation is used here to address the current issues. Key areas of the PoPM addressed are the value-driven process strategy with its prioritization approach, process and data governance, a process model based simplification and standardization approach and several people enablement initiatives. Existing capabilities are linked to specific outcomes to achieve step by step a value-driven approach to BPM.

Immediate result is the adjustment of budgets and the re-definition and re-scoping of ongoing initiatives. Tangible results are expected after six to eight months.

The experience with the first 26 organizations shows that organizations looking for the systematic implementation of a BPM-Discipline through the process of process management fall into three groups:

1. Organizations have launched one or even multiple process improvement initiatives but the results are not sustained. Every new improvement initiative starts from scratch, not using existing knowledge about business processes systematically. There is no real management discipline in place. BPM is considered a set of tools for improvement projects.
2. Organizations put in place many components of a BPM infrastructure (e.g. process execution environments) but have not achieved real business value through their BPM activities. Components of management discipline are in place but they are not aligned and not used in a value-driven way so that they don't realize their full potential.
3. Organizations launched some improvement initiatives and built some BPM infrastructure but both do not really fit together, it is unclear what the next steps and priorities are. The produced business value is limited. A BPM-Discipline is attempted but not really achieved since there is not clear direction defined.

Organizations of the first group establish the "project-focused" sub-processes of the PoPM but forget about the activities and infrastructure necessary to keep the improved processes on track and to be able to create synergies between different initiatives over time. In those cases "asset-focused" sub-processes need to be addressed. In most of the cases this results in a combination of governance, enterprise architecture and people enablement processes, combined with the development of an appropriate value-driven BPM agenda.

The second group of organizations gets lost in all the available methods, tools and technologies but forgets to identify how to create business value through them. The link of BPM activities to strategic value-drivers and the launch of initiatives effecting those value-drivers is key here. Hence, the "project-focused" sub-processes of the PoPM need to be addressed. The launch of a process strategy initiative is here most important: identifying high impact low maturity processes, the required BPM capability and based on those the development of the BPM agenda. This needs to be combined with the launch and execution of improvement projects and the consequent value-realization. BPM capabilities can be adjusted according to the requirements identified in the BPM agenda.

Most organizations belong to group three. They have some BPM capabilities and improvement initiatives in place but the BPM journey is missing direction, focus and clear business impact. They don't have a BPM-Discipline in place but know how to apply a number of methods and tools, e.g. Six Sigma. Instead of strategy execution, BPM activities result in operational fixing of symptoms. Here a combination of a real outcome-focused process strategy, the management of the process knowledge in an enterprise architecture and a well defined (but simple) governance approach are good starting points to move towards a value-driven BPM-Discipline.

Here some key lessons learned from first practice experiences:

- Get top management support. Establishing a value-driven BPM-Discipline requires the top-down support, best for the entire company, but at least for the business unit in scope.

- Identify business processes where you can deliver immediate benefits while building the required lasting BPM capabilities. Otherwise sponsors will lose patience.
- Set clear priorities, don't try to "boil the ocean". Organizations who launch too many initiatives at once often fail.
- Keep things simple, "less is often more". This is especially true for the use of tools and technologies.
- Encourage innovation and creativity instead of punishing people for making mistakes.
- A value-driven BPM Discipline is an enabler of growth and strategic agility, not just a cost reduction engine.
- People are key for success. You need to treat them accordingly.
- A value-driven BPM-Discipline and its leadership recognizes the business value potential of technology and digitalization and makes it transparent to the organization. It enables real business value from digital initiatives.

The first experiences with the BPM-D Framework and the reference model of the process of process management have demonstrated the business impact of the approach and enabled the continues improvement of the reference model. The reference model allows to identify and establish the appropriate BPM capabilities in the company-specific context quickly and at low cost while applying them immediately to achieve fast business benefits.

A company can use the individualized reference model as basis for the definition of the company-specific BPM processes. The process of process management is transferred into an operational business process. It becomes part of the enterprise architecture of the company. The owner of the process of process management, a "Chief Process Officer", oversees this process.

6 The Journey Goes on

Business Process Management (BPM) has become a value-driven management discipline that transfers strategy into people and technology based execution – at pace with certainty. This management discipline is implemented through the process of process management. It enables an organization to master the new normal in a digital world and reach optimal performance.

The BPM-D Framework with its sub-components and the reference model for the process of process management help organizations to establish a value-driven BPM-Discipline efficiently and effectively. The reference model and the tools behind it are continuously improved based on practice experience as well as newest academic thinking.

Most powerful for the practical application has been the addition of execution tools and templates related to the PoPM reference model, e.g. the development of the process prioritization tool, the capability assessment tool, the weak point analysis for rapid process simplification and improvement or the process governance and BPM Center of

Excellence job aids. New tools and templates need to be continuously developed and linked to reference model.

The BPM-Discipline and the underlying process of process management enables companies to create an end-to-end "value network" around the existing organizational structure. This is the basis for high performance and productivity in the new normal of our digital world. The BPM-Discipline becomes the strategy execution engine of an organization.

We expect the importance of a well-established BPM-Discipline will continue to increase through the influence of digitalization in general and "the cloud" in specific [24]. The fact that more and more of the classical information technology moves outside the organization and is procured through the cloud makes processes the key assets that stay within the company boundaries. They become the "secret sauce" of the organization. Companies need an appropriate management discipline to address those process assets and drive them towards optimal performance regarding the overall business strategy. The impact of the cloud is visualized in Fig. 13.

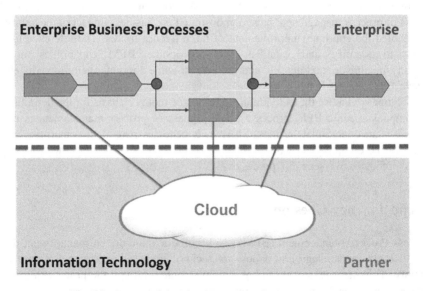

Fig. 13. Impact of the cloud: processes become a key asset

References

1. Sinur, J., Odell, J., Fingar, P.: Business Process Management: The Next Wave – Harnessing Complexity with Intelligent Agents. Meghan-Kiffer Press, Tampa (2013)
2. Ismail, S., van Geest, Y., Malone, M.: Exponential Organizations – Why new organizations are ten times better, faster, and cheaper than yours (and what to do about it). Diversion Books, New York (2014)
3. Mitchell, C., Ray, R.L., van Ark, B.: The Conference Board – CEO Challenge 2015: Creating Opportunity Out of Adversity: Building Innovative, People-driven Organizations. The Conference Board Whitepaper, New York (2015)

4. Kirchmer, M., Franz, P.: Targeting Value in a Digital World. BPM-D Whitepaper, Philadelphia, London (2014b)
5. Rummler, G.A., Ramias, A., Rummler, R.A.: White Space Revisited – Creating Value thorugh Processes. Wiley, San Francisco (2010)
6. Kirchmer, M., Lehmann, S., Rosemann, M., zur Muehlen, M., Laengle, S.: Research Study – BPM Governance in Practice. Accenture Whitepapers, Philadelphia (2013)
7. Franz, P., Kirchmer, M., Rosemann, M.: Value-driven Business Process Management – Which values matter for BPM. Accenture / Queensland University of Technology BPM Publication, London, Philadelphia, Brisbane (2011)
8. Kirchmer, M., Franz, P.: The BPM-Discipline – Enabling the Next Generation Enterprise. BPM-D Training Documentation, Philadelphia/London (2013)
9. Alkharashi, B., Jesus, L., Macieira, A., Tregear, R.: Establishing the Office of Business Process Management. Leonardo Consulting Publication, Brisbane (2015)
10. Von Rosing, M., Hove, M., von Scheel, H., Morrison, R.: BPM center of excellence. In: von Rosing, M., Scheer, A.-W., von Scheel, H. (eds.) The complete Business Process Handbook – Body of Knowledge from Process Modeling to BPM, Amsterdam, Boston, vol. 1, pp. 217–240 (2015)
11. Franz, P., Kirchmer, M.: Value-driven business Process Management – The Value-Switch for Lasting Competitive Advantage. McGraw-Hill, New York (2012)
12. Swenson, K.D., von Rosing, M.: What is Business Process Management. In: von Rosing, M., Scheer, A.-W., von Scheel, H. (eds.) The complete Business Process Handbook – Body of Knowledge from Process Modeling to BPM, Amsterdam, Boston, vol. 1, pp. 79–88 (2015)
13. Scheer, A.-W.: ARIS – Business Process Frameworks, 2nd edn. Springer, Berlin (1998)
14. Kirchmer, M., Franz, P., von Rosing, M.: The chief process officer: an emerging tope management role. In: von Rosing, M., Scheer, A.-W., von Scheel, H.: The complete Business Process Handbook – Body of Knowledge from Process Modeling to BPM, Amsterdam, Boston, vol. 1, pp. 343–348 (2015)
15. Kirchmer, M., Franz, P.: Chief Process Officer – The Value Scout. BPM-D Whitepaper, Philadelphia, London (2014)
16. Scheer, A.-W.: Business Process Engineering – Reference Models for Industrial Enterprises, 2nd edn. Springer, Berlin (1995)
17. Packowski, Gall, Baumeister: Enterprise Process and Information Governance – Integration of business process and master data governance as competitive advantage – Study Results. Camelot Consulting, Germany (2014)
18. Kirchmer, M.: High Performance through Process Excellence – From Strategy to Execution with Business Process Management, 2nd edn. Springer, Berlin (2011)
19. Fettke, L.: Reference Modelling for Business Systems Anlysis. ICI Global, London (2007)
20. Cantara, M.: Start up your business process competency center. In: Documentation of The Gartner Business Process Management Summit, National Harbor 2015
21. Kirchmer, M.: Business process management in a digital world – trends and predictions. In: Proceeding of the International Conference on Modeling and Simulation in Engineering, Economics and Management, Santiago de Chile, 20–22 January 2016
22. McDonald, M.: Digital Strategy Does Not Equal IT Strategy. Harvard Business Review, 19 November 2012
23. Kirchmer, M.: Enabling high performance through digitalization – the BPM-discipline as value-switch. In: CIO Review, 14 January 2016
24. Abolhassan, F.: Was treibt die Digitalisierung? Warum an der Cloud kein Weg vorbeifuehrt. Wiesbaden (2016)

Author Index

Printed in the United States
By Bookmasters